BLACKSTONE'S GUIDE TO

The Charities Act 2006

BLACKSTONE'S GUIDE TO

The Charities Act 2006

Alison Maclennan

OXFORD
UNIVERSITY PRESS

OXFORD
UNIVERSITY PRESS

Great Clarendon Street, Oxford OX2 6DP

Oxford University Press is a department of the University of Oxford.
It furthers the University's objective of excellence in research, scholarship,
and education by publishing worldwide in

Oxford New York

Auckland Bangkok Buenos Aires Cape Town Chennai Dar es Salaam Delhi Hong Kong Istanbul Karachi
Kolkata Kuala Lumpur Madrid Melbourne Mexico City Mumbai Nairobi
São Paulo Shanghai Singapore Taipei Tokyo Toronto

with an associated company in Berlin

Oxford is a registered trade mark of Oxford University Press
in the UK and in certain other countries

Published in the United States
by Oxford University Press Inc., New York

British Library Cataloguing in Publication Data

Data available

Library of Congress Cataloging-in-Publication Data

Maclennan, Alison E.
Blackstone's guide to the Charities Act 2006 / Alison MacLennan.
  p. cm. — (Blackstone's guide)
Includes bibliographical references and index.
ISBN 978-0-19-921479-2 (pbk. : alk. paper) 1. Charity laws and legislation—Great
Britain. I. title. II. Title: Charities Act 2006.
  KD1487.M33 2007
  346.42'064—dc22

                                                    2007005197

Typeset by Laserwords Private Limited, Chennai, India
Printed in Great Britain
on acid-free paper by
Ashford Colour Press Limited, Gosport, Hampshire

ISBN 978–0–19–921479–2

1 3 5 7 9 10 8 6 4 2

Contents—Summary

Contents—Detailed

Table of Cases

References are to Paragraph Numbers

Table of Legislation

References are to Paragraph Numbers

Introduction

Charities in England and Wales are increasing in importance in society, and there are around 600,000 organizations, including 188,000 registered charities, operating in the not-for-profit sector. The United Kingdom is unique in having a strong tradition of charity-encouraging activity and innovation in a wide variety of activities. The bodies carrying out such activity are diverse and range from organizations with ancient roots to modern organizations seeking to address purely modern concerns. The diversity of the sector reflects the changes in society for over 400 years. Society continues to change though, and charity law needs to keep pace with those changes whilst facilitating action by charities.

Generally, the voluntary sector has recently enjoyed greater prominence and has been the subject of a government review.[1] Whilst it has been reviewed before,[2] the current policy of achieving closer partnerships between central and local government, and achieving the full potential of the sector, has helped to provide the necessary initiative to equip the sector with a modern legal framework, embodied in the Charities Act 2006. The review of the law is part of a wider review which includes examining the role of the voluntary sector in public service delivery and improving access to public regeneration funding.

The voluntary sector has remained independent from the Government, and the Review document (see note 1) stresses that that is vital to its success. The legal reform in the Charities Act 2006 is aimed at increasing the dynamism of the sector whilst preserving the existing considerable public trust in its voluntary nature. The five main areas of change concern:

(a) the modernization and restatement of charitable purposes or objects;
(b) an express obligation on charities to ensure that they provide public benefit;
(c) changes to the composition of, and function of, the Charity Commission;
(d) the establishment of a Charity Tribunal; and
(e) the improvement of the range of legal forms available to charities and social enterprises.

Whilst the purpose of new legislation generally is to change the law, many of the provisions of the Charities Act 2006 restate and modernize the current law in statutory form. (Much of the current law is contained in case law and piecemeal

---

[1] See *Private Action, Public Benefit. A review of charities and the wider not for profit sector*, Cabinet Office Strategy Unit Report, September 2002.
[2] Deakin Commission 'Meeting the Challenge of Change, Voluntary Action into the 21st Century' and also 'The Report of the Deakin Commission on the Future of the Voluntary Sector' London NCVO 1996.

statutory amendments, which will retain relevance in interpreting the Charities Act 2006.) Traditionally, the issue of recognizing new charitable purposes has been an exercise dependent on arguing that new objects clauses are analogous to previously decided cases. The volume of decided and reported cases has dwindled as the cost of litigation in the High Court has risen and the value of the decided cases to modern circumstances has declined. Additionally, matters concerning the administration of a charity are largely within the jurisdiction of the Charity Commission and only rarely require a ruling in the High Court. The result is that charity law in modern practice is comparatively inaccessible. By introducing new legislation the law becomes more accessible to all and the importance of decisions made by the Charity Commission is recognized. The enhanced role of the Charity Commission itself, but also the innovation of having a Charity Tribunal, ought to make charity law and practice more transparent, accountable, and publicly available.

1

THE MEANING OF 'CHARITY'

A. DEFINITIONS

Part 1, s 1(1) of the Charities Act 2006 defines 'charity' as an institution which is   1.01
established for charitable purposes only and which falls to be subject to the control
of the High Court in the exercise of its jurisdiction with respect to charities. The
Charities Act 1993 contained an almost identical definition (see para 1.02 below).
Despite the apparent similarity of the meaning of the term in the two Acts, there
have been some cases where the essential issue under the 1993 legislation was
whether or not an institution was a charity, under the law of England and Wales, at
all. The Charities Act 2006, s 1(1) addresses and clarifies this issue.

The issue of whether an institution was or was not a charity began with ss 96 and   1.02
97 of the 1993 Act. A charity was an institution which was established for charitable
purposes and subject to the control of the High Court. A charitable purpose was a
purpose which, judged according to the law of England and Wales, was one which
was exclusively charitable. Historically, the problem has not lain in identifying
whether the particular purposes and activities of an institution were 'charitable' or
not, but in whether the Charity Commission and the High Court had jurisdiction
to register and regulate the charity or branch of a foreign charity operating in the
United Kingdom.[1]

The new s 1 changes the emphasis from judging the institution against current   1.03
English law to stating what charity means 'For the purposes of the law of England
and Wales'. *Dreyfuss (Camille and Henry) Ltd v IRC*[2] concerned the Income Tax Act
1918, s 37. The Dreyfuss Foundation was incorporated in the state of New York
and the objects of the institution were exclusively charitable according to the law of
England and Wales. It was held by the Court of Appeal that the word 'established',
which is also used in s 1 of the 2006 Act, meant bodies regulated by and subject to

---

[1] 'Jurisdiction in Charity Law', PCB 2004, Issue No 4, 240.   [2] [1954] Ch 672.

the law of the United Kingdom. There must be a trust taking effect and enforceable under the law of the United Kingdom which creates an obligation enforceable in the courts of the United Kingdom. In the above case the corporation would not have been 'resident' in the United Kingdom under the principles of private international law.

1.04   It is arguable that there are two limbs to jurisdiction or showing that a charity is 'established' in England and Wales. First there is a concern about securing the administration of the charity and the practical matter of enforcing the trust, if necessary, against the trustees in breach. Secondly, there is a question as to the true 'residency' of a charity under international law.

1.05   The first question—enforceability—may be the subject of proceedings, and the court may enjoy a limited jurisdiction as in *Provost of Edinburgh v Aubrey*[3] and *Attorney General v Lepine*,[4] where the court simply declared the trust charitable and directed that the gift was to be applied and administered elsewhere. In *Gaudiya Mission v Brahmachary*,[5] Mummery LJ began his assessment of the principles and practice to be followed by citing Dicey & Morris,[6] repeating the principle that

> the English Courts will not administer a foreign charity under the supervision of the Court, nor will they settle a scheme for such a charity. It is clear that the Court cannot effectively control trustees who will probably hold property outside England, and if it appointed trustees for a charity both within and without England the English trustees would have difficulty in controlling their co-trustees.

1.06   More recently, in the Armenian Patriarch of Jerusalem[7] case, property was held by a bank in England for certain charitable purposes in Jerusalem, where the detailed application of the income within those purposes was to be determined by the Patriarch of Jerusalem. The Charity Commission stated that the bank was a nominee only and did not fall within the definition of a charity trustee under s 96 of the Charities Act 1993. The court disagreed and stated that there was a trustee in this country, and the charitable trust was therefore subject to the supervision of the English court.

1.07   The Charities Act 2006, s 1(2) further defines 'charity' by stating that the meaning of the term in s 1(1) does not apply for the purposes of an enactment if a different definition of that term applies for those purposes by virtue of that enactment. In other words, another Act may expressly declare whether or not an institution is to be treated as a charity, eg an Education Act. If that is the case then the basic definition in s 1(1) is not to be applied. In *Construction Industry Training Board v Attorney General*,[8] it was argued that the court did not have jurisdiction over the charity as the Act establishing it appointed the Minister as the controlling body. It was held that the relevant provision of the Charities Act 1960 dealt with

---

[3] (1754) Ambler 256.   [4] (1818) 2 Swan 181.   [5] [1998] Ch 341.
[6] *The Conflict of Laws.*
[7] *His Beatitude Archbishop Torkum Manoogian, the Armenian Patriarch of Jerusalem v Yolande Sonsino and Others* [2002] EWHC 1304.
[8] [1973] Ch 173.

a charitable institution established in terms which provided for control from outside the institution, such as the executive in a statutory body, and where the extent of that control was such that the jurisdiction of the court was substantially ousted, the charitable institution was not a charity within the statutory definition.

The Charities Act 2006 recognizes the principle that a charity may well fall within the definition of 'charity' in s 1(1) but be primarily regulated by some body other than the Charity Commission. The concept of a 'principal regulator' is expressly included in the 2006 Act[9] for the first time. It has been introduced in conjunction with the power of the relevant Minister to make orders which can specify that particular institutions, or particular classes of institutions, either cease to be, or become, exempt charities. The circumstances in which this power may be used by the relevant Minister are not given. Potentially, whole classes of charities may be principally regulated by a body other than the Charity Commission. The Charity Commission may still regulate[10] the charity, but in a secondary or supplementary way. 1.08

Consistent with the intention of preserving the current law and merely modernizing it, any reference to a charity within the meaning of the Charitable Uses Act 1601, or the preamble to it, is to be construed as a reference to a charity within s 1 of the Charities Act 2006. The references are to be in an enactment or document. The 1601 Act is often referred to as the 'Statute of Elizabeth I'.[11] In the 19th century the Statute was interpreted further[12] and four heads of charitable purposes were established. These were: 1.09

(a) the relief of poverty;
(b) the advancement of education;
(c) the advancement of religion; and
(d) other purposes beneficial to the community.

The government review took the view that the four heads of charity and the Statute of Elizabeth I produced uncertainty and confusion, and did not accurately represent the full range of different types of organization enjoying charitable status today. The intention of the Charities Act 2006 is to clarify what constitutes 'charity' in the 21st century and change the parameters of charitable status to include organizations which provide public benefit but which are currently either borderline cases or denied charitable status.

B. THE MEANING OF 'CHARITABLE PURPOSE'

The Charities Act 2006, s 2(1) defines 'charitable purpose' as being a purpose which falls within the list in s 2(2) and which is for the public benefit. The Act thus 1.10

---

[9] Charities Act 2006, ss 13 and 14.   [10] See para 4.08 below.
[11] For a longer discussion of the foundations of charitable purposes and the Statute of Elizabeth, see *Tudor, Charities*, 9th ed (Thompson, Sweet & Maxwell, 2003), chap 1.
[12] *Income Tax Special Purposes Commissioners v Pemsel* [1891] AC 531, at 583.

contains a two-part test: (i) the purpose itself; and (ii) a requirement to provide public benefit. The inclusion of a specific element of public benefit in the statute is an innovation and is further defined in s 3 of the 2006 Act (see further paras 2.21 to 2.31).

1.11   Section (2) lists descriptions of purposes which are charitable. The first three—the prevention or relief of poverty, the advancement of education, and the advancement of religion—are familiar. Of the next three—the advancement of health or the saving of lives, the advancement of citizenship or community development, and the advancement of the arts, culture, heritage, or science—only the second is relatively new. 'Citizenship' is not defined. The seventh and new charitable purpose is the advancement of amateur sport.[13] Human rights, conflict resolution or reconciliation, religious and racial harmony or equality and diversity are all included in the eighth charitable purpose under the Charities Act 2006. Environmental protection and improvement and animal welfare are also expressly included in the list in s 2 of the Act. The promotion of the efficiency of the armed forces of the Crown and the emergency services also appears. Section (2)(j) refers to the relief of those in need and covers such activities as the provision of care homes, facilities for the disabled, and social housing. The final charitable purpose included in the list in s 2(2) of the Charities Act 2006 is given as 'any other purpose within subsection (4)'. Section (4) states that those purposes are 'any purposes not within paragraphs (a) to (l) of subsection (2) but recognised as charitable purposes under existing charity law or by virtue of section 1 of the Recreational Charities Act 1958 ... '. Further, they include any purposes which may be 'reasonably' regarded as analogous to, or within the spirit of, any of those purposes listed in s 2(2). All these charitable purposes are discussed further in Chapter 2.

---

[13] *Re Nottage* [1895] 2 Ch 649.

2

THE TWO-PART TEST FOR CHARITY

A. CHARITABLE PURPOSES

1. The Prevention and Relief of Poverty

The relief of poverty as a charitable purpose is well established, and gifts as indefinite   2.01
as those 'for the good of poor people forever'[1] have been held to be valid charitable
gifts. The relief of poor people appears in the Statute of Elizabeth itself and has
continued to be charitable. If an institution or gift is expressly established for the
relief of the poor of a class of people or geographical area, it will still be charitable.
The types of classes of preferred beneficiary include the poor families of the armed
forces or of a particular regiment, servants, poor pious persons, and 'youths of
merit'.[2] Relieving the poverty of people of a specific religious denomination is also
charitable. Classes of beneficiary may be described by reference to particular places
(eg a particular parish or town). Traditionally, relief of the poor has enjoyed tolerant
treatment in the courts. There is no 'test' of what constitutes poverty.[3] Orphans,
widows, and almost every description of a person who may be poor, may be found
in extensive case law. In the case of relieving poverty, the existence of public benefit
as required under the Charities Act 2006 may easily be met. Modern examples of
the Charity Commission recognizing new methods of relieving poverty can also
easily be found.[4] Although relieving poverty is obviously in the public benefit, the
imposition of the statutory public benefit requirement may lead to publication of
specific guidance by the Charity Commission in future. There are some cases[5] where
it has been doubted that the class of beneficiaries constitutes a sufficient section of

---

[1] *Att-Gen v Peacock* (1676) Rep. T. Finch 245.
[2] See *Tudor, Charities*, 9th ed (Thompson, Sweet & Maxwell, 2003), at para 2-011.
[3] See eg *In re Coulthurst* [1951] Ch 661, at 665.
[4] (1995) 4 Ch Com Dec, pp 1–7, The Fairtrade Foundation; (1994) 4 Ch Com Dec, pp 13–16.
[5] *Dingle v Turner* [1972] AC 601; cf *Oppenheim v Tobacco Securities Trust Co Ltd* [1951] AC 297,
Re Cox [1955] AC 627.

the public, or where the class of beneficiaries enjoys a personal nexus which excludes the benefit of the public. The current anomalous 'poor relations' cases[6] will probably continue to enjoy charitable status, for now, as the Charities Act 2006 seeks to preserve the existing law; however, in the light of the public benefit requirement, any new registration of charities for the relief of poverty will have to satisfy the Charity Commission. It is not clear whether quantitative or qualitative judgements will be made.

2.02   The use of the word 'prevention' appears to be an innovation in the Charities Act 2006, but indirect means of relieving poverty have historically been recognized. Providing land, houses, and almshouses, and providing houses to be let at affordable rents, all have been recognized as charitable purposes but could equally be interpreted as methods for the prevention of poverty. Issues such as unemployment may be addressed under this head. The relief of unemployment was found to be charitable in *IRC v Oldham Training and Enterprise Council*,[7] but under the fourth head of charity in *Pemsel* (see para 1.09 above). The Charity Commission has produced guidance since 1999 on what, in its judgement, would be charitable. It remains possible for a charity to fall within more than one of the listed charitable purposes in the Charities Act 2006, s 2(2).

2. The Advancement of Education

2.03   The advancement of education also features in the Statute of Elizabeth and has long been recognized as charitable. The extent of this recognition is shown by the principle, operating prior to the Charities Act 2006, that institutions established for this purpose were presumed to be for the public benefit and therefore charitable. This presumption has been removed expressly in s 3(2) of the 2006 Act. Educational purposes are similar to the relief of poverty in that the court has been tolerant towards quite widely expressed purposes and declared them charitable.[8] 'Education' itself remains undefined, both in the law prior to the Charities Act 2006 and after it. Any guidance in the cases is vague, but it could be said that to be educational something must improve knowledge and be of some value to society. The promotion of information and knowledge should not be carried out in a campaigning or propagandist way, or be political.

2.04   The establishment of schools, the payment of schoolteachers, the provision of scholarships and prizes, and the provision of facilities (eg books or whole libraries) for educational purposes are all charitable.[9] Physical education is also included.[10] Aesthetic education is considered to be charitable,[11] as is the provision of education in institutions or societies which could not be defined as schools or colleges.

---

[6] See Lord Cross in *Dingle v Turner*, above, n 5, at 623.
[7] [1996] STC 1218.
[8] See *Re Ward* [1941] Ch 308.
[9] See *Tudor*, above, n 2, paras 20–21 to 20–25.
[10] See *IRC v McMullen* [1981] AC 1.
[11] *Royal Choral Society v IRC* [1943] 2 All ER 101.

Education is not confined to educating children but may include general education of the public. Currently, independent schools enjoy charitable status; but where high fees are charged this may change, unless such institutions can prove that they provide sufficient public benefit to satisfy s 3 of the 2006 Act (see further para 2.21 below).

3. The Advancement of Religion

This purpose was presumed to be charitable prior to the Charities Act 2006. As 2.05 in the case of education, s 3(2) of the Act removes any presumption of public benefit. In s 2(3), religion is further defined as including a religion which involves belief in more than one god and a religion which does not involve belief in a god. This approach is consistent with the modernizing of charity law. In *Re South Place Ethical Society*,[12] two essential attributes of a religion were given as faith in a god and worship of that god. Other characteristics which were important before the 2006 Act included submission to the object worshipped and the veneration of it.[13] In Australia it has been established since 1983 that belief in a supreme being is not necessary to a religion, nor even that a religion should necessarily be theistic.[14] The new Act makes it clear that English law now accepts a wider view of what constitutes a religion. One element of a religion which is still undefined in the Charities Act 2006, though, and which may remain as an essential element in defining what is a religion, is 'worship'. It is clear that as currently interpreted, English law requires a form of worship within a religion, although the official recognition that belief in a deity is not essential could lead to change.[15] Thus, whilst the Charities Act 2006 has modernized the law, in that it provides a statutory definition of what is not necessary in a religion, it has not attempted to define exactly what *is* necessary in a religion. It may be predicted that organizations which have been refused registration as religions may renew their attempts to become registered.[16]

4. The Advancement of Health or the Saving of Lives

The relief of the sick is a well-established charitable purpose, but the idea that it is 2.06 only the 'sick' who may benefit under this head is too narrow. The advancement of health is a wide term which includes the prevention of disease, whether by preventative medicine or the education of the public. The change in the expression of this head of charity reflects the modern position which is much more open and liberal. Even spiritual healing has been recognized as charitable.[17] The advancement of health includes the provision of hospitals and other therapies, including those

---

[12] [1980] 1 WLR 1565. [13] *R v Registrar General, ex p Segerdal* [1970] 2 QB 697.
[14] See *The Church of the New Faith v Commissioners for Payroll Tax* (1983) 154 CLR 120.
[15] See the Charity Commission decision on the Church of Scientology, [1999] Ch Com Dec.
[16] For a discussion concerning human rights and the freedom of religion, see *Tudor*, above, n 2, at paras 2–049 to 2–051.
[17] [2002] Ch Com Dec, 15 August.

directed at mental health as well as physical health. It is also an ingredient in the recognition of the advancement of amateur sport as charitable. It is clear that the saving of lives is also charitable and long-established, eg through the recognition of organizations such as the Royal National Lifeboat Institution.

5. The Advancement of Citizenship or Community Development

2.07   In various framework documents the Charity Commission has argued for the recognition of new charitable purposes which were difficult to argue as being analogous to the Statute of Elizabeth. The promotion of urban and rural development and 'community' building may all be considered under this charitable purpose.[18] The concept of 'citizenship' is not defined, but s 2(3) states that the promotion of 'civic responsibility, volunteering, the voluntary sector or the effectiveness or efficiency of charities' would be included. Whilst it is clear that encouraging participation in socially or economically deprived areas produces public benefit, it may be less clear in some other circumstances, and organizations operating in well-off communities may have difficulty in showing the necessary public benefit. Included under this head are organizations such as the National Council for Voluntary Organizations, which exists as a body established for the purpose of helping other charities to run more effectively, and to provide services to them. The 'community' being developed does not have to be only a geographical community but can be a community of interest too.[19]

6. The Advancement of the Arts, Culture, Heritage, or Science

2.08   The inclusion of this charitable purpose is again uncontroversial in that all the activities listed have already been recognized as charitable. The requirement of public benefit may cause difficulties if the organization wishes to charge large amounts for access to such facilities. The Royal Opera House and other similar organizations may have to demonstrate that public access to their productions is not too restrictive and out of the reach of the majority of the public. 'Science' itself is not defined, but it is extremely unlikely that it is restricted only to natural science, being wide enough to include other previously recognized charitable purposes.[20] The inclusion of heritage as a charitable purpose has long been recognized in practice, with bodies such as the National Trust being familiar to all. There may be scope to argue about the quality of any heritage which some may think worth preserving but others consider worthless. The word itself is undefined in the Charities Act 2006, as is the word 'culture'.

---

[18] See Charities for the Relief of Unemployment (1999) RR3, and also Promotion of Urban and Rural Regeneration (1999) RR2.

[19] For further examples of charities of this type, see *Tudor*, above, n 2, at pp 103 and 113.

[20] An example of this is *Re Pleasants* (1923) 39 TLR 675, in which horticulture was advanced.

7. The Advancement of Amateur Sport

Amateur sport was recognized as a charitable purpose shortly before the Strategy   2.09
Unit Report which led to the Charities Bill. It was an innovative change in the
law. Previously it had been recognized that there might be some public benefit
in advancing sport but that the private enjoyment of participants outweighed
that public benefit.[21] If sport was encouraged to enable organizations such as the
police or the armed forces to function better, or as part of the curriculum in a
school or college,[22] such sport was recognized as being a charitable purpose. The
inclusion of sport as a charitable object recognizes the change in society which now
considers sport to be integral to a healthy lifestyle and the prevention of illness. The
provision of facilities for the community, including sports facilities, was recognized
as charitable in 1958 in the Recreational Charities Act of that year. It is now clear
that the promotion of community participation in healthy recreation is charitable.

'Sport' itself is defined in s 2(3)(e) of the Act as meaning 'sports or games which   2.10
promote health by involving physical or mental skill or exertion'. Community
amateur sports clubs, which are not charities, are entitled to favourable tax treatment
under Sch 18 to the Finance Act 2002. There is guidance from HM Revenue &
Customs which defines terms such as 'amateur', and it might be thought likely
that these definitions might be used in the context of charities too. Some sports
clubs may remain non-charitable if they consider that it would be difficult to meet
the public benefit requirement, or that their subscriptions prevented them from
providing sufficient public benefit. To avoid dual regulation, the Act provides that
if a community amateur sports club is registered under Sch 18 to the Finance Act
2002, it is not a charity.[23]

The Recreational Charities Act 1958 is amended by s 2(4)(a) of the Charities Act   2.11
2006. The amendment is aimed at clarifying s 1 of the 1958 Act. Section 1(2) of
the Recreational Charities Act now reads:

(2) The requirement in subsection 1 that the facilities are provided in the interests of social
welfare cannot be satisfied if the basic conditions are not met.

(2A) The basic conditions are—

(a) that the facilities are provided with the object of improving the conditions of life for the
persons for whom the facilities are primarily intended; and

(b) that either—

   (i) those persons have need of the facilities by reason of their youth, age, infirmity or
   disability, poverty or social and economic circumstances, or

   (ii) the facilities are to be available to members of the public at large or to male, or to
   female, members of the public at large.

The special conditions for miners' welfare trusts are abolished.[24]

---

[21] *Re Nottage* [1895] 2 Ch 649.   [22] *IRC v McMullen* [1981] AC 1.
[23] See s 5(4), (5) of the Charities Act 2006.
[24] See the Miners Welfare Act 1952 and *Wynn v Skegness UDC* [1967] 1 WLR 52.

8. The Advancement of Human Rights, Conflict Resolution or Reconciliation, or the Promotion of Religious or Racial Harmony or Equality and Diversity

2.12   These purposes are new and represent some very modern concerns in society. The Charity Commission has already recognized the promotion of human rights as a charitable purpose.[25] Similar to the promotion of citizenship, the types of organization registered under this head do not have a body of case law to aid the interpretation of the statute. Most of the relevant decisions have been made by the Charity Commission.

9. The Advancement of Environmental Protection or Improvement

2.13   This purpose reflects the growing concern for the protection and the improvement of the environment, and may be considered to be an expanding area of activity for charitable organizations.[26]

10. The Relief of Those in Need by Reason of Youth, Age, Ill-health, Disability, Financial Hardship, or Other Disadvantage

2.14   This purpose is widely drafted and will include organizations such as almshouses, hospices, hostels, etc. Section 2(3)(e) specifically provides that this purpose includes relief given by the provision of accommodation or care to the persons mentioned in this head of charity. 'Care' itself remains undefined. Although this purpose includes the provision of accommodation, it does not exclude other activities designed to aid the people described under this purpose. The provision of advice, advocacy, or day care would all be included here.

11. The Advancement of Animal Welfare

2.15   The inclusion of animal welfare as a directly charitable purpose is new. Prior to the Charities Act 2006, the public benefit in protecting animals was held to be charitable on the grounds that it promoted feelings of humanity and repressed brutality. The public benefit was therefore indirect. In *Re Wedgewood*,[27] it was stated that gifts for animal welfare

> tend to promote and encourage kindness towards them, to discourage cruelty, and to ameliorate the condition of brute creation, and thus to stimulate humane and generous sentiments in man towards the lower animals, and by these means promote feelings of humanity and morality generally, repress brutality, and thus elevate the human race.

---

[25] There are currently 28 registered charities concerning human rights.
[26] See, eg, Agriforestry and Environmental Protection, registered in 1996. Also see the National Society for Clean Air and Environmental Protection, which was registered in 1963.
[27] [1915] 1 Ch 113, at 122.

Animals' usefulness to mankind is also recognized, and therefore their utility 2.16
provides another reason justifying the protection of animals being considered
charitable.[28] Many of the most publicly recognized charities exist for this purpose.
Not all organizations which could be formed for this purpose have been held to be
charitable, though, and there were some notable exceptions prior to the Charities
Act 2006.[29] Sanctuaries for the protection of wild animals against man have been
held not charitable;[30] however, in practice many charities provide nature reserves,
and it is arguable that the protection of wildlife may be included in the advancement
of environmental protection or improvement (see para 2.13 above).

12. The Promotion of the Efficiency of the Armed Forces of the Crown, the Police, Fire, and Rescue Services

The promotion of the efficiency of the armed forces of the Crown has traditionally 2.17
been recognized as charitable.[31] It has been held that sport, if designed to improve
the fitness of forces personnel and therefore their efficiency, does provide public
benefit. Any gift designed to encourage boys (or girls) to become officers within the
forces would have been charitable. Whilst assessments of which activities promote
efficiency in the forces have been liberal, there are limits to what is acceptable.
Learning to shoot alone is now not enough to produce sufficient public benefit[32]
as, in some circumstances, the activity was recreational and produced insufficient
public benefit.

The specific inclusion of the police, fire, and rescue services under this head is 2.18
new. However, the provision of fire services was recognized as charitable in 1951.[33]
Whilst the inclusion of the rescue services under this head is also new, it is possible
to foresee that some organizations will be able to qualify as organizations for the
'saving of lives' and also promote the efficiency of the rescue services.

13. Any Other Purposes within Subsection (4)

This charitable purpose is inclusive and is intended to cover all institutions and 2.19
purposes which are currently recognized as charitable. Anything already recognized
but not included in the list set out in s 2(2) or under the Recreational Charities Act
1958 remains a charitable purpose. Further, any purposes which could be regarded
as analogous to the purposes listed in s 2(2)(a)–(l) will be charitable purposes. The
wording of s 2(4)(b) states that such a purpose should 'reasonably be regarded as
analogous'. This suggests that an objective test will be applied in deciding whether
there is sufficient analogy to a purpose listed in s 2(2)(a)–(l). Initially, such a test
will be applied by the Charity Commission when a charity applies for registration. If

---

[28] *London University v Yarrow* (1857) 1 De G&J 72.
[29] See eg *National Anti-Vivisection Society v IRC* [1948] AC 31.
[30] *Re Grove-Grady* [1929] 1 Ch 557.   [31] *Re Driffill* [1950] Ch 92.
[32] See gun clubs at (1993) 1 Ch Comm Rep, App A.
[33] *Re Wokingham Fire Brigade Trusts* [1951] Ch 373.

either a body or the potential trustees of a charity are refused registration, an appeal may be brought to the Charity Tribunal.[34] If a purpose has been recognized as being charitable as it is for the public benefit, but it is not included in (or analogous to) the listed charitable purposes in s 2(2)(a)–(l), it will still be charitable under the Charities Act 2006.

2.20   The interpretation of the charitable purposes and words used to describe the listed charitable purposes is to remain the same as prior to the 2006 Act.[35] This interpretation effectively means that any words having a particular definition in charity law will continue to have that definition and be interpreted accordingly. Charities established by statute (which declares them to be charitable) will remain charitable.[36] Some charities may be established by Act of Parliament or by Royal Charter,[37] and those continue to enjoy charitable status. In s 2(6), 'documents' referring to charitable purposes are to be interpreted as referring to a charity within s 2(1). Only documents or enactments made before the 2006 Act fall into this category. If a will is made which refers to charitable purposes, and that will was made prior to the Act coming into force, it will be construed as referring to charitable purposes after the Act comes into force.

B. PUBLIC BENEFIT

2.21   The requirement that charitable purposes should be for the public benefit is set out in s 2(1)(b) of the Charities Act 2006. Section 3 applies a public benefit 'test'. However, the Act does not contain any new definition of 'public benefit' or suggest how charities should demonstrate public benefit. Decisions on how the public benefit test will operate will rest with the Commission as the independent regulator for charities in England and Wales, based on underlying case law.

2.22   The document reproduced in Appendix 2 sets out the Charity Commission's approach to the public benefit test in more detail, including the process for consultation and issues concerning fee-charging charities.

2.23   The public benefit test not only applies at the time of registration but also represents a continuing obligation which must be demonstrated by all existing charities in their day-to-day activities and their reporting arrangements. Generally, all existing charities should already be operating for the public benefit in order to take advantage of tax exemptions granted to charities.[38] However, this is the first time such a requirement has been codified in statute.

2.24   The difference is in emphasis. The removal of the presumption of public benefit[39] and the commitment to testing the actual activities of an organization represent a radical change. It is clear that benefits to specific individuals would not qualify;

---

[34] See Sch 4, Charities Act 2006.   [35] Section 2(5).   [36] Section 2(6).
[37] However, see s 15 of the Charities Act 1993, allowing amendments by the court, and also s 16 of the Charities Act 1993.
[38] See *Jones v Williams* (1767) Amb 651.   [39] Charities Act 2006, s 3(2).

but the quantity of benefits may not be the only measure, and it is expected that qualitative judgements will be made and that indirect types of benefit will be taken into account.

Charities which may be affected include those which need to charge substantial   2.25
fees. For example, independent schools, private hospitals and homes, and perhaps institutions such as opera houses. The substantial fees charged by this type of organization have the effect of excluding the less well-off. It is likely that if an institution is charging such fees, it will be found to be unduly restrictive.

Section 3(3) states that references to public benefit are references to public benefit   2.26
'as that term is understood for the purpose of the law relating to charities in England and Wales'. It is therefore necessary to assess some of the cases when there has been an issue relating to the value to the public of various activities. Generally, charities should be for the benefit of the public or a sufficiently large proportion of the public. It has been the function of the court to assess whether or not there is sufficient public benefit to be found.[40] The motive or views of the founder are irrelevant in assessing public benefit.[41] If there was a potential disbenefit to the public, the court would weigh the benefit against the disbenefit in deciding whether or not an organization or body was charitable.[42] Equally public benefit as against private benefit was also measured.[43]

Prior to the Charities Act 2006, charitable purposes were divided into four   2.27
heads.[44] Trusts for the relief of poverty, for the advancement of education, for the advancement of religion, and for other purposes beneficial to the public, were all charitable. The first three purposes could be said to enjoy a presumption that they were established for the public benefit. The court would assess the value or utility to the public of the activity in question and the section of the public who would benefit from that activity. The judgments made involved some qualitative testing and also a quantitative test. It might be thought that there could be a threshold in monetary terms or as to the numbers benefited, but the requisite public benefit often varied according to the type of organization involved. In *IRC v Baddeley*[45] Lord Samervell of Harrow stated that

I cannot accept the principle ... that a section of the public sufficient to support a valid trust in one category must as a matter of law be sufficient to support a trust in any other category. ... There might well be a valid trust for the promotion of religion benefiting a very small class. It would not follow that a recreation ground for the exclusive use of the same class would be a valid charity.

Charity law has developed incrementally by analogy, and it would be surprising   2.28
to find that there was already a definitive test of public benefit to be applied in

---

[40] *Re Hummeltenberg* [1923] 1 Ch 237; *Gilmour v Coates* [1949] AC 426.
[41] *Hoare v Osborne* (1866) LR 1 Eq 585.
[42] *National Anti-Vivisection Society v IRC* [1948] AC 31; and see para 1.09 above.
[43] *Oppenheim v Tobacco Securities Trust Co Ltd* [1951] AC 297.
[44] *Income Tax Special Purposes Commissioners v Pemsel* [1891] AC 531.
[45] [1955] AC 572, at 615.

every situation.[46] It is clear that the Charity Commission intends to follow the approach taken by the court in assessing the presence or absence of public benefit. Particular regard will be paid to the social and economic context within which an organization operates, as well as to the relevant charitable purposes and activities of the organization. An example of changing social contexts can be seen in the case of the General Medical Council, which originally existed as an organization to recover the fees of doctors but which has evolved into a regulatory body. The public benefit in regulating medical education and the standards of medical practice had increased sufficiently to allow a change of status from a private organization to a charity.

2.29   It is possible to foresee that there will be disagreements between the promoters of a potential charity and the Charity Commission as to what is in the public benefit. Lacking public benefit is, of course, grounds for the refusal of registered status.[47] The arts, heritage, and other similar bodies where matters of taste may be important, may have to attempt to show the value of their activities to the public. The type of evidence required to satisfy the Charity Commission is unknown. It is equally foreseeable that 'expert' evidence will be relied on by advisers in seeking to persuade the Charity Commission. The potential for organizations to be innovative or original may be reduced significantly, and there is a danger that innovation will be replaced by the prevailing public opinion at any one time. The removal of the presumption of public benefit combined with the statutory requirement to show public benefit places a positive burden on promoters of potential charities.

2.30   The Charity Commission will be undertaking reviews of various types of charity with a view to assessing public benefit. It is not clear what the consequences will be for charities currently registered but judged to provide inadequate public benefit. The possibility is that they may be regarded as having been included on the register by mistake,[48] and as such as never having been charities. Alternatively, it might appear that an institution was charitable at its inception but has since ceased to be regarded as such. If that happens then there will be a cy-près situation[49] and the assets of the former charity could be applied to some other purpose which is clearly charitable. The Charity Commission is highly likely to encourage and help trustees to remedy the situation and increase the public benefit provided by the charity threatened with de-registration. Potentially, a charity may increase the public benefit it provides by merging with another charity, thus diluting any perceived disproportionate private benefit.

---

[46] The 'poor relations' cases are an example of an anomaly created by this approach which would now fail to satisfy the public benefit test. See *Dingle v Turner* [1972] AC 601.

[47] Disagreement on this issue is not novel; see *Re Pinion* [1965] Ch 85, where it was stated that there was no public utility in 'foisting on the public this mass of junk'.

[48] This happened in 1965 when the Eclusive Bretheren was registered by mistake when registration first began.

[49] See Chapter 10.

Section 4 of the Charities Act 2006 provides that the Charity Commission must   2.31
provide guidance in pursuance of its public benefit objective.[50] That objective is
described in the Act as being to promote awareness and understanding of the
public benefit test in s 3. The guidance may be revised from time to time, and
the Charity Commission is required to carry out public consultations or 'other'
consultations before issuing any guidance or revising such guidance. Any guidance
must be published, but the manner of such publication is as the Charity Commission
considers appropriate. It seems likely that the guidance will be available on the
website of the Charity Commission.[51] There is an obligation on charity trustees,
when exercising any powers or duties to which the guidance is relevant, to have
regard to it. On making decisions in board meetings trustees may wish expressly to
consider the issue of public benefit and state whether or how the current guidance
might affect their decisions.

---

[50] See Chapter 3 and s 7 of the Charities Act 2006 for a complete list of the Charity Commission's
objectives.
[51] See <http://www.charity-commission.gov.uk>.

3

THE CHARITY COMMISSION

A. ESTABLISHMENT OF THE CHARITY COMMISSION

The Charity Commission occupies s 1 of the Charities Act 1993, which states   3.01
that there shall be a body of Charity Commissioners for England and Wales.
Section 1(2) of the 1993 Act incorporates Sch 1 to the 1993 Act, which provides
for the constitution of the Charity Commission. The Charities Act 2006 inserts
new ss 1A–1E after s 1 of the 1993 Act.[1] The new s 1A(6) states that both s 1
of and Sch 1 to the 1993 Act cease to have effect. All references to the Charity
Commission prior to the 2006 Act are deemed to apply to the newly incorporated
Charity Commission.

The Charity Commission will, from the date when the relevant section comes   3.02
into force, be a corporate body, and there will be a Welsh name for the Charity
Commission too. The Commission will perform its functions on behalf of the
Crown, but shall not be subject to the control of any Minister or other government
department. The Charity Commission will maintain its independence from the
Government in this respect. Ministers have no capacity to direct or reverse any of
the Commission's decisions, and it is perceived in the voluntary sector that the
Commission acts in promoting public awareness of the sector and the Government's
awareness of charities and their concerns. The Commission remaining independent
may help to insulate the sector from political interests, despite the move towards a
greater provision of public services by the voluntary sector. In the 'partnership' of
the voluntary sector and the Government[2] the Charity Commission occupies part
of the middle ground, helping the sector but also regulating it, and reporting to the
Government[3] when required.

---

[1] A consolidating statute is expected in the near future which should allow for much easier reading
of the various amendments made to the Charities Act 1993 by the Charities Act 2006.

[2] See Introduction, p xvii above.

[3] See also the Office of the Third Sector.

3.03   Nevertheless, independent, administrative control over the Commission's expenditure is reserved to the Treasury,[4] and the Commission's role may be affected 'by or under any enactment'. It may be that the Charity Commission could be or become merely the secondary regulator for certain types or classes of charity. Section 13(2) of the 2006 Act sets out the duty of the principal regulator, and s 13(4) defines the principal regulator as 'such body or Minister of the Crown as is prescribed as its principal regulator by regulations made by the Secretary of State'.[5]

3.04   The composition of the Charity Commission is set out in Sch 1A which is inserted into the 1993 Act. There will be a Chairman and between four and eight other members. If all the posts are filled, there will be nine members of the Commission including the Chairman. All are appointed by the Minister. The aim of the appointments should be to ensure that those appointed have relevant experience in the sector. There should be two legally qualified members of over seven years' standing. Additionally, at least one member who knows about conditions in Wales should be appointed following consultation with the National Assembly for Wales. Members are expected to have knowledge of the law relating to charities, charity accounts and the financing of charities, and of the operation of different charities. Appointment as a member of the Charity Commission is normally for a three-year term and the only grounds (other than resignation) for removal of a member are incapacity or misbehaviour.[6] The maximum total length of service is ten years. The members of the Commission may establish committees, and it not necessary that the members of such committees should be members of the Charity Commission.

3.05   Schedule 1 to the Charities Act 2006 provides for the procedure and mechanics of actually running the Charity Commission. Provisions for the delegation of functions and powers to staff, the execution of documents, and the validity of documents are included. Deeds executed by the Commission are to be effective from the date of their delivery and it is presumed that delivery took place simultaneously with execution.[7] The Act also defines who is a 'purchaser' of property. A purchaser is a purchaser in good faith for valuable consideration.

3.06   It is a mandatory requirement for the Charity Commission to issue an annual report[8] at each year end. In common with many public bodies, the end of the financial year is stated to be 31 March. There is some flexibility on the date for the publication of each report, as such report is to be published at the year end but also as soon as 'practicable'. The contents of the report should comment on the discharge of the functions of the Charity Commission and whether, in the opinion of the Commission, the objectives of the Commission have been met. The management of the Commission will also be addressed in the report. The report

---

    [4] Charities Act 1993, s 1B(5).
    [5] The scheme of the 2006 Act envisages 'block exemptions' from regulation by the Charity Commission. See s 11.
    [6] Sch 1 to the 2006 Act, which also makes provision for the staffing of the Commission and its structure.
    [7] Charities Act 1993, Sch 1A, para 10(4).
    [8] This is similar to the current annual report issued by the Charity Commission.

will be laid before Parliament each year. Under Sch 1A, para 12 to the 1993 Act, the Charity Commission is obliged to hold a public meeting, within three months of the date of publication of the report, for the purpose of considering the annual report. This requirement is new and quite innovative, and is designed to increase the transparency and accountability of the Charity Commission to the public. It is envisaged in the Act that the Charity Commission will allow a general discussion of the contents of the annual report and provide an opportunity for attendees to put questions to the Commission on matters to which the report relates.

Apart from allowing general discussion and questions, the Charity Commission   3.07
may otherwise organize the public meeting in any way it considers appropriate. Reasonable notice of the meeting should be given to every registered charity and notice of the annual meeting should also be publicized to the general public. Public notice should be calculated to bring the meeting to the attention of the public, but there are no other specific methods prescribed for giving notice. The notices are required to state the time, place, duration, and agenda of the meeting, and to give details which are designed to enable people to attend. Although such an opportunity to discuss the contents of the annual report is a welcome initiative, and may increase public knowledge and participation in matters connected with charity or the voluntary sector, the agenda may be restricted as the public meeting concerns the contents of the annual report. The quality of each annual report is therefore a significant factor in dictating the content and general interest in attending the public meeting. Initially, it can be predicted that the reports and meetings will be unremarkable. Eventually, the report may include statistics, such as the number of reviews requested by charities and the results of referrals to the Charity Tribunal, which may provide an interesting insight into the evolution of the role of the Charity Commission under the Charities Act 2006.

The Charities Act 2006, Sch 2 contains mainly transitional provisions to ensure   3.08
that acts done by or on behalf of the Charity Commission continue to be valid during the period of commencement of the new Act. Existing office holders continue to hold office but in the new Commission.

B. THE COMMISSION'S OBJECTIVES, GENERAL FUNCTIONS, AND DUTIES

1. The Commission's Objectives

The Charities Act 2006 inserts an entirely new concept into the Charities Act 1993.   3.09
The new s 1B sets out the Charity Commission's objectives. The five objectives and whether the Charity Commission has met them are matters to be included in the annual report.[9] The five objectives are:

(a) the public confidence objective;

---

[9] See para 3.07 above.

(b) the public benefit objective;

(c) the compliance objective;

(d) the charitable resources objective; and

(e) the accountability objective.

3.10   'Public confidence' is defined as increasing public confidence and trust in charities. As noted earlier, the voluntary sector enjoys a privileged position in society. The privilege is not only fiscal; the concept of charity is widely approved of and supported by the general public. Aggressive fundraising techniques may have slightly tarnished the public perception of charity, but most charities already occupy an indulged position in the minds of the public.[10] In the absence of large-scale or widespread exploitation and fraud, it is difficult to predict how the 'increase' in public trust and confidence is to be achieved. Measuring such an increase may be difficult too, and other than the annual commissioning of public opinion polls, it may be difficult to show that this objective is being met. The recent, quick Charity Commission response to disasters may show where such an increase in public trust is being experienced. By responding quickly in setting up committees of charities or new charitable funds in response to disasters, natural or even financial,[11] the public wishing to give aid can be confident that any gifts will reach their target. Generally, fundraising also continues to be regulated.[12]

3.11   The public benefit objective is to promote awareness and understanding of the operation of the public benefit requirement.[13] The Charity Commission has published an indicative programme entitled 'Taking forward public benefit',[14] which sets out a consultation programme. There will be a Citizen's Forum exploring research, public perceptions, and expectations of what 'public benefit' is. From January 2007 there will be public consultation on public benefit, the principles, how to demonstrate it, and how it might be assessed. By March 2007 it is anticipated that analysis of the findings will be undertaken by the Charity Commission, and this will be followed by discussions between charity sub-sectors on the application of the principles. The principles of public benefit are not expected to be published until June 2007. Detailed guidance appropriate to different sectors of charities will be issued from September 2007. The assessment of public benefit in September 2007 is described as a 'pilot assessment' and formal assessment will not be undertaken before April 2008. A report to Parliament is expected to be made in the summer of 2008. Any interested members of sub-sectors of the voluntary sector may wish to consider

---

[10] In oral evidence to the Joint Committee on the Draft Charities Bill, Fiona McTaggart MP told the Committee that, 'I think the purpose of the Bill is, the fundamental purpose of the Bill is to protect from the risk of decline' and 'the best time to protect a brand is when it is still all right, not when it is seriously at risk' (in answer to questions 976 and 967).

[11] Tsunami disaster appeal committee, and the 'Farepak' savings scheme collapse.

[12] See Charities Act 2006, Pt 3, Ch 1, ss 45 to 66.

[13] See Chapter 2. Section 1B(4) relates this objective directly to the public benefit test in s 2.

[14] See <http://www.charitycommission.gov.uk>.

providing input during the consultation phases to ensure full understanding by the
Charity Commission of issues which may be specific to their types of charity.

The compliance objective is to promote compliance by charity trustees with their   3.12
legal obligations in exercising control and management of the administration of
charities. This objective is designed to 'promote compliance' with legal requirements
rather than actually to regulate, as much more detailed provisions concerning items
such as accounts are included later in the Act.

The charitable resources objective is defined as the promotion of the effective use   3.13
of charitable resources—an obligation already placed on the Commissioners by the
Charities Act 1993.

The accountability objective is designed to increase the accountability of charities   3.14
to donors, beneficiaries, and the public.

2. The Commission's General Functions

Section 1C is also inserted into the Charities Act 1993 and describes the Charity   3.15
Commission's six general functions. These functions are described very widely and
include matters such as deciding whether an organization or institution is a charity,
encouraging and facilitating better administration, identifying and investigating
misconduct or mismanagement, giving advice, information, or proposals to any
Minister of the Crown, obtaining information in relation to the performance of its
own duties, and determining the issue of public collections certificates. The fifth and
sixth general functions are expressed to be the maintenance of an accurate register[15]
and responding to Minister's requests for information and/or advice.

3. The Commission's General Duties

The Charity Commission's general duties are contained in new s 1D of the 1993 Act.   3.16
At first sight the duties appear to be expressed as mandatory, but the description
of the methods of carrying out such duties is so widely drafted that there is a
large degree of discretion. The general duties all relate to the performance of the
functions of the Charity Commission. The Commission must act in a way which
is compatible with its objectives in so far as this is 'reasonably practicable', and in
a way which is most appropriate for the purpose of meeting the objectives. There
is a duty, with the same qualifications as above, to encourage charitable giving
and voluntary participation in charity work. The Charity Commission must 'have
regard' to the need to use its own resources effectively in the performance of its
functions. Section 1D(2)4 introduces a statutory form of public duty expected of
a public body such as the Charity Commission. In performing its functions the
Commission must have regard to the principles of best regulatory practice and
to the concepts of proportionality, accountability, consistency, and transparency.
Any action should be aimed only at cases in which action is needed. Concern that

---

[15] See Chapter 4.

regulation may stifle innovation is addressed by the inclusion of the duty of the Commission to have regard to the desirability, in appropriate cases, of facilitating innovation by charities. There is no guidance in the Act as to what may or may not be an appropriate case, but the Charity Commission publishes operational guidance on its website, and this may be a topic for such guidance in future.

4. The Commission's Incidental Powers

3.17   The insertion of s 1E into the Charities Act 1993 provides that the Charity Commission 'has power to do anything which is incidental to the performance of any of its functions and general duties'. Any act must merely be calculated to facilitate that performance. The Commission's incidental powers are very wide in pursuit of its objectives, and are limited only by the qualification in s 1E(2) which states that nothing in the Act authorizes the Commission to exercise functions corresponding to those of a charity trustee or otherwise act in the actual administration of a charity. This limitation is consistent with current Charity Commission practice and not novel. The limitation itself is, however, further qualified. It does not apply in cases where the powers of the Charity Commission are utilized under s 19A or 19B of the Charities Act 1993.[16] Section 19A applies after an inquiry into the charity has been instituted and some misconduct or mismanagement has been found. In those circumstances the Charity Commission may make directions for the protection of charity.[17] A similar power is contained in s 19B.[18] The Charity Commission may direct the application of charity property in some circumstances.[19]

---

[16] See later, Chapter 5.
[17] See Charities Act 2006, s 20, which inserts s 19A into the Charities Act 1993.
[18] See Charities Act 2006, s 21, which inserts s 19B into the Charities Act 1993.
[19] See also the increased regulation of exempt charities contained in Sch 5 to the Charities Act 2006.

4

REGISTRATION OF CHARITIES

A. THE REGISTER OF CHARITIES

The established register under the Charities Act 1993 will continue to operate. 4.01
Under the 1993 Act (s 3), the legislation sets out the scheme of the registration.
The Commission is given the duty of maintaining the register of charities and the
power to remove charities if they cease to be charitable or cease to act. A list of
exempt charities is given in Sch 2 to the 1993 Act. Other significant exemptions
derive from other enactments. An example of this would be education corporations
within the meaning of the Further and Higher Education Act 1992. The scheme
of the provisions on registration is therefore that there will be a register, with the
Commission deciding how best to maintain that register; there will be specific
exemptions from the requirement to register listed in a schedule; and there are
certain enactments which give a 'block' exemption from registration. Under the
1993 Act certain very small charities[1] were also exempt from registration. Under
the Charities Act 2006, all charities whose gross income does not exceed £5,000 are
exempt from registration.[2]

---

[1] Those having an income of less than £1,000.
[2] Section 3A(2)(d) of the Charities Act 1993, inserted by s 9 of the Charities Act 2006.

4.02   The Charities Act 2006 substitutes a new s 3 for the old s 3 of the 1993 Act. The essential scheme of the new provision is the same as under the 1993 Act. There will continue to be a register of charities, which may be kept by the Commission in such manner as it thinks fit. The name of every registered charity should be on the register, plus such other particulars and information relating to every charity as the Commission thinks fit. The Commission must remove from the register any institution which it no longer believes to be a charity and those ceasing to exist or operate. If an institution changes its trusts and is consequently removed, the date of removal is taken to be the date of the change in the trust.

4.03   Section 3(7), (8), and (9) of the Charities Act 2006 exactly replicate existing provisions in the 1993 legislation. These provisions relate to the public accessibility of the register. The register shall be open to inspection by the public at all reasonable times, and any information should be in legible form. The current practice is that the register is available electronically. The governing documents of a charity are not currently available in electronic form, but it is anticipated that the amount of information appearing on the electronic version of the register will expand. Entries which have been cancelled shall also be included on the register but the Commission may determine exactly what information concerning cancelled entries is to be available. At the moment, copies of all registered charities' governing documents which are held by the Charity Commission are available for public inspection. This remains the same under the new legislation. The ability of the public to inspect the trusts of a registered charity is limited by an exception. If the relevant Minister makes regulations concerning specified charities or charities of a certain description or type, the right of the public to inspect the trusts may be limited. It is envisaged that in some 'circumstances as are so specified' in regulations, the right to inspect could be limited.

B. REGISTRATION OF CHARITIES

4.04   Following the previous scheme of registration under the 1993 Act, s 3A, inserted into the 1993 Act by s 9 of the Charities Act 2006, provides a general duty to register charities with the Charity Commission. Every charity must be registered, unless it falls within the categories specified in s 3A(2).[3] Exempt charities (those listed in the new Sch 2 replacing the old Sch 2), smaller excepted charities, and small charities do not have to register.[4]

C. DUTIES OF TRUSTEES IN RELATION TO REGISTRATION

4.05   An express statutory duty is placed on charity trustees to apply for registration under s 3B as inserted by s 9 of the Charities Act 2006. In accordance with the duty to

---

[3] It is the duty of the charity trustees to apply for registration; see s 3B of the Charities Act 1993 as inserted by s 9 of the Charities Act 2006.
[4] See later at paras 4.05–4.07.

apply is a corresponding duty on the trustees to supply the Charity Commission with the required documents and information considered necessary to decide the whether the body should or should not be registered. Copies, or particulars, of the charity's trusts are required. The trustees' (or promoters') duty includes providing the Commission with 'such other documents as may be prescribed by regulations made by the Secretary of State' and 'such other documents or information as the Commission may require' for the purposes of the application for registration.

If the institution ceases to exist, or if there are changes in the trusts or a change in the particulars registered, then it is the trustees' duty to inform the Charity Commission and to supply details of the changes. This duty, which already applies under the existing law, aids the Charity Commission in the performance of its general function in maintaining an accurate register. Any scheme made with respect to a charity is not included in this duty unless the scheme is settled by the court. This is because, generally, it will be the Charity Commission that will make such a scheme in any event. Schemes will be open to inspection by the public too.[5]

D. INTERIM CHANGES IN THE THRESHOLD FOR REGISTRATION OF SMALL CHARITIES

At any time before the commencement of s 9 (and therefore the provisions of the new s 3), the relevant Minister may, by order, change the threshold of registration for small charities under the existing s 3 of the 1993 Act. Small charities are defined by reference to their gross income in any year. It is arguable that all new charities being established and applying for registration will be unable to show a figure in accounts for gross income. Section 3A(10) provides that the expression 'gross income' is to be construed in relation to a particular time, ie the gross income in the financial year immediately preceding that time, or, if the Commission determines, as an estimate by the Commission as to the likely amount of the gross income of a charity. Any order made pursuant to the interim measures in s 10 of the Charities Act 2006 cannot be made after the day on which s 9 comes into effect.

E. CHANGES IN EXEMPT CHARITIES

As stated at para 4.04 above, various types of charities are exempt from registration with the Charity Commission. Schedule 2 to the Charities Act 1993 lists various charities which were exempt prior to the Charities Act 2006. There are 28 categories of exempt charity listed in that schedule (less after various amendments) but it is difficult to classify the listed charities in any particular way. Certain listed universities are exempt from registration, such as Oxford and Cambridge, among

4.06

4.07

4.08

---

[5] See s 3B(5) of the Charities Act 1993 as inserted by s 9 of the Charities Act 2006.

others. Universities established by the Queen, which are declared as exempt, are included. Higher education corporations are also exempt, as are the Boards of Trustees of various nationally important museums such as the Victoria and Albert Museum. Church Commissioners, Industrial and Provident Societies, and Friendly Societies are exempt, as is the National Lottery Charities Board. Winchester College and Eton College were also exempt from registration with the Charity Commission.

4.09   Exempt charities are charities not registered with the Commission for the reason that they are already being supervised by other regulators, such as government departments or public authorities. Examples of this type of exempt charity are housing associations and some schools. Such bodies have charitable status and enjoy fiscal benefits like any other charity, it is simply the exemption from registration which is different. The principles of charity law apply to exempt charities as to registered charities, but some of the powers exercised by the Charity Commission under the 1993 Act related only to registered charities. Such charities may be thought to be less transparent and less accountable in comparison with registered charities. Evidence presented to the Joint Committee on the Draft Charities Bill estimated that there were around 10,000 exempt charities.

4.10   Evidence showed that the regulators of some exempt charities were often unaware of the requirements of charity law, and there was no mechanism for the monitoring and compliance of exempt charities with charity law. Additionally, it was suggested that such charities ought to demonstrate that they continue to merit the benefits obtained by having charitable status, such as fiscal advantages. Such potential anomalies were thought by the Strategy Unit Review to confuse the public and threatened the integrity of the status of charities.

4.11   The Home Office estimates that changes to the regulation of exempt charities will bring around 7,800 such charities within the Charity Commission's powers to investigate, albeit at the request of their principal regulator. The concept of the principal regulator is not new[6] but has taken on a greater importance in the new Act. Specific amendments to Sch 2 to the 1993 Act are contained in s 11 of the Charities Act 2006. From the list of exempted charities, the Colleges of Winchester and Eton and the colleges of the Universities of Oxford, Cambridge, and Durham are omitted. Higher education corporations and further education corporations continue to be exempt. The Church Commissioners and institutions administered by them are no longer exempt from registration. Registered social landlords under Pt 1 of the Housing Act 1996, if charitable, are exempt, but other charitable Industrial and Provident Societies have lost their exemption. Even though many universities are exempt, the students' unions attached to them will be registrable. Section 11(12) allows the relevant Minister to make further amendments to Sch 2 'as he considers appropriate' for securing that specific institutions, or institutions of a particular description, cease to be exempt. The schedule may be amended further if one of the listed institutions ceases to exist.

---

[6] See eg *Construction Industry Training Board v Attorney General* [1973] Ch 173; [1972] 2 All ER 1339.

At the time the Draft Bill was being debated, concern was expressed at the   4.12
position of voluntary schools established under the Education Reform Act 1988.
Objections were raised that these schools, which were part of the state schools
system and (if charitable) were previously excepted, would have to register and
would bear extra administrative costs in complying with additional accounting
and audit requirements. A second issue concerning the nature of the principal
regulator's role and the role of the Charity Commission, and the relationship
between them, was raised, particularly in relation to higher education. A third
concern was voiced by some charities whose activities may fall to be regulated by a
different principal regulator. It was thought that various bodies acting as principal
regulator would not be familiar with charity law, and the idea that they would then
go to the Charity Commission when regulation failed was thought to be unrealistic.
A principal regulator would probably be most reluctant to consult with the Charity
Commission in the light of its own failed regulation. Certain charities considered
that all regulation of charities ought to be undertaken by one regulator. It was
recommended that voluntary and foundation schools should continue to be exempt
and that the Home Office should consider designating a principal regulator for
these types of schools.

F. INCREASED REGULATION OF EXEMPT CHARITIES

Schedule 5 to the Charities Act 2006 contains provisions which increase the   4.13
regulation of exempt charities under the 1993 Act. Section 12 of the 2006 Act
inserts the new schedule. The Charity Commission may require the name of an
exempt charity to be changed. It may institute an inquiry into an exempt charity
where this has been requested by the principal regulator of that charity. Other
powers include the power to call for documents. The provisions in Sch 5 alter the
1993 Act and they operate effectively by omitting many of the references in the
1993 Act which have had the effect of excluding exempt charities from various
obligations under the Act. Schedule 5, para 4 establishes the Charity Commission's
jurisdiction over exempt charities. Section 18 of the 1993 Act is important, as it is
this section that establishes the use of the Charity Commission's powers where there
has been an inquiry into the charity's affairs. Under this section the Commission
may make a range of orders for the protection of the charity. Section 18(16)
had provided that the section did not apply to exempt charities. This is now
substituted by Sch 5, para 6, which has the effect of bringing exempt charities
within these extensive powers. Where there are proceedings, exempt charities will
now need the permission of the Commission under s 33 of the Charities Act
1993 as amended by the 2006 Act. Similarly, any such proceedings must also be
within the jurisdiction of the Attorney-General. Various other powers are extended
to exempt charities, such as the power to give directions about dormant bank
accounts and the power to order disqualified persons to repay money received from
a charity.

G. GENERAL DUTY OF THE PRINCIPAL REGULATOR IN RELATION TO EXEMPT CHARITIES

4.14   Section 13 of the Charities Act 2006 applies to any body or Minister of the Crown who is the principal regulator in relation to an exempt charity. The section places a duty on such regulators to meet the compliance objective in relation to the charity.[7]Principal regulators are not placed under the same extensive objectives as the Charity Commission as the section concentrates on legal compliance only. The standard of the regulator's duty is set out as having to do 'all that it or he reasonably can' to meet the compliance objective.[8] The regulator should promote compliance with legal obligations in exercising control and management of the administration of the charity. The principal regulator is defined in s 13(4)(b) as such body or Minister of the Crown as prescribed as its principal regulator by regulations made by the relevant Minister. A Minister may make regulations for the purpose of facilitating or discharging the duty under this section.

H. CHARITY COMMISSION DUTY

4.15   Following the recommendation by the Joint Committee on the Draft Charities Bill, the Charity Commission is to consult with the principal regulator of exempt charities prior to exercising any of the powers granted under Sch 5 to the Charities Act 2006.[9]

I. EXCEPTED CHARITIES

4.16   Excepted charities are charities which are excepted from the requirement to register with the Charity Commission but which otherwise are technically subject to its supervision. Registration of charities began in the 1960s, and some charities were already registered with their own umbrella or support groups. Examples of such charities are Guide and Scout groups. Some armed forces charities also fall within this category. Similar to exempt charities, in not being registered, these organizations also have to comply with the principles of charity law, but it was also perceived that transparency and accountability were lacking and that the Commission's regulation of them was in many cases inadequate.

4.17   Charities may be excepted 'permanently or temporarily' by order of the Commission. It is envisaged that exceptions may have conditions attached. It is likely that such conditions will relate to achieving the legal compliance objective. Any

---

[7] See above, para 3.12.   [8] Charities Act 2006, s 13(2).
[9] A new s 86(A) is inserted into the 1993 Act by s 14 of the Charities Act 2006.

charity which would be excepted but has an income of over £100,000, would have to be registered. It is likely that in future the threshold figure which would trigger registration of an otherwise excepted charity will be lowered. The figure of £100,000 was chosen until the costs to such charities in complying with the registration requirement have been assessed in practice. The administrative burden on the Charity Commission in the year immediately after the passing of the 2006 Act will also be great, and setting the threshold at such a level may be realistic in the circumstances. Charities may also be excepted in the same way by regulations made by the relevant Minister. Orders by the Commission, and regulations made by the relevant Minister, must be made prior to the day that the relevant provision comes into force, as s 3A(3) and (4) impose a general prohibition on new exception orders.

5

COMMISSION ASSISTANCE AND SUPERVISION OF CHARITIES BY COURT AND COMMISSION

A. GENERAL

The Charity Commissioners were first established in 1858 and the institution has 5.01 evolved into its new corporate form.[1] The powers of the Charity Commission have increased over time, and there has also been an increase in the monitoring and control of charities. The Charities Act 2006 for the first time states the objectives of the Charity Commission in statutory form. The existing powers of the Charity Commission under the Charities Act 1993 are extensive, and the provisions of the Charities Act 2006 are designed to enhance those existing powers. In order to appreciate the extent of the role played by the Charity Commission in assisting and supervising charities at present, reference must be made to the provisions of the 1993 Act. The additions in the Charities Act 2006 enhance these powers in nine specific areas. The power to suspend or remove trustees and members from charities in certain circumstances, the power to act for the protection of charity, the power to direct the application of charity property, and the power to make schemes, all are altered in some way under the Charities Act 2006. The power to remove or discharge trustees without their consent, the power to give advice and guidance, and the power to determine the membership of a charity all appear in the new provisions in the Charities Act 2006. Enhanced powers to enter premises for certain purposes, and the power to approve mortgages by charities, have also been altered.

---

[1] See Chapter 3.

B. THE EXISTING POWERS OF THE CHARITY COMMISSION

5.02   The Charity Commission is responsible for the maintenance of an accurate register,[2] and the decision whether or not to enter an organization or institution on the Register of Charities rests with the Charity Commission under ss 3 and 3A of the Charities Act 1993.[3] The new s 69E, inserted by the Charities Act 2006, includes the power of the Charity Commission to register a Charitable Incorporated Organization ('CIO').[4] Equally, removal of a body from the register lies with the Charity Commission. The contents of the register, other than those required by legislation, also rest with the Charity Commission. The Commission may require a charity to change its name if necessary, and such a power may be used if it is felt that there is confusion, or likely to be confusion, about the true identity of any organization.

5.03   Inquiries[5] with regard to a particular charity or class of charity may be instituted by the Charity Commission, either generally or for particular purposes. In conducting an inquiry the Commission may undertake the inquiry itself, or appoint someone else to carry out the inquiry. The obtaining of documents and financial records and the taking of evidence under oath are all within this power. The results of such inquiries may be published by the Charity Commission.[6] Section 9 of the Charities Act 1993 grants the Commission a power to call for documents and to search records. These types of powers are supervisory in nature.

5.04   Many powers which concern the administration of a charity are within the jurisdiction of the Charity Commission. Section 16 of the Charities Act 1993 states that the Charity Commission shares concurrent jurisdiction with the High Court for certain purposes. Those purposes include establishing a scheme for the administration of a charity, appointing and removing trustees, vesting or transferring property, and settling the terms of schemes ordered by the High Court. Limitations to these powers are built into s 16 and generally the Commission may not exercise the powers in cases which are very contentious and more appropriate for determination by the court. The powers are exercisable at the request of the trustees.

5.05   The Charity Commission may act for the protection of charities where an inquiry has revealed misconduct or mismanagement and it is thought desirable to act for that purpose. The powers include the removal of trustees and ordering the repayment of money to a charity. Unlike the purely administrative powers, the powers exercised in the context of evidence of misconduct can be exercised by the Charity Commission on its own motion rather than on application by the charity or charity trustees. Appointment of a new trustee may be ordered under s18 of the Charities Act 1993. The Commission is at liberty to review and discharge orders made under s 18.[7]

---

[2] See Chapter 4.   [3] Ibid.   [4] See Chapter 7.
[5] See s 8 of the Charities Act 1993.
[6] These are currently published on the Commission website, <http://www.charitycommission.gov.uk>.
[7] Charities Act 1993, s 18(13).

The power to make common investment schemes is also within the remit of 5.06
the Charity Commission under s 24 of the Charities Act 1993. Similarly, the
Commission may refuse to make a common deposit scheme under s 25 of the same
Act. Additional powers of the Charity Commission which are commonly used in
the administration of charities can be found in s 26 of the 1993 Act. Trustees may
apply to the Charity Commission for approval of acts which they wish to undertake
in administering the charity. Particular transactions may be authorized and general
authority may also be sought. Particular expenditure may be sanctioned under this
section. If an order is given then the action is deemed to have been properly done
by the trustees. Ex gratia payments may be authorized by order of the Charity
Commission. Dormant bank accounts containing charitable funds may be ordered
to be transferred and directions as to the application of such funds can be made.[8]

A general power to advise charity trustees is contained in s 29 of the Charities Act 5.07
1993, and in the absence of bad faith or misleading information, any written advice
given under this section is deemed to be sufficient discharge of the trustees' duty
and to have been done in accordance with the trusts of the charity. The safe custody
of documents is also within the power of the Commission.[9] The Commission
has a specific power to order the taxation of solicitors' bills and to authorize the
taking of proceedings by charity trustees or other interested persons.[10] In certain
circumstances the Commission may consent to the disposal of charity land and to
the mortgaging of land held by a charity.

Accounts of a charity may be ordered to be audited[11] and independent examina- 5.08
tion of accounts may be directed.[12] The Charity Commission may grant a certificate
of incorporation to the trustees of a charity under s 50 of the Charities Act 1993,
and it may also amend such a certificate.[13] Any conditions associated with such
incorporation may be enforced by the Charity Commission. If such a body has no
assets, does not operate, and has effectively ceased to exist, the Commission may
dissolve the incorporated body.

Charitable companies may apply to the Charity Commission for consent to alter 5.09
their objects clauses,[14] setting out the purpose of that company, and for consent
to ratify[15] acts or transfers to associated or connected persons.[16] Under s 69(1) of
the Charities Act 1993, the Charity Commission may require an investigation and
audit of a charitable company's accounts, and appoint a company auditor[17] for this
purpose. Such an appointed auditor may ask questions and request explanations
from any charity trustee, past or present. Directions can be made to secure that any

---

[8] See s 28 of the Charities Act 1993; this power is now extended to exempt charities under Sch 5
to the Charities Act 2006.
[9] Charities Act 1993, s 30.   [10] Charities Act 1993, s 32 and s 33.
[11] Charities Act 1993, s 43(4).
[12] But also see Charities Act 1993, s 46, applying to exempt and excepted charities, and Sch 6, paras
11 and 12 to the Charities Act 2006 concerning group accounts for these charities.
[13] Section 56(4) of the Charities Act 1993.
[14] Charities Act 1993, s 64(2).   [15] Charities Act 1993, s 65(4).
[16] See s 35A of the Companies Act 1985 and also s 322A of the Companies Act 1985.
[17] See s 25 of the Companies Act 1989.

default is made good. Various other powers already exist under the Charities Act 1993, which are exercised by the Charity Commission in its role as supervisor of and adviser to charities.[18]

C. CHANGES IN THE CHARITIES ACT 2006

5.10 Apart from the necessary alterations which extend the powers of the Charity Commission in some circumstances under the Act,[19] there are some specific changes to the powers of the Charity Commission.

1. Power to Suspend or Remove Trustees

5.11 Section 18 of the Charities Act 1993 is amended by the inclusion of a new s 18A. As seen at para 5.05 above, this section concerns the Charity Commission's power to act for the protection of charity at any time after an inquiry has been instituted and where the Charity Commission is satisfied on two different matters. First, the Commission may act if it is satisfied that there has been misconduct or mismanagement in the administration of the charity. Secondly, the Charity Commission may act for the protection of charity if it is considered necessary or desirable for the purpose of protecting the property of that charity, or for securing the proper application of that property or property coming to the charity.

5.12 The Charity Commission may order the following actions on its own motion. The Commission may:

(a) suspend any trustee, charity trustee, officer, agent, or employee of the charity from the exercise of his office or employment, pending the consideration of his removal;

(b) appoint additional trustees by order, and vest any property held in trust for the charity in the official custodian;[20]

(c) order any person to transfer such property to the official custodian.[21] If such an order has been made under s 18 then any trustee may not deal with the property of the charity without the prior consent of the Charity Commission. Payments of money, both into and by the charity, may require the consent of the Charity Commission under s 18 of the Charities Act 1993; and

(d) appoint a manager and receiver in respect of the property and affairs of the charity.

---

[18] See Charities Act 1993, ss 72, 73, 79, 80, and 96.

[19] Such as the amendments to the registration sections concerning the institution of the new form of charitable incorporated organization.

[20] See ss 21 and 22 of the Charities Act 1993.

[21] The official custodian simply holds the property on behalf of the charity and does not exercise any of the functions of trustees with respect to the management and control of the charity.

The actions are not mutually exclusive and the Charity Commission may order one or more of the actions specified in s 18 at once.

The suspension of trustees or persons responsible for or privy to the misconduct may lead to their removal under s 18. The Commission may make a scheme for the administration of the charity. Any of the powers under s 16 of the Charities Act 1993 can also be used in the context of s18 and the protection of charity. A suspension of a trustee is subject to a one-year limitation. The Commission is under an obligation to review the order made under s 18, and if appropriate it may discharge such order.

    5.13

Prior to the enactment of the Charities Act 2006, the Charity Commission only had the jurisdiction to suspend or remove 'trustees, charity trustees, officers or agents and employees' from the exercise of their office. Any person so suspended or removed could remain as a member of the charity. The new s 18A empowers the Commission to suspend the membership of the charity of a person who has been suspended from office. The suspension of membership applies during the period that the officer is also suspended from office or employment.

    5.14

If a person is removed from his office or employment under the provisions of s 18 then an order terminating that person's membership of the charity can now also be made. Resumption of membership may be made only with the consent of the Charity Commission. After five years the person whose membership was terminated may apply to rejoin the charity as a member, and it is presumed that he should be allowed to do so, unless the Charity Commission is satisfied that in any special circumstances the application should be refused.

    5.15

2. Power to Give Specific Directions for the Protection of Charity

Section 20 of the Charities Act 2006 inserts a new s 19A into the 1993 Act. The new section applies only after a s 8 inquiry into the charity has been instituted. If the Charity Commission is satisfied that there has been misconduct or mismanagement, or that it is otherwise desirable to act in the administration of the charity, the Commission may, by order, direct certain persons to act. The persons capable of being directed in such a way are the charity trustees, any trustee for the charity, any officer or employee of the charity, or, if the charity is a body corporate, the charity itself. Prior to this change the Charity Commission could act through its appointed receiver and manager to take any action required by the Commission. This new section allows the Charity Commission to make directions in situations where no receiver and manager is appointed. Any directions given should be expedient in the interests of the charity. If the trusts of the charity give only limited powers to act, the order of the Charity Commission directing an action will override the limitations of the charity trustees in relation to the administration of the charity. No order may require a person to act in a way which is expressly prohibited by an Act of Parliament or in a way which is expressly prohibited in the trusts of the charity. Further, the Charity Commission, even in these circumstances where there has been misconduct, etc, may not require any person to act in a way which is inconsistent with the purposes of the charity.

    5.16

5.17   If an order made under s 18A is complied with then any person or body acting in such a way is deemed to have acted properly in the administration of the charity.

3. Power to Direct Application of Charity Property

5.18   Section 21 of the Charities Act 2006 inserts a new s 19B into the Charities Act 1993. This section applies in cases where the Charity Commission is satisfied that a person or persons in control or in possession of any property held on charitable trusts, is or are unwilling to apply it properly for the purposes of the charity. This power is new and quite radical. There does not have to be any element of bad faith, dishonesty, misconduct, or mismanagement. The basis of the intervention in this situation is simply that the Commission considers the trustees to be 'unwilling' to apply the property 'properly'. This introduces a very subjective element to interventions in the charity's affairs by the Charity Commission, and it is arguable that they are in danger of acting in the administration[22] of the charity as they have substituted their view of what is 'proper' for that of the trustees.

5.19   In order to intervene the Charity Commission must be satisfied not only that the trustees are 'unwilling' to act properly, but also that it is necessary or desirable for them to make an order 'for the purpose of securing a proper application of that property for the purposes of the charity'. Section 19 of the Charities Act 1993 concerns supplementary provisions relating to a receiver and manager appointed for a charity under s 18(1)(vii) of the 1993 Act, and although it is not entirely clear how the new provision in s 19B will feature, it may be supposed that such a power will be used in circumstances where an investigation has begun but conduct causing concern, but which does not amount to misconduct, has been found. It is to be anticipated that any order made under this section by the Charity Commission will be quite specific, as an order may direct that the property is applied 'in such manner' as the order specifies.

5.20   It may be the case that many trustees, particularly those with older constitutional documents, lack the power to act in the way in which the Charity Commission wishes them to. There may be restrictions on how the trustees can apply the property. An example might be that they may be unable to dispose of certain types of land, as they may lack the power to sell or transfer it. If the trustees' powers are limited, the Charity Commission order may require an action to be taken, 'whether or not it would be within the powers exercisable by the person or persons concerned in relation to the property'. Alternatively, the receiver and manager appointed to conduct the inquiry may be ordered to act in a particular way. This would have the effect of the receiver and manager being placed in the position of trustee when all formal appointment procedures under the terms of the trust have not been exercised. This would streamline the efficiency of the inquiry procedure and address the issue of what happens in inquiries where the misconduct is difficult to prove by

---

[22] See s 1E inserted into the Charities Act 1993 by s 7 of the Charities Act 2006.

conventional evidential methods. It may provide a result or remedy which would be difficult to achieve without litigation under the current situation.

The limitations on the exercise of this power are that it may not be used in contravention of an Act of Parliament, or if the act is expressly prohibited by the trusts of the charity.[23]

5.21

4. Relaxation of Requirements Relating to Schemes

Under s 16 of the Charities Act 1993, the Charity Commission enjoys concurrent jurisdiction with the High Court for the purposes of making schemes for the administration of a charity.[24] Section 20 of the Charities Act 1993 is completely replaced by a new provision. Administrative schemes may be directed in a number of different situations. A scheme may be used if there has been misapplication of funds by the person administering the charity,[25] or if for any other reason it is deemed that better regulation is required,[26] and in a variety of other situations.[27] A modern example of a cy-près[28] scheme being used is in the case of *Versani v Jesani*,[29] where different groups of a charity could no longer worship together. A scheme was used to divide the funds between the purposes of the two different groups. Administrative schemes have also been used to allow the administration of more than one charity under one administrative scheme. In the case of small charities or charities of a similar nature, a scheme would have been required to allow this.[30]

5.22

Under the old s 20, all schemes had to be notified to the public for at least one month before they were submitted to the court or the relevant Minister. Representations could be made by the public within one month of the date of the notice. Under the new s 20, the one month time limits have been omitted. The timing of the notice, the time for representations, and the period for making representations are now all within the control of the Charity Commission. Further, it is open to the Charity Commission to disapply the publicity requirements if it considers that 'by reason of the nature of the scheme, ... or for any other reason' compliance with the requirements is unnecessary. It is not clear on the face of the statute how this provision will be used. If publicity is given and representations are made then the Commission must take into account those representations (if made within the time specified) but may proceed with the proposals either without modifications or with such modifications as it thinks desirable. Again, this provision includes an element of discretion given to the Charity Commission which it did not enjoy under the previous legislation. The important factor is what the Commission

5.23

---

[23] See s 19B(3)(b) of the Charities Act 1993, as inserted by s 21 of the Charities Act 2006.
[24] For cy-près schemes, see Chapter 10.
[25] *Att-Gen v Coopers' Co* (1812) 19 Ves 186.
[26] *Att-Gen v Dedham School* (1857) 23 Beav 350.
[27] See *Tudor, Charities*, 9th ed (Thompson, Sweet & Maxwell, 2003) at para 10-008.
[28] See Chapter 10.
[29] [1999] Ch 219
[30] Also see s 44 of the Charities Act 2006 with respect to mergers.

'thinks' is desirable. The Commission is obliged to make copies of any scheme publicly available for a period of one month after the order is published. Schemes affecting local charities must be displayed in a convenient place in the area of the charity. There is a power to disapply the publication of the scheme locally if the Commission thinks this is unnecessary. The notices are not in any prescribed form, save that an address for making representations should be given.[31]

5.24   The old version of s 20 under the 1993 legislation stated that the Commission must give public notice of schemes removing trustees from their position, with the exception that the publicity requirements did not apply in cases after an investigation had been conducted. Under the old s 20, there was a discretion to disapply the publicity of this type of order. Under the new s 20 the position is the same, in that any publicity of the removal of a charity trustee may be dispensed with. If a charity trustee is to be removed, he, she, or it must be given notice of the proposed order. This applies only if the trustee is within the jurisdiction of the United Kingdom. A removed trustee may make representations concerning the order, but the Commission may proceed with an order nevertheless. There is no requirement to modify the order to take representations into account.

5.25   Generally, all notices under the new s 20 are to be in a form which the Commission considers to be sufficient and appropriate. Orders removing a trustee must be notified by post to the trustee's last known address in the United Kingdom. Although not vastly different from the provisions of s 20 under the Charities Act 1993, there has been a slight widening of the Charity Commission's discretion which may make it more difficult for the people in a local area to object to any scheme.

5. Participation of Scottish and Northern Irish Charities in Common Investment Schemes

5.26   The administration of assets of a charity is often more efficient if investments are controlled by professionals such as fund managers, and many charities participate in this form of investment. A common investment fund is classed as a charity in its own right and is therefore exempt from tax. The Charities Act 2006 amends the 1993 Act by making it possible for Scottish and Northern Irish charities to participate in common investment funds established by schemes of the Charity Commission.

6. Power to Give Advice and Guidance

5.27   Another section which is replaced by a new provision is s 29 of the Charities Act 1993. The first part of the section remains the same, in that the Commission may, on the written application of a trustee of a charity, give that person its opinion or advice in relation to the performance of any duties of the trustee or matters which otherwise relate to the proper administration of the charity. On receipt of such

---

[31] Section 20(7) of the Charities Act 1993, as inserted by the Charities Act 2006.

advice and guidance (if followed), a trustee may be deemed to have acted properly in administering the trust, unless that person knew of facts not known to the Commission. If such a trustee had reasonable cause to suspect that the advice by the Commission was given in the absence of material facts then he will not necessarily be deemed to have acted properly. In this context, a decision of the court takes precedence over anything which the Commission advises, and if proceedings are pending it is unlikely that the Commission will advise other than in general terms.

In the new s 29 there is a cross-reference to the functions of the Charity 5.28
Commission contained in s 1C as inserted by the Charities Act 2006 into the Charities Act 1993. This allows or reinforces the role of the Charity Commission in giving general guidance to charities. In practice the Charity Commission produces guidance on various topics to trustees on its website and through its publications. Trustees ought regularly to review the guidance of the Charity Commission generally, or that on any particular topic concerning them.

An innovation in the new s 29 is that the Charity Commission may issue advice 5.29
or guidance which is specifically directed at charities generally, at any class of charity, or at any particular charity. This allows the Commission to give advice of its own motion rather than only on the written application of a trustee. Whilst there are no specified sanctions for trustees who fail to follow such guidance (however it is published or issued), the implication must be that they will be failing properly to discharge their duties as trustees if they are unaware of it.

7. Power to Determine Membership of a Charity

A new s 29A is inserted into the Charities Act 1993, which allows the Charity 5.30
Commission to determine who are the members of a charity. This power may be used at the request of the charity, or at any time after the institution of an inquiry under s 8 of the Charities Act 1993. The Commission may appoint a person to undertake this task; and if there is an inquiry, the person conducting the inquiry on behalf of the Charity Commission may do this.

This power will be very useful in cases where internal trustee disputes are in 5.31
danger of paralyzing a charity. The appointed person can simply determine the qualifications for membership, such as the payment of subscriptions, or the signing of the constitution or rules of the charity and an agreement to abide by those rules. Many internal arguments may be settled by the appointment of a person with authority, who can be brought in to conduct elections or whatever else may be needed to restore the charity to a functioning body. Arguments concerning the identity of the proper trustees of a charity often degenerate into, or are complicated by, arguments as to who are the proper members of a charity.

8. Power to Enter Premises and Seize Documents, etc

A new s 31A is inserted into the existing provisions of the Charities Act 1993 by 5.32
s 26 of the Charities Act 2006. This new section gives the Charity Commission's staff

power to require documents to be provided by certain persons. The power is not a new one as it appeared in other legislation prior to the 2006 Act. The inclusion of this is therefore a consolidation of the Charity Commission powers. As might be expected, the Commission's powers with respect to the entering of premises are limited by several requirements before they can be exercised.

5.33   First, a warrant must be obtained from a Justice of the Peace. To obtain such a warrant, the Commission must provide evidence on oath that there are reasonable grounds for believing that the following conditions are satisfied:

(a) an inquiry must have been instituted under s 8 of the Charities Act 1993;

(b) there must be reasonable grounds to believe that there is a document or information relevant to the inquiry on the premises;

(c) it has to be shown that there is reason to believe that without a warrant the trustees would refuse to produce the document, even if its production was ordered by the Commission; or

(d) there should be grounds for the belief that if such a document or information is not seized it will be destroyed.

5.34   Secondly, the warrant must name a member of the Commission's staff and authorize that person to search the specified premises (with such aid as is necessary) and take possession of the document or information. Computerized information or documents may be required, and the Commission may take copies of anything which it considers to be necessary. Any person on the premises is required to assist the Commission staff in taking copies and providing any explanation of documents found. Entry into the premises must be made within one month of the date the warrant was issued and at a reasonable time of day.

5.35   Any occupier of premises is entitled to request that the Commission staff member conducting the search produces identification evidence showing that he or she is a member of the Commission staff, and to inspect the warrant itself. A full record must be kept which specifies the time of the search, the number of people accompanying the Commission staff member, the time taken, the actions taken at the premises, and any document or device which was possessed by the staff member as a result of the search. Any person occupying the property may request a full record of the search and the Commission is obliged to provide this. The record must be completed and a copy supplied to the occupier of premises before the Commission staff member leaves the premises. Both documents and devices (such as computers) may be retained for as long as the Commission considers that they are relevant, for the purposes of the inquiry into the charity's affairs under s 8 of the Charities Act 1993. Intentional obstruction of such a search is a summary offence liable to be punished by a 51-week term of imprisonment or a fine not exceeding level 5 on the standard scale. Section 50 of the Criminal Justice and Police Act 2001[32] applies to the powers of seizure in this section.

---

[32] See Pt 1 of Sch 1.

9. Restrictions on Mortgaging

Generally, trustees wishing to mortgage land as security for a loan to the charity   5.36
may do so if they have written advice from a financial expert on the necessity of the
mortgage, that its terms are reasonable, and on the ability of the charity to repay
the sums under the terms of the mortgage. Otherwise they must have the consent
of the Charity Commission or the court to enter such an arrangement. If advice is
sought, that advice must be independent and from someone who has no financial
interest in advising positively or otherwise. A finance officer, if suitably qualified,
could provide such advice. The difficulty in the current climate with the restrictions
on mortgaging derives from the issue of funding by way of grant. Large sums
may be given by grant makers for the purposes of facilitating activities undertaken
by a charity. Grant funding may derive from a number of sources, such as other
charities, government bodies, the National Lottery Charities Board, etc. Often the
grant funding is secured by a charge over the premises of the charity, so that should
the charity fail, an element of clawback for the funder is present. The Commission
has indicated that trustees cannot rely on the statutory power to give a charge over
charity property in these circumstances and will therefore require the Commission's
express consent. Another problem arises where a charity wishes to enter into an
all-moneys mortgage with a lender, in which case the initial advice about the loan
and its terms will not cover all the situations designed to be covered by the charge.

The new s 38 is expressed to include charges to secure grants as well as loans.   5.37
Generally, a mortgage requires the permission of the Commission unless proper
advice has been taken, as above. The inclusion of grants in this section ought
to facilitate the provision of funding in many charities. Such charities may be
dependent on such funding for their existence. Provided the correct advice has been
obtained, charities may enjoy greater freedom to charge their property in return
for essential funding. Although this is a welcome change, trustees must still take
full advice and consider very carefully if such a charge could potentially destroy the
charity. Even grant funding is subject to a 'reasonableness' test before the trustees
accept it and execute the charge in favour of the grantor. In addition, new rules are
provided in relation to all money charges.

6

THE CHARITY TRIBUNAL

A. GENERAL

It has often been said that no public body other than the Charity Commission enjoys   6.01
such freedom with respect to deciding what a person or trustee should do and also
in regulating the persons and institutions it advises. Whilst the two functions of the
Charity Commission could be described as advisory and regulatory,[1] there appeared
to be a lack of accountability for decisions made and actions taken, and it could
have been perceived that trustees were treated unfairly in some circumstances. Other
criticisms were that the Commission was not transparent or accountable enough
and that decisions lacked consistency. Whether this was true or not, or merely
a perception, it was recognized that unless there was a process for complaint or

---

[1] See Chapter 3.

redress, the Commission would always be open to such criticism. The provision of a Charity Tribunal in the Charities Act 2006 seeks to address this fundamental deficit in accountability and to ensure that the Commission's procedures comply with the Human Rights Act 1998. Taking into account the new discretions contained in the extended powers highlighted in the previous chapter, such a provision is welcome. Reporting of decisions of the Tribunal may help to make actions of the Charity Commission more predictable, and it should become clearer to trustees precisely where their duties lie.

B. INTRODUCTION OF THE TRIBUNAL

6.02   Section 8 of the Charities Act 2006 inserts several new provisions into the Charities Act 1993—ss 2A to 2D. Much detail is also contained in Schs 1B to 1D. Section 2A covers jurisdiction and the matters which are within the remit of the Tribunal. Section 2B concerns the practice and procedure to be adopted with respect to the work of the Tribunal. Section 2C provides for appeals from the Tribunal to the High Court. Section 2D concerns intervention by the Attorney-General, who has historically represented the public interest in ensuring the proper application of charitable funds.[2] Whilst the purpose of the Tribunal is to make charity law accessible to all, as well as enabling it to develop, the inclusion of the Tribunal in such complicated provisions may make that purpose very difficult to achieve.

C. SECTION 2A

6.03   Under s 2A(3), Sch 1B is incorporated into the Charities Act 1993. This schedule describes the constitution of the Tribunal and other matters relating to it. The matters within the jurisdiction of the Tribunal are contained in Sch 1C, incorporated by s 2A(4)(a). This subsection deals with 'appeals and applications' in respect of decisions, orders, or directions of the Commission.

6.04   Section 2A(4)(b) concerns such matters as are referred to the Tribunal under Sch 1D either by the Charity Commission itself or by the Attorney-General. It can be seen, therefore, that there will be two different types of cases under this particular provision. First, cases in which a person[3] applies, perhaps if he or she disagrees with some order, decision, or direction made by the Commission; and, secondly, cases where the Commission or Attorney-General considers it important to have a determination on a specific issue.[4]

---

[2] See *Tudor, Charities*, 9th ed (Thompson, Sweet & Maxwell, 2003) at para 10-018, for a fuller description of the role of the Attorney-General with respect to charities.

[3] See the provisions of the Table in Sch 1C as to who may apply.

[4] The third type of case is a review, see para 6.13 below.

D. LEGAL AID

In a letter responding to concerns raised by Lord Phillips of Sudbury,[5] the Attorney-   6.05
General said that even if a matter might be of public importance and there was
a need to establish a body of case law within the Tribunal, the Government was
unable to envisage circumstances where it would be possible to certify that the costs
of such proceedings could be paid out of public funds. It was admitted that charity
cases would, at least initially, require significant legal input, but it was asserted that
the purpose of the Tribunal was to allow greater access to the public and litigants
in person. It was estimated that the vast number of cases would be the type of
case described in s 2A(4)(a). The Attorney-General considered that it was only in
'one or two' cases annually where legal costs would debar an individual litigant.
As the cases would not concern liberty and the fundamental rights of individuals,
such legal assistance could not be given as it would establish a precedent in other
tribunals where legal aid was not given. It may be thought that referrals made by the
Charity Commission and the Attorney-General will be matters of law or of public
importance, and that in those circumstances individual litigants may not be in a
position to be represented.

E. PRACTICE AND PROCEDURE

Section 2B gives the Lord Chancellor the power to make rules regulating the exercise   6.06
of the rights to appeal or apply, or alternatively make references, to the Tribunal.
Such rules have not been made at the time of publishing but might be expected
to follow reasonably quickly after the Charities Act 2006. The rules will specify
the steps to be taken prior to an application, appeal, or reference. It is envisaged
that these steps will have to be taken within a specified period of time. The rules
are not therefore unusual, in that most of the Civil Procedure Rules concern the
actual process of making an application to a tribunal of one description or another.
The difficulty may be that the tribunal system as it currently stands prescribes
different sets of rules for different tribunals, depending on the subject matter of the
applications. The rules for employment matters are very different from rules in, say,
leasehold valuation tribunals.

F. DRAFT TRIBUNALS, COURTS AND ENFORCEMENT BILL

One of the purposes of this Bill is to create and introduce a new, simplified statutory   6.07
framework for tribunals to provide coherence and enable future reform. Whilst it

---

[5] Given to the Joint Committee on the Draft Charities Bill, dated September 2004.

is by no means certain that this Bill, or any subsequent Act, will be forthcoming soon, and apply directly to the Charity Tribunal, it may be instructive to consider the effect of proposals which may be of general application to all tribunals. Much research and effort has been put into assessing the capabilities of tribunals generally.[6] The White Paper does state that all new tribunals will be included in the new system. A review of existing tribunals and the establishment of a new system will begin in early 2007. It may be supposed that regulations concerning the Charity Tribunal, even if not immediately incorporated into a new system, will be drafted in order to coincide with any such new system. The Cabinet Office has released a paper, 'Charities Act 2006: Implementation Plan', in which it is stated that the Charity Tribunal provisions will not be implemented until the third Commencement Order, expected in early 2008.[7]

6.08 Ultimately, any appeal from the Charity Tribunal will be to the High Court on a point of law, and it is likely that such an appeal will be a statutory appeal under the Civil Procedure Rules, Part 52. If so, there may be either a review or a rehearing of matters. At present there is no unified system: different appeals reach the High Court by different routes and each statute tends to prescribe its own rules.

6.09 The rules when made will include rules as to the determination of preliminary, interlocutory, or ancillary matters[8] which will be decided by the President or a legal member of the Tribunal.[9] In certain circumstances there need not always be a hearing, and there may be a fast-track procedure in some urgent situations. Disclosure of documents, evidence, the representation of parties, the withdrawal of cases, the recording of cases, and publicity will all be dealt with in the rules. They may confer discretions either on the Tribunal, or on a member of the Tribunal, or on some other person in relation to such matters.

G. COSTS

6.10 One issue which is usually a discretionary matter for the judge is costs. In relation to the Charity Tribunal, costs orders are restricted to only two situations. Section 2B(6) states that if a tribunal considers that any party to proceedings before it has acted 'vexatiously, frivolously or unreasonably' then the Tribunal may order that party to pay the costs of any other party to the proceedings. There is a discretion to award part or all of the costs. If the Tribunal considers that any order made by the Charity Commission was unreasonable, it may order the Commission to pay, to any other party to the proceedings, all or part of that party's costs.[10] The costs of the Attorney-General are not expressly mentioned in the new provisions.

---

[6] White Paper; 'Transforming Public Services, Complaints Redress and Tribunals', published July 2004. The Draft Tribunals, Courts and Enforcement Bill was published on 25 July 2006.

[7] See Appendix 3.

[8] See s 2B as inserted into the Charities Act 1993 by s 8 of the Charities Act 2006.

[9] See para 1(2)(b) of Sch 1B for a definition of a legal member.

[10] Section 2B(7) as inserted by the Charities Act 2006.

H. COMPOSITION OF THE TRIBUNAL

Schedule 1B sets out the constitution of the Charity Tribunal, which consists   6.11
of the President and its other members. Appointment of the President is by the
Lord Chancellor, as is appointment of legal members of the Tribunal and its
ordinary members. The President or a legal member must have had a seven-year
general qualification within the meaning of the Courts and Legal Services Act
1990. A general qualification is one where the holder has a right of audience in
the Supreme Court, or the county court or magistrates' court. Ordinary members
may be appointed only if they appear to the Lord Chancellor to have appropriate
knowledge or experience relating to charities. The Deputy President will also be
appointed to act with the President and in his absence. The terms of their respective
appointments are within the discretion of the Lord Chancellor. Similar to all
judicial offices, removal, other than by resignation, is possible only on the grounds
of incapacity or misbehaviour. Retirement is at the age of 70. The Tribunal members
will sit as panels for the purpose of discharging their functions.

I. PANELS OF THE TRIBUNAL

Decisions of the Tribunal will be made by a panel sitting at times and in places that   6.12
the President directs. It is not clear whether there will be one central building where
the Tribunal will sit, or what arrangements may be made to take panel sittings to
different regions. More than one panel may sit at a time, and the composition of a
panel will be determined according to rules made by the Lord Chancellor and the
issues in a case. There are six different possible constitutions of the panels:

(a) the President may sit alone;
(b) a legal member may sit alone;
(c) the President and two other members may sit;
(d) a legal member may sit with two other members;
(e) the President may sit with one other member; and
(f) a legal member may sit with one other member.

Decisions are taken by a majority vote, but if the President is sitting with another
member he will have a casting vote. Similarly, if the panel consists of a legal member
and another member then the legal member will also have a casting vote. If two
legal members sit together then there will be rules as to who has a casting vote.
Without such an arrangement, differences in opinion between two legal members
could cripple decision making. There are various other amendments to statutes
to take account of the new Tribunal, but perhaps the most significant is that the
Charity Tribunal is now included in the Tribunals and Inquiries Act 1992.[11]

---

[11] See Pt 1, Sch 1 to the Tribunals and Inquiries Act 1992.

J. DETERMINATION OF THE APPEAL

6.13 Schedule 1C deals with appeals and applications to the Tribunal in respect of decisions, orders, and directions made by the Charity Commission. Schedule 1C, para 1(1) begins with a general proposition stating that an appeal may be brought to the Tribunal against any decision, direction, or order listed in column 1 of the table found in Sch 1C. An example is the refusal to register an organization as a charity. The table is extensive and very prescriptive, and refers directly to the precise statutory provision under which the Charity Commission purports to act. Column 2 describes the persons who have locus standi to apply or appeal. The Attorney-General has an unfettered right to apply.[12] Whilst the table system appears daunting, particularly for lay applicants, if orders of the Commission attribute their actions to precise powers or statutory provisions, it should be easy for all to follow. Unless this happens it will be very difficult to assess whether or not there is a right to apply or appeal.

K. EXCEPTIONS TO THE RIGHT TO APPLY OR APPEAL

6.14 Schedule 1C, para 1(1) is inclusive, in that it states that orders, etc may be appealed against unless the type of order made is reviewable. Certain acts of the Charity Commission are therefore not appealable but are reviewable. The reviewable matters are set out in para 3 of Sch 1C. They are:

(a) the decision to institute an inquiry under s 8 into a particular charity;

(b) the decision to inquire under the same section into a class of charities;

(c) a refusal to make a common investment scheme;

(d) a decision not to make a common deposit scheme;

(e) a refusal to make any order under s 26 of the Charities Act 1993; and

(f) a decision not to make an order under s 36 or s 38 of the Charities Act 1993.

The last two provisions are those allowing the disposition of land (possibly to connected persons) and allowing the trustees to take a mortgage or secure a charge over land.

L. DETERMINATION OF THE APPEAL

6.15 The Charity Commission will be the respondent to appeals. The Tribunal will consider the decision, direction, or order afresh, and may take into account new

---

[12] Sch 1C, para 1(2)(a).

evidence which was not available to the Charity Commission when it made its order. The possible results of determination by the Tribunal are also specified, this time in column 3 of the table in Sch 1C. Generally, the Tribunal may affirm the order, or quash the Charity Commission decision or order and substitute a different order. Alternatively, some orders may be remitted to the Commission for reconsideration after a determination by the Tribunal.[13] The exception to the general rule concerns the power of the Charity Commission to call for and search records. In that case the Tribunal must consider the specific question of whether or not the document in question relates to a charity and is relevant to the discharge of its functions by the Charity Commission or the official custodian for charities. Although this is an important exception in principle, there is an obvious flaw, in that a person having control of a document which the Commission wishes to inspect, who is ordered to produce it but then an appeal is launched, will almost inevitably have to disclose the document during the appeal so that the Tribunal may consider its relevance. From the perspective of the Charity Commission, a decision will have to be taken as to the most efficient method of obtaining documents or records. It may be easier in some circumstances to institute an inquiry and use the powers of search described in the previous chapters. It may be less costly to order production and wait for the appeal to inspect the requested documents.

M. REVIEWS

As seen in para 6.14 above, certain matters are 'reviewable' matters. In these cases 6.16 an application to the Tribunal may be made by the Attorney-General, or by the persons listed in column 2 of the table in Sch 1C. In such cases the determination of the Tribunal must follow the principles established by the High Court in cases of judicial review.[14] Making decisions of the Charity Commission reviewable (even if the list of reviewable matters is relatively short) is a welcome innovation and introduces a new level of accountability of the Charity Commission for the decisions it makes, and for the way in which it makes them.

N. AMENDMENTS

The provision of a prescriptive table showing those matters which are appealable 6.17 and by whom, and the results of a successful appeal, is very specific, and it may be thought that some omissions from or alterations to the table will become necessary. This can be done by order of the relevant Minister, but such orders must be approved by Parliament.

---

[13] See Sch 1C, para 5.
[14] For the current position on judicial review and human rights in charity cases, see *Tudor*, at para 10-033.

O. REFERENCES

6.18   Section 2A(4)(b), inserted into the Charities Act 1993 by s 8 of the Charities Act 2006, gives jurisdiction to the Charity Tribunal to hear matters which are referred to it by the Charity Commission and/or the Attorney-General. The issues that may be so referred are restricted. Schedule 1D describes such referable matters as questions arising in connection with the Charity Commission's functions and which also involves the operation of charity law in any respect, or its application to a particular state of affairs. In other words, this represents cases where the underlying issue is one of law. The Charity Commission may refer matters only with the consent of the Attorney-General. The trustees of a charity or any affected persons are entitled to be represented at such hearings. Presumably, it was with this class of case in mind that Lord Phillips[15] advocated help for charities with the costs of the hearing.

6.19   The Attorney-General may refer a matter to the Tribunal. If this is done, the Charity Commission will be made a party to the proceedings, but trustees of the charity concerned, and the charity itself (if a corporate body), will be joined as parties only with the Tribunal's permission. All matters concerning such a reference will be stayed and time will not run until the Tribunal has determined the reference. Time limits for the trustees to apply or appeal will be suspended during the period after a reference has been made but before the determination of it by the Tribunal. The exception to this is where the parties to a reference agree to steps being taken.

6.20   It is important to note that the Charity Commission and Attorney-General will be parties to a reference, but not necessarily the charity trustees or the charity itself. Trustees may be wise to apply to the Tribunal in any event for permission to be a party, even if the reference develops in a way which does not require actual representation at a hearing. Simply by being a party the trustees will be kept informed when their time for appealing begins to run, and they may be in a better position to object to acts done in the interim. It is open to trustees to agree to steps proposed by the Charity Commission during the reference period.

P. APPEALS AND REFERENCES

6.21   At first sight it appears that trustees may become parties to a reference, if given permission by the Tribunal, and contribute to the determination of the question of law to be decided. However, if they do this, their further rights to appeal are then excluded.[16] This is an important limitation which forces trustees to make a choice. They may join as a party to the reference, but if they do and the decision goes against the Charity Commission, the Charity Commission is not obliged to

---

15 See 'Legal Aid' at para 6.05 above.   16 Sch 1D, para 6(2)

50

change any decision it has already made which has been found to be incorrect.[17] The crucial question therefore becomes exactly who is a party to proceedings, as this question may determine their rights to appeal a particular decision or participate in a reference. Procedural rules will define this important issue.[18]

---

[17] Sch 1D, para 3(3).   [18] Those issued under Sch 2B(1).

7

CHARITABLE INCORPORATED ORGANIZATIONS

A. GENERAL

A radical innovation in the Charities Act 2006, s 34, which inserts Sch 7, concerns   7.01
the creation of a new incorporated form which may be adopted by charities. Charities
have, until now, had to choose from a range of different forms. Some charities
(including some very large ones) remain as unincorporated associations. Others may
choose to adopt the structure of a company (usually limited by guarantee) or a trust.
Often a charity may have an excessive administrative burden if it has to comply
with more than one regulatory regime. This is particularly obvious in relation to
companies. If a trust is chosen then there may be problems with acting effectively,
as several individuals may be required to sign documents, etc. The new Charitable
Incorporated Organization ('CIO') is specifically designed to meet charities' needs
and is available to charities only.

7.02   A CIO must have a constitution, be a body corporate, and have a principal office in England and Wales.[1] It may have one or more members, and the members' liability to contribute on a winding up may be limited to a maximum amount. Alternatively, such members may not have to contribute at all. The constitution must state all of the above matters, and also the name and the purposes of the CIO. Regulations are expected to prescribe which other matters will be required in the constitution of a CIO.[2] The Act contains provisions on requirements for membership and eligibility for membership, the appointment of one or more persons to be charity trustees, and directions as to what will happen to the charity's assets on dissolution or winding up. Currently, winding-up provisions of charitable bodies generally provide that the net assets should be transferred to other charities or applied for charitable purposes. The constitution must be in English or Welsh (as appropriate). The person who is charity trustee does not necessarily have to be a member of the charity and the membership of the CIO can be wider than just the charity trustees. There is a general requirement to comply with matters prescribed in the regulations.

B. NAME AND STATUS

7.03   The name of the CIO has to appear in legible characters on all business letters, notices, and other official publications. Conveyances, bills, receipts, invoices, and letters of credit all have to include the name of the CIO. Similar to the use of 'Limited' in company law, a CIO must include 'CIO' or 'Charitable Incorporated Organization' in its name. The Welsh version will be *sefydliad elusennol corfforedig* (or 'SEC'). Using the initials CIO when the organization is not a bona fide CIO will be an offence, as is signing documents without revealing the status of the body at the time of signing.

7.04   Registration of the CIO lies with the Charity Commission only. Consistent with the functions of the Commission in registering charities under s 3,[3] the Commission may determine the charitable status of the organization. Compliance with the regulations concerning the constitutional documents will be checked and the name of the CIO will be approved. If the name chosen is likely to cause confusion with another CIO then the Commission may require a different name to be registered. Once registered the CIO automatically becomes a body corporate, and any property vested in persons for charitable purposes becomes vested in the corporate body. The register must state the date of the charity's registration and the fact that it is a CIO.

---

[1] The concept of a 'principal office' is based on company law, and until any reported decisions are made on this issue it may be instructive to consider cases on this issue under the Companies Acts 1985 and 1989.

[2] Draft regulations have been produced and run to around 35 pages. See Cabinet Office, Office of the Third Sector website: <www.cabinetoffice.gov.uk/the_third_sector>.

[3] See Chapter 3.

C. CONVERSION INTO A CIO

There are two types of organization that can apply to the Charity Commission for 7.05
conversion into a CIO. These are charitable companies and charities in the form
of Industrial and Provident Societies under the Industrial and Provident Societies
Act 1965. Any company which does not have fully paid-up capital cannot apply
and neither can exempt charities.[4] If an application for conversion is made, the
Charity Commission will inform the relevant registrar, or such other person as the
Commission thinks fit. Companies are registered with the Registrar of Companies,
and Industrial and Provident Societies are currently registered with the Financial
Services Authority.

Certain items must accompany the application for registration as a CIO. There 7.06
must be a copy of the resolution of the company, a proposed constitution for the
CIO, and any other documents either prescribed in regulations or requested for
information by the Charity Commission. The same criteria apply to Industrial and
Provident Societies. If a company or society decides to apply to become a CIO then
the resolution making that decision should be a special resolution, or a unanimous
written resolution signed by or on behalf of all members entitled to vote on a special
resolution.[5] If the application for conversion is by a company limited by guarantee,
the members of the CIO will remain liable to contribute to its assets on winding
up, and this provision must remain in the new constitution of the CIO. Usually,
companies limited by guarantee provide that each member is liable up to £1. If this
is the case, and the total amount of each member's liability to contribute does not
exceed £10, then on conversion that guarantee will be extinguished.[6]

D. THE CHARITY COMMISSION'S DECISION

By the provisions of new s 69H of the 1993 Act, the Charity Commission, after 7.07
consultation with the relevant registrar and any other interested person, will satisfy
itself that the organization is a charity, that the constitution complies with the
provisions discussed above, and that the regulations have been complied with. The
Commission may require a name change if it is necessary at this stage,[7] and may
also consider any other representations from those consulted on the application. If
for any reason registration as a CIO is refused then the Commission will inform the
relevant registrar.

Section 69I contains the detailed provisions about registration of the new CIO. 7.08
The registration will be provisional until any old registration is cancelled, and it is at

---

[4] See new s 69G in Sch 7 of the Charities Act 2006.
[5] See s 53(3) of the Industrial and Provident Societies Act 1965.
[6] See Sch 7, para 1.
[7] See Charities Act 2006, Sch 7, new s 69H(3).

the time of such cancellation by the relevant registrar that the new corporate body comes into being. The register will show the name of the CIO, the fact that it is a CIO, and the date it became one (ie the date the alternative or old registration was cancelled).

E. CONVERSION OF COMMUNITY INTEREST COMPANIES

7.09 Regulations may make provision for community interest companies to convert into CIOs.[8] In particular, if such a conversion is to be undertaken, the accounting provisions of the Companies (Audit, Investigations and Community Enterprise) Act 2004,[9] ss 53 to 55 will be modified or disapplied.

F. AMALGAMATION OF CIO WITH ANOTHER CIO

7.10 Applications for amalgamation may be made to the Charity Commission by two or more CIOs. If successful, a new CIO will be created. The application is made in the CIO's name and should be supported by copies of special resolutions by both or all CIOs applying. Seventy-five per cent of those voting at a general meeting of the CIOs should have voted in favour of amalgamation. Alternatively, a unanimous vote in favour of amalgamation can be agreed, and if this is the case a general meeting is not required. Resolutions to amalgamate are either effective the date of the meeting at which 75 per cent or more approved the amalgamation, or, if there is no meeting, on the last date specified in the constitution or in regulations, provided that this date is not earlier than the last vote to have been received.

7.11 There are detailed provisions for the giving of notice in cases where there is a proposed amalgamation, and provisions for interested persons to make representations. If an application has been submitted, the Charity Commission may refuse to approve such an amalgamation if it considers that the new CIO would not be a charity, or if there is a serious risk that the new CIO would be unable properly to pursue its purposes. It is not clear what types of considerations might lead the Charity Commission to the conclusion that the charity could not properly pursue its purposes. It may be that in creating an amalgamated charity the trustees will be faced with a significant number of members who have dissented and plan to disrupt the activities of the new CIO. Alternatively, governance arrangements might be thought to be inadequate. It is clear that the constitution of the amalgamated charity must be agreed prior to the application. Under Sch 7 to the 2006 Act, which inserts the new s 69K(9) into the 1993 Act, not having a constitution which complies with all the CIO requirements is a ground on which the Charity Commission can refuse to allow the amalgamation.

---

[8] See Charities Act 2006, Sch 7, new s 69J.
[9] Establishing community interest companies or 'CICs'.

G. OBJECTS CLAUSES

If a CIO wishes to amalgamate with another CIO, the Charity Commission may   7.12
refuse unless certain conditions are met. First, the purposes of the CIOs should be
the 'same or substantially the same' as those contained in the constitutions of both
or all of the old CIOs. The old constitutions should be the same or similar in the
provision for transfer of assets on dissolution or winding up, and the authorization
in the constitutions with reference to any benefit obtained by charity trustees,
members, or persons connected with them. These three factors should be the same.
The requirement that trustee benefits should be regulated to the same extent in
amalgamating CIOs is intended to avoid amalgamations being proposed with a
view to gaining more generous benefits by adopting the more liberal provisions of
one CIO than are provided for in the other.

Supplementary provisions for the registration of the newly amalgamated CIOs   7.13
are contained in s 69L. On registration of the new CIO, all property vests in the
new CIO and each of the old CIOs is dissolved. Any gift (including gifts in wills)
which is expressed to be in favour of the old CIOs takes effect (after the date of
registration) as a gift to the new CIO. This provision avoids much uncertainty and,
at least in the case of CIOs, obviates the need to retain any record of the old CIO
other than as a charity removed from the register. Currently, if a charity wishes
effectively to wind up or dissolve for any reason, it is usually advised to retain a legal
presence, at least on the register, in order to take advantage of legacies coming to it
after the date of its dissolution.[10]

H. TRANSFER OF CIO'S UNDERTAKINGS

In some cases charity trustees may consider that their best course of action would   7.14
be to transfer the CIO's undertakings to another CIO. This type of situation might
occur where a small independent charity has been administered perfectly correctly
but, by virtue of some change of circumstance, it becomes obvious that the CIO will
have difficulty achieving its aims or objects. An example could be where a small local
charity becomes subject to new regulations, say, regarding care homes, hospitals,
etc, making it too expensive to adapt the charity's current activities. Alternatively, a
particular charity may have difficulty recruiting sufficient trustees to act effectively
under its constitution. In these types of circumstances, the trustees may be advised
to transfer the charitable property to another charity to enable the remaining funds
to be utilized more efficiently.

---

[10] See the problems historically caused by the winding up or dissolution of charities under the
following cases: *Re Lucas* [1948] Ch 424, *Re Roberts* [1963] 1 WLR 406, *Re Faraker* [1912] 2 Ch 488.
However, the provisions in s 44 of the 2006 Act, relating to the merger of non-CIO charities, will
enable this to be avoided in future.

7.15   The procedure is relatively straightforward, in that both CIOs resolve either to transfer assets, or to receive assets. Copies of the resolutions should be sent to the Charity Commission, which will, if necessary, direct that notice be given of the proposed transfer and a time (28 days) be allowed for representations to be made. It is envisaged that representations will be made by persons interested in the transferor, but not by the transferee. If the constitution of the transferee is in good order and the Commission considers there is little risk that the transferee could not properly carry out its purposes then it is unlikely that the Commission will refuse such a transfer. The same conditions as in the amalgamation of two CIOs are required—the same or similar purposes, the same level of trustee benefit, and the same or similar provisions for the application of assets on a winding up. Once the copies of resolutions have been sent to the Charity Commission, there may be no positive or negative response from the Charity Commission. If so, within a period of six months the Commission may extend the time for representations to be accepted. Reasons must be given for the extension of time. This may happen if there is some resistance to the transfer, or if a business plan needs to be drawn up. If no extension is made then the resolutions will be treated as confirmed by the Commission on the day after their receipt by the Charity Commission. Express confirmation may be given too. After the date of confirmation, any gift expressed as being in favour of the transferor takes effect as a gift to the transferee CIO.

I. FURTHER PROVISIONS ON A WINDING UP

7.16   It is expected that there will be regulations concerning the winding up of a CIO and the consequent transfer of assets from the CIO. It is envisaged that the regulations will cover matters such as the transfer of any charity property from persons or nominees holding it for the purposes of the charity, the possible application of property cy-près, the liability (if any) of the trustees to contribute to any liabilities of the CIO, and the reversal, on a revival of a CIO, of anything done on its dissolution.

J. MISCELLANEOUS

7.17   There is a general power to the Cabinet Office Minister[11] to make regulations concerning the conversion of bodies and organizations into CIOs. Unincorporated associations may specifically be enabled to transfer assets to a CIO. Further provisions set out the theoretical basis and underlying concepts governing CIOs. The powers of the trustees are not limited, other than by the provisions of the organization's own constitution. The powers must of course be exercised in pursuit of the purposes of the CIO. If there is a provision in the constitution which provides for members to

[11] See Sch 7, which inserts new s 69Q into the 1993 Act.

contribute on winding up then the constitution and its terms take effect as a contract between the CIO and its members to abide by the terms of that constitution. Any debt owed by a member to the CIO is to be in the nature of a specialty debt.[12]

The doctrines of ultra vires and ostensible authority are enshrined in Sch 7 to the Charities Act 2006, which inserts Sch 5B into the Charities Act 1993. No act done by the CIO can be challenged on the grounds that it lacked constitutional capacity to act, and the power of the trustees to bind the CIO cannot be called into question on the grounds of any lack of authority.[13] These provisions apply only to bona fide purchasers for value acting in good faith. A third party is presumed to be acting in good faith and need not inquire as to the authority under which the CIO is purporting to act in a transaction.[14] If a third party acts in good faith and pays full consideration for property, it does not invalidate that transaction if it is later revealed that the CIO or the trustees lacked capacity to enter that transaction. This principle applies in all cases where the third party had no notice that the CIO was acting outside its capacity. If a person[15] uses the fact that the third party knew that the CIO did not have power to act then whichever person raises that question must prove that assertion. If it becomes obvious, prior to a transaction being entered, that there may be some doubt about the capacity of the CIO to act, proceedings to prevent the unauthorized transaction may be brought. If, however, there is an agreement or other legal obligation that the CIO will enter a transaction, and before it finalizes the transaction it becomes clear that the CIO cannot act, an injunction to prevent the completion of that transaction cannot be sought.

7.18

These provisions may have been drafted in contemplation of land transactions or other transactions which involve several steps. The provisions attempt to clarify the position of third parties dealing with a CIO and the level of authority that such a third party is entitled to expect when dealing with a CIO. Many of the concepts and duties of those involved with charities in other forms have been addressed in the provisions of the Act relating to CIOs. This may make the CIO the form of choice for those considering the establishment of a new charity. Such clarity may be adequate persuasion (if the conversion regulations are clear enough) for existing charities to convert into a CIO. The new form is likely to be attractive. The success of the new form is not assured, but the clear drafting and fearless addressing of problematic areas for trustees will, it is hoped, increase the number of charities choosing this form. An example of this clarity is the expression of the trustees' duties with reference to potential personal benefits. It is expressly stated that a trustee may not benefit personally from any transaction entered into by the CIO if the trustee's interest in the matter was not disclosed to the other members of the trustees in advance. This is in addition to the general requirement that a trustee may not

7.19

---

[12] The type of debt determines the limitation period during which the CIO could recover the debt due. See McGee (ed), *Limitation Periods*, 4th ed (Thompson, Sweet & Maxwell, 2002).

[13] Many charities have similar provisions in their current constitutions which derive from company law provisions.

[14] See *Omar Hugh Bayoumi v Women's Total Abstinence Educational Union Ltd* [2003] Ch 283.

[15] Perhaps the trustees themselves.

receive any personal benefit unless this is expressly permitted by the constitution, the Charity Commission, or the court.

7.20   A certain degree of flexibility to amend the constitution of the CIO is included, and detailed provisions provide a procedure to do this. The exceptions are the same as often appear in charitable companies now. The winding-up or dissolution provisions must be regulated, as must any change to the purposes or objects clause of the CIO, and any amendment which could result in personal benefits to trustees. Regulation is by Charity Commission consent to the regulated amendments. Any resolutions to amend should be sent to the Charity Commission for registration, and the Charity Commission may refuse to register amendments in some circumstances.

K. DRAFT REGULATIONS CONCERNING CIOS

7.21   Thirty-two pages of draft regulations have been issued. The regulations are not yet in force but provide great detail about how the existence of a new legal form will be recognized in other existing legislation, such as the Insolvency Act 1986 and the Companies Act 1985. The detailed constitutional provisions which ought to be found in the documents of a CIO are further defined. There are fifteen items which should be adequately addressed in the constitution of the CIO.[16] The duties of the trustees on a dissolution are also expanded. A power is included to restore to the register a removed CIO after a hearing in the Tribunal, as are detailed regulations concerning the execution of documents by a CIO, internal procedures, administration of the charity, and the power to delegate or appoint nominees and custodians. Electronic communications with the Charity Commission may be allowed, subject to provisions concerning the application of time limits in such 'correspondence'. Applications and appeals concerning CIOs (not currently in the table referred to in Chapter 6, para 6.13) are also allowed for under the draft regulations. It will be necessary to check the eventual form of the regulations when they are published.

---

[16] Some legal publishers have already begun drafting model constitutional documents, and the Charity Commission is also expected to produce a model form of constitution for a CIO.

8

CHARITY TRUSTEES

A. GENERAL

The position of trustee of a charity is essentially a voluntary one,[1] and the principle   8.01
of volunteering remains strongly supported. The position is one of trust,[2] however,
and charity trustees are placed under an increasing duty not only to preserve the
charity property they hold on trust, but also actively to govern and supervise
the management of their charities. Principles of good governance and proper
administration which is efficient and makes the best use of resources are increasingly
important. Whilst this is recognized and reflected in the expression of the Charity
Commission's functions and duties (see para 3.09 above), it is also reflected in the
revision and clarification of the duties of charity trustees. Among other obligations,
trustees have a duty to comply with the terms of the trust, a duty of prudent
investment, a duty to conserve trust property, and a duty to apply for a scheme if
necessary.[3] Section 1 of the Trustee Act 2000 sets out the duty of care which trustees
should fulfil when exercising certain powers. They should exercise such care and
skill as is reasonable in all the circumstances, having regard to any special knowledge
or skills enjoyed by the trustees. What is reasonable will be assessed against what it
is reasonable to expect of anyone in that business or profession.[4]

---

[1] Although the Charity Commission recently authorized the remuneration of two-fifths of the
trustees in a particular charity (CfTB Education Trust) where a case was made for this exceptional step;
see *Third Sector*, 25 October 2006.
[2] See Underhill and Hayton, *The Law of Trust and Trustees*, 17th ed (Butterworths, 2006).
[3] See also *Tudor, Charities*, 9th ed (Thompson, Sweet & Maxwell, 2003), chap 6.
[4] *Bartlett v Barclays Bank Trust Co Ltd* [1980] Ch 515.

8.02   Several areas of concern to trustees are addressed in the provisions of the new Charities Act. Consistent with the legislative scheme, the 2006 Act inserts new sections into the Charities Act 1993. The areas persistently requiring either clarification or reform concern matters such as trustees providing services to charities and the remuneration they receive from such activities. Many charities require permanent members of staff to manage their day-to-day activities, and the employment of people who are or have been trustees can create problems. Although the reality may be that the founder of a charity, or a trustee closely connected with the charity, may be the best person to take on the task of managing it, it may appear that the person concerned is in receipt of some direct or indirect private benefit from his association with the charity, or is subject to a conflict of interest and duty. It may also be frustrating for the trustees of a charity, who can identify skills among the membership of the board of trustees which they need to use, but who perhaps feel unable to do so for fear of a conflict of interest arising.

B. TRUSTEES MAY PROVIDE SERVICES TO A CHARITY UNDER CONTRACT

8.03   Trustees have always been able to enter into contracts to provide paid services to the charities of which they are trustees, provided that there is either an express provision in the governing document or express permission from the Charity Commission or the court. However, the inclusion of a new s 73A in the Charities Act 1993 confers a statutory power to receive such remuneration, subject to specified conditions. It is important to note that the power applies only where the trustee is supplying goods or services to the charity; it does not sanction or otherwise concern payment of the trustee for holding the office of trustee, attending meetings, etc. It does not apply where a trustee is employed by the charity, or where the situation is governed by an order of the Charity Commission or the court, or where there are express provisions contained in the trusts of the charity which would allow payment of the trustee. Nor does it apply to any express provision in an Act of Parliament allowing payment of trustees.

C. CONDITIONS TO BE MET WHEN CONTRACTING WITH A CHARITY

8.04   Two conditions must be met before any agreement is entered. First, remuneration may be paid by the charity from its funds only if the maximum amount of remuneration is set out in an agreement in writing. That sum should not exceed what is reasonable in the circumstances for the provision of services to the charity. Secondly, the trustees must be satisfied that it is in the best interests of the charity to enter such an agreement and for the services to the charity to be provided by that person for the maximum remuneration to be agreed.

If, after the agreement has been signed, there is more than one trustee contracting   8.05
with the charity, the number involved in such agreements must remain in the
minority on the trustee board. No such contract can be entered in any case
if there is an express prohibition in the trusts of the charity preventing such
arrangements.

Two further requirements which must be satisfied are that the trustees should   8.06
have regard to any published Charity Commission guidance concerning the making
of such agreements, and the duty of care embodied by the second condition applies
to decisions concerning such agreements. This duty of care continues during the
period for performance of the contract and until all of the obligations under it
have been discharged. It is not enough to consider these matters only prior to
entering the agreement. This implies that continuous reviewing of whether or not
it remains in the best interests of the charity to continue such agreements must be
undertaken.

'Remuneration' includes any benefits in kind, and such a benefit may be direct   8.07
or indirect. All the above principles apply to trustees, but they also apply to people
who are 'connected' with a trustee. Relations of a trustee, companies owned or
controlled by a trustee, business partners of a trustee, and spouses are all connected
with that trustee.

Section 73C sets out what trustees should do if a contract is desired. The trustee   8.08
providing such services or goods is disqualified from acting with respect to the
agreement. If the trustee does so act, this does not necessarily render an agreement
void but the trustee is liable to reimburse to the charity the whole or part of
the remuneration received. The reimbursement may be ordered by the Charity
Commission. Benefits in kind received by the trustee will be valued and that sum
may be ordered to be reimbursed.

D. TRUSTEES, AUDITORS, AND PERSONAL LIABILITY FOR BREACH OF TRUST

A trustee who commits a breach of trust, or a person appointed to audit or examine   8.09
the accounts of a non-company charity who makes a mistake, may be relieved
from personal liability. Under the Charities Act 2006,[5] the Commission will be
empowered to excuse the breach and order that there should be no personal liability,
provided the trustee or other person concerned has acted honestly and reasonably.
Under the previous law the Charity Commission were unable to provide such relief
in any circumstances. This statutory provision is a welcome extension to the Charity
Commission's jurisdiction in this regard as previously it was only the court which
was enabled to do this. This jurisdiction to provide relief from liability does not
exclude the operation of s 61 of the Trustee Act 1925 or s 727 of the Companies
Act 1985 which are unaffected by it.

---

[5] See s 38, inserting a new s 73D and a new s 73E into the Charities Act 1993.

E. TRUSTEES' INDEMNITY INSURANCE

8.10 Charity trustees may now[6] arrange for the purchase of insurance designed to indemnify the trustees against personal liability in cases where they may have been negligent or acted in breach of trust in carrying on the activities of the charity. The funds of the charity may be used to purchase this insurance. Previously this was possible only where the charity's constitution expressly provided for the charity to pay for such insurance, and it was necessary to obtain the Commission's consent to the alteration of the constitution to include such a provision because indemnity insurance was perceived as a benefit to the trustees concerned. Under the new Act, even if a trust document or constitution contains an express prohibition preventing the trustees from gaining a personal benefit from the trust, the statutory provisions on the taking of trustee indemnity insurance will still apply.

8.11 The terms of the insurance to be obtained should indemnify against negligent or inadvertent breaches of trust only and not extend to deliberate acts of dishonesty, fraud, or wilful or reckless misconduct by a trustee. The insurance should not indemnify against fines or penalties for criminal offences incurred by the trustees. The decision to take out such trustee indemnity insurance is to be made by the trustees, who must be satisfied that it is in the best interests of the charity to do so. The power to excuse trustees' breaches of trust and the power to buy such insurance are both useful provisions which ought to help charities to find trustees willing to act on their behalf.

---

[6] See s 39, inserting a new s 73F into the Charities Act 1993.

9

FUNDRAISING FOR CHARITABLE, BENEVOLENT, OR PHILANTHROPIC INSTITUTIONS

A. GENERAL

Fundraising itself is not a charitable activity but may be necessary to enable   9.01
charities to do their charitable work. The public collection of funds is often the
most obvious interface with the general public, and there has been regulation of
fundraising for some time.[1] Fundraising activities were one of the factors mentioned
in the Cabinet Office Strategy Unit Report.[2] As public fundraising directly impacts
on the public perception of the voluntary sector, this was considered to be an
important area for strong regulation. The regulation of fundraising activities will
aid in achieving the stated aim of preserving public confidence and trust in
charities.

---

[1] See Pts II and III of the Charities Act 1992; and see the Charitable Institutions (Fund Raising)
Regulations 1994 (SI 1994/3024).
[2] See Introduction, p xvii above.

9.02   Four areas of concern were identified:

(a) the self-regulation of fundraising;
(b) public collections;
(c) the participation of commercial fundraisers; and
(d) trading by charities.

9.03   The Institute of Fundraising[3] has already adopted a code of conduct for fundraisers to abide by which describes good practice for fundraising professionals. The Charities Act 2006 institutes a new regime of regulation for fundraising. There are several new definitions which define types of fundraising activity—public charitable collections, door-to-door collections, and the sale of items (see para 9.04 below). Charitable appeals are also included in the new provisions. Conducting charitable collections and appeals without the necessary authority is sanctioned by conviction of a criminal offence.[4]

B. PUBLIC CHARITABLE COLLECTIONS

9.04   Public charitable collections are defined in s 45(1) of the 2006 Act as including collections in a public place and door-to-door collections. A public place is widely defined as 'any public place' but the concept is considerably more complicated than that.[5] 'Door-to-door' collections include collections by means of visits to houses or businesses. A 'charitable appeal' is an appeal to members of the public requesting them to give money or other property, but also includes offering items or services for sale. This wide definition of public collections and appeals is intended to encompass many of the usual fundraising activities, for example the offering of services at charity auctions would fall within this definition. Charitable appeals are further defined as appeals for money or property accompanied by a representation that the whole or any part of the proceeds will be applied for charitable, benevolent, and philanthropic purposes. The inclusion of benevolent and philanthropic purposes reflects previous legislation, such as the Charities Act 1992, and avoids the need to draw technical distinctions between charitable appeals (where tax relief would apply) and non-charitable appeals which nevertheless share an altruistic motivation (where tax relief would not be available). The 'giving of money' is defined as giving by any means, so telephone pledges or collections via the internet, for charitable purposes, would be included in this definition. Whilst it might be thought that 'giving' implies that the gift would be unilateral and the giver would not expect anything in return, this is not the definition adopted in the Act, which states that 'it does not matter' that the giving of money or property is in return for something

---

[3] Established in the mid-1980s
[4] See *Jones v Attorney-General* (1976) *The Times*, 10 November.
[5] See para 9.05 below.

of value.[6] The definition of 'appeal' also includes the exposing of or offer of goods or services for sale. The main criterion is that any such offers are made to members of the public.

Both 'business' and 'house' are given wide definitions, and a 'public place' means highways, public areas at stations, shopping precincts, or other similar areas. The definition of 'public place' is therefore simply defined as any area to which the public have access. The definition does, however, exclude areas which are within a building and places where access results from the specific sale of tickets to allow admission to that place. One-off access to a place given for the purposes of an appeal is also outside the definition of a 'public place'. · 9.05

C. OTHER CHARITABLE APPEALS

A charitable appeal will not be a public charitable collection within the meaning of s 45 if it is made in the course of a public meeting, or on land used as a place of public worship or adjacent to it. The phrase used in s 46 of the Charities Act 2006 includes land which is contiguous to, or adjacent to, a place of worship. Churchyards or burial grounds are thus not public places for the purposes of public collections. Enclosed land (whether in a building or within walls) is not included. The traditional church fête, or fundraising activities at any other place of worship, such as within the precincts of a mosque, etc, will not be regarded as 'public collections'. · 9.06

It might be thought that excepting these types of fundraising events or activities is both pragmatic and proportionate to achieving the aim of preserving public confidence. The exception implies that the funds will be given by those attending that type of land, and the physical presence of the donor is assumed. The number of attendees is therefore limited to the land in question, and most people will need to be associated with the place of worship in order to know about such events. Any land to which the public must be invited or permitted to enter by the occupier is not 'public' for the purposes of the Charities Act 2006. Any land which is expressly excluded by another enactment is also not a public place for these purposes. Unattended collection boxes are not included if such a box is not in the possession or custody of a person acting as a collector. An example of this could be collection boxes at nature reserves or in churches. · 9.07

D. PUBLIC COLLECTIONS CERTIFICATES

There is a general prohibition on holding public collections in the absence of a valid public collections certificate which has been issued to the promoter of the collection. A promoter is a person who organizes or controls, either alone or with others, the · 9.08

---

[6] See s 45(3) of the Charities Act 2006.

conduct of a charitable appeal. If there is no person organizing and controlling the collection then 'promoter' is defined as the collector himself.[7]

9.09   The Act authorizes public collections via two steps: by the issue of public collections certificates; and by the issue of public collections permits. Short-term local collections[8] do not require certificates or permits. Any collection in a public place made by a promoter without authorization is a summary offence punishable by a fine not exceeding level 5 on the standard scale. Door-to-door collections must not be conducted without a public collections certificate. Further protection on the doorstep is provided in that even if the promoters hold the necessary certificate, they must also inform the local authority, before the collection, that they will be conducting such a collection. Promoters must provide a copy of the certificate to the local authority prior to beginning the collection. This provision is directly aimed at protecting vulnerable people from bogus charity collections on their doorsteps. Local short-term collections are also exempt from this provision. If a doorstep collection is undertaken, the information to be given to the local authority includes the purposes of the appeal, the dates of the collection, and the locality where the collection will take place. Further requirements may be prescribed. A further distinction is made with relation to doorstep collections. If the appeal is for goods only (eg clothing or unwanted items) and does not include either money or cheques, the punishment for contravening the requirements listed above is a fine at level 3 on the standard scale. If money and goods are collected then the punishment is set at level 5 on the standard scale.

E. SHORT-TERM LOCAL COLLECTIONS

9.10   As seen above, this type of charitable collection is exempt from the provisions regulating public charitable collections. Short-term local collections are not totally free from regulation, though. A short-term local collection is one in which the nature of the appeal is local and is of limited duration. If such a collection is proposed then the promoters must inform the local authority in the area in which the collection is to be made. The local authority must be told what the purpose of the collection is, the dates on which the collection will take place, and the area in which the collection will be made. The local authority may object to the holding of such a collection, and if this is the case it must serve a notice to that effect on the potential promoters of the collection. There are certain grounds on which the local authority may object. If it seems that the collection is not a local short-term collection, or that the persons conducting the collection have at any time breached regulations concerned with public collections, or have previously been convicted of an offence concerning fundraising, the local authority may object to the holding of such a collection. If this happens, the local authority is obliged, in communicating that decision, to include a notice which informs the potential promoter of the right to

---

[7] See ss 47 and 48 of the Charities Act 2006.
[8] Defined in s 50 of the Charities Act 2006.

appeal against that decision. To hold a short-term local collection in a public place, or by visits from door to door, without notifying the local authority is an offence.

F. APPLYING FOR PUBLIC COLLECTIONS CERTIFICATES

Public collections certificates are to be issued by the Charity Commission. This is a completely new power for the Commission. The application must be made prior to the time of the collection. Regulations will specify the length of time which is required. Alternatively, the Commission may specify the time at which such an application should be made. The maximum period for which a certificate will be valid is five years. Single collections may be the subject of an application for a certificate. The form of application for a certificate and the expected regulations will govern the application procedure. Once an application is received, the Charity Commission may make inquiries and then either grant or refuse the application. If granted, the certificate will be in force for the time specified in it. In view of the expected number of applications, it is likely that transitional arrangements will be put in place. Certificates may include conditions. 9.11

The grounds for the Charity Commission to refuse the grant of a public collections certificate are set out in s 53 of the Charities Act 2006. Generally the person applying must be authorized by the charitable, benevolent, or philanthropic body concerned. A fundraiser should be shown not to have acted in the past without due diligence, and the proportion of funds collected which is to be directly applied to charitable activities must be sufficient. The remuneration (if any) of the fundraiser must not be excessive and any information previously supplied for the purposes of an application for a public collections certificate must not have been misleading. Further grounds for the refusal of a certificate include persistent breaches of any conditions attached to such a certificate in the past, or the provision of false information to the Charity Commission. Conviction of a relevant offence is a ground on which a certificate may be refused. The relevant offences include all offences of dishonesty, offences under the Charities Act 2006 (see, eg, para 9.09 above), and any offence which would be facilitated by the issuing of a certificate.[9] Failing to observe due diligence, another ground for refusal, includes a failure to ensure that collectors authorized for the purposes of the collection are fit and proper persons, failing to ensure that regulations are followed, and failing to ensure that badges cannot be taken by unauthorized persons. 9.12

If more than one person applies for a certificate, they must all be suitable. It is probable that all badges authorizing collectors will have to include prescribed details under regulations to come. An applicant or certificate holder is required to furnish documents to the Charity Commission relevant to fundraising if the Charity 9.13

---

[9] Offences under some specific Acts are also included. There are three relevant Acts listed in s 53(8): the Police and Factories etc (Miscellaneous Provisions) Act 1916, the House to House Collections Act 1939, and the Civic Government (Scotland) Act 1982.

Commission requests to see them. Transfers between the trustees of unincorporated charities should be by application to the Charity Commission, and such applications should be approved by all the other trustees of such a body.

G. WITHDRAWAL OR VARIATION OF CERTIFICATES

9.14 In certain circumstances the Charity Commission may either withdraw or vary public collections certificates. A change of circumstances which, had it occurred at the time of the application, would have meant that the Charity Commission would have either refused to grant a certificate or attached different conditions to it, allows the Commission to withdraw the certificate. Alternatively, the Commission may suspend the certificate. This applies where the Commission believes that any information supplied to it was false or misleading, or where a request for information is not complied with. Breach, or threatened breach, of conditions attached to the certificate also allows the Commission to make changes to the certificate or withdraw it completely. If the Commission does attach new conditions to the certificate then those conditions must be of a type that is normally part of the certificate. There is currently no guidance on the types of conditions which may be attached to certificates.

9.15 Trustees or holders of certificates which have been varied or withdrawn should expect to be notified by the Charity Commission under s 56(7). The notice of suspension, withdrawal, or variation must inform the holders of the certificate that they have a right of appeal and also state the time period for bringing any appeal. If the Commission believes that it is in the public interest, it may suspend or withdraw the order with immediate effect to prevent any further harm from being caused. This is consistent with the Commission's commitment to preserve the public trust in charities. In less serious cases the certificate will continue until an appeal has been brought or abandoned. It is not clear from the terms of the statute which circumstances will lead to the Commission taking the view that an appeal has been abandoned, but it may be assumed that if a time limit is not complied with the Commission could view the appeal as abandoned. Until regulations are drafted it is not clear exactly what procedural steps will be required in regard to this appeal or any other.

9.16 Appeals are made to the Charity Tribunal under s 57 of the Charities Act 2006. The Tribunal has the power to reconsider the issues raised and consequently alter or quash the decision of the Charity Commission. Suspension of a certificate will continue until the Commission informs the holder that the certificate is in force again, or for a period of six months.

H. APPLICATIONS FOR PERMITS TO CONDUCT COLLECTIONS IN PUBLIC PLACES

9.17 Permits apply to specific fundraising activities where the promoters of a public collection wish to act in a particular area or locality. Application for a permit is made to the local authority, and it is envisaged that promoters will already have been issued with a public collections certificate by the Charity Commission since an application for a fundraising permit must be accompanied by a copy of the public collections certificate. Certificates are general authorities to charities or fundraisers judged by the Commission to be suitable; permits operate on a local scale. This system ought to ensure that only proper persons who hold a certificate can carry out fundraising activities, and that if there is to be any such activity, the local authority knows and approves of it. There will be prescribed periods for notifying the local authority of the proposed public collection and the application should specify the dates on which a collection is to be made. If more than one date is requested then those dates must not span more than one year. As it is also necessary to hold a public collections certificate as a precondition to applying for a permit, there is a degree of flexibility in the Act to cover those cases where the application for a certificate is still outstanding. In such cases the application for a permit should be made as early as practicable before the day of the first collection.

I. DETERMINATION OF APPLICATIONS AND THE ISSUE OF PERMITS

There will be a prescribed period during which the local authority must determine whether to issue a permit. There are limited grounds for refusal to issue a permit. These are that the collection would cause inconvenience to members of the public if it were conducted on the dates applied for, or at the time applied for. If a local authority considers that the frequency of the collections or the locality of the collections would inconvenience the public then it may refuse to issue a permit. This should prevent the situation where there are multiple collections happening simultaneously on particular streets or in particular areas. If a public collection is to be made on land to which the public must be invited, and the occupier consents to a collection being undertaken, the frequency of collections, and the fact that there may be multiple collections, should not be taken into account. Large events may attract many applications for permits and the efficient administration of the permit system is crucial to its success. It should be remembered that public collections which do not comply with the provisions regarding certificates and permits may lead to a criminal conviction, and charities should not be tempted to attempt public collections in these circumstances. 9.18

Local authorities have the same powers with respect to permits as the Commission does as regards certificates (see para 9.14 above). Permits may be withdrawn or varied, or may have conditions attached (which may also be varied), and the local authority must notify the applicant of its decision. The reasons for refusal should be stated, and there will be specified period during which to appeal against that decision. Appeals against refusals of a permit, or appeals concerning any conditions attached to the permit, are brought under s 62 of the Charities Act 2006. This specifies that such appeals are within the jurisdiction of the magistrates' court in 9.19

the local area and must be brought within 14 days of the date of service of the notice notifying the applicant of the decision to refuse the application. Decisions of the magistrates are then appealed to the Crown Court if necessary. It is expected that detailed regulations concerning the issue of both public collections certificates and permits will be put in place quite quickly. Misuse of a charity's badge, etc is a criminal offence. Sections 45 to 66 of the Charities Act 2006 are expected to be brought into force by the year 2009.

9.20   The difficulty with imposing criminal sanctions on corporate bodies has been addressed in the Charities Act 2006. If it is shown that an offence has been committed by a corporate body, and it is proved that the offence was committed with the consent, connivance, or neglect of a director, manager, secretary, or other person holding a similar office, they too will be liable with the corporate body to conviction and punishment.[10]

J. AMENDMENTS TO THE EXISTING PROVISIONS

9.21   Section 60 of the Charities Act 1992 concerns professional fundraisers and commercial participators.[11] Regulation has been undertaken for some time of the relationships between charities and people or organizations conducting fundraising on behalf of charities as a professional activity. The remuneration of professional fundraisers and the benefits to commercial participators have been scrutinized to ensure that a sufficient proportion of the funds raised is transferred to the charity concerned. In an effort to increase the transparency of these arrangements, s 67 of the Charities Act 2006 imposes a requirement to disclose the method by which the remuneration of the fundraiser is determined. Exact accounting for sums raised is required, and items such as the costs of promotional material must be included.

9.22   A person may not be a professional fundraiser but may still be rewarded or paid for collecting for charity. The provisions of s 60 now apply to these people too. A fundraiser must state the name of the institution proposed to benefit from the funds, whether he or she is being paid by the charity, and whether he or she is an office holder in that charity. Low-paid collectors are exempt from these requirements. A person is low-paid if he or she earns less than £5 per day or £500 per year from the fundraising activity.[12] Charities using paid collectors may expect to see further regulations concerning this type of solicitation.

9.23   Trustees, charities, and persons connected with charitable, benevolent, or philanthropic bodies are required to adopt 'good practice' with relation to fundraising activities. The Charities Act 2006 defines good practice as taking all reasonable steps to ensure that there is no unreasonable intrusion on the privacy of those

---

[10] Charities Act 2006, s 65.

[11] For the definition of 'professional fundraiser' and 'commercial participators', see s 58 of the Charities Act 1992.

[12] This has remained the same and there is no change to these thresholds.

approached, that the approaches are not unreasonably persistent, that no undue pressure is applied on those solicited, and that no false or misleading representations are made about the urgency of any need for funds by a charity or the use of such funds by the charity. No misleading representations should be made about the achievements or finances of a charity either. Primary purpose trading is excluded from these provisions.

10

TRANSFER OF PROPERTY AND MERGERS

A. GENERAL

Prior to the Charities Act 2006, trustees might have had difficulty winding up a   10.01
charity, or otherwise transferring assets to other charities. Trustees might feel the
need to do this if the purposes of the charity could not be carried out effectively
either because of lack of income, or because the type of property concerned restricted
its use. The Charities Act 1993 already contained provision for small charities to
transfer their assets in certain circumstances. This power has been extended and a
new s 74 substituted by the Charities Act 2006. The power applies only to small
charities, which are now defined as charities having an income of less than £10,000
per year. It applies only to unincorporated charities having no designated land.
('Designated' land is land held on trusts which stipulate that the land must be used
for the purposes of the charity.) The trustees should pass a resolution by not less
than a two-thirds majority vote, stating their intention to transfer the property to
an organization having substantially the same purposes as their charity. They must
also state that they consider that such a transfer is expedient and in the interests of
furthering the purposes for which they were established.

B. TRANSFERS

The new s 74 is more relaxed than the same provision as it appeared in the 1993 Act.   10.02
Trustees must try to ensure, 'so far as is reasonably practicable', that the property
is used or applied for the correct purpose, or for one which is substantially similar
to those of the transferring charity. In these circumstances the Charity Commission
will facilitate the transfer by making vesting orders as necessary. There is a power

for the Charity Commission to require further information if a transfer is requested by the trustees of a charity. The type of information most likely to be requested is a final account and any information concerning the trustees' compliance with regulations. In some circumstances the Charity Commission may direct that public notice is given of the transfer, and that time is allowed for representations from interested parties to be received and considered.

C. PERMANENT ENDOWMENT

10.03   The Charity Commission is currently reviewing its guidance on permanently endowed charities. The current guidance is contained in Charity Commission publication CC 38, which provides that if a charity wishes to use assets which it is unable to sell or dispose of, it may apply to the Charity Commission for express permission to use those assets in the way it wishes. Provided the Charity Commission is satisfied that this is the best use of the capital assets of a charity and that the charity itself is not put in jeopardy, it may allow that use. Conditions designed to maintain the capital level of the trust, eg provision for recoupment out of future income, are commonly imposed.

10.04   Section 74B considerably extends a small charity's ability to transfer its property, including its permanent endowment. This represents a slight relaxation of the law. Rather than being 'reasonably satisfied' that the transferee charity has purposes similar to those of their own charity, the trustees must be 'satisfied' that the transferee has purposes substantially similar to those of their own charity. This imposes a slightly higher threshold on trustees than that contained in s 74 (see para 10.02 above), to ensure that the original purposes of the trust will be respected. Further guidance on the transfer of permanent endowments is expected.

10.05   Section 74C allows small charities to change the purposes of their trust to other purposes if they are satisfied that it is no longer expedient in the interests of the charity to continue with those purposes. Any change must be to a purpose which is substantially similar to the original purpose. This section applies only to small, unincorporated charities having no permanent endowment. The same provisions as to resolutions and notices (if required) apply in these circumstances (see para 10.02 above).

10.06   There is a general relaxation of regulation and a greater flexibility for small unincorporated charities under the Charities Act 2006. Subject to the required resolution by two-thirds majority of the trustees but also the members in general meeting (in the case of an unincorporated charitable association with a membership), small charities are given a general power to amend the administrative provisions in their constitutional rules.

10.07   The new s 75 of the Charities Act 1993, as inserted by s 43 of the Charities Act 2006, allows unincorporated charities to spend capital. However, larger charities whose trustees wish to spend capital will be governed by s 75A. In these cases, the test of whether such an action is justified is that the trustees must be satisfied that the purposes of the charity are more effectively carried out if the capital as well as the income is spent. In the case of larger (unincorporated) charities, the

Commission may require notice to be given to the public, or that the larger charity should demonstrate why it has decided that capital should be released from the previous restriction on its application. Some charities do not have any limits on the spending of capital in their constitutional documents and these sections apply only if no power to do this has already been given. Some gifts to charity are specified to be used for particular purposes. In certain circumstances these gifts create special trusts within a charity. Section 75B may apply if the trustees are satisfied that the use of the property is better served, or carried out more effectively, if the special trusts are relaxed or removed. This can now be done, subject to the concurrence of the Charity Commission.

D. MERGERS

The new s 75C of the Charities Act 1993[1] contains a radical new power under which the Charity Commission may approve mergers of charities. This section applies to both small and large charities. Trustees may from time to time decide to merge their charities, either by transferring the property of one charity to another or by the creation of a new charity to which both the original charities transfer their property. If this is done, the merger itself can be registered with the Charity Commission. The only charities excepted from this provision are CIOs, which have their own provisions for amalgamation.   10.08

There are detailed provisions concerning the transfer of property and the vesting of it in the new charity created by the merger. The most helpful effect of registering a merger is that s 75F allows gifts made to any participant charity to take effect as gifts to the new charity.   10.09

E. CY-PRÈS

In some cases it becomes obvious that it has become impossible or impracticable to carry out the purposes of a charity. Alternatively, there may be a gift to an institution which has ceased to exist. In these circumstances a cy-près scheme may be used to direct how such gifts are applied for charitable purposes. The assets or gift will be used for a purpose as close as possible to the 'spirit of the gift' which was intended. The Charities Act 2006 amends the existing provisions,[2] modernizing some of the language used.   10.10

Section 17 of the 2006 Act inserts a new s 14A into the Charities Act 1993. In some appeals, where funds have been raised for particular purposes, eg in response to a disaster or event, the purpose can be fulfilled by using only a portion of the funds raised. Prior to the Charities Act 2006 it was necessary for the trustees to apply for   10.11

---

[1] Inserted by s 44 of the Charities Act 2006.
[2] Currently ss 13 and 14 of the Charities Act 1993.

a cy-près scheme to allow the surplus funds to be used for an associated purpose or a similar purpose. If this was not done, the surplus donations would be returnable to the original donors. If an appeal is made, it is not always possible to trace each and every donor to offer to return the surplus donations. This is particularly the case where small cash donations have been made. Under the new provisions it is assumed that if a cy-près situation arises, the donor intended the gift to be applied cy-près for charitable purposes. It remains open to a donor expressly to declare that if for some reason the gift cannot be applied for the specific purpose for which it was intended, its return to the donor is required. This change effectively reverses the presumption that gifts should be returned to the donor and replaces it with a presumption that, unless expressly stated, the gift was intended to be an outright gift for charitable purposes.

11

IMPLEMENTATION AND CONCLUSION

The Office of the Third Sector (Cabinet Office) has recently released the Charities 11.01
Act 2006 implementation plan, indicating how the various new provisions will
be brought into force. The Office of the Third Sector is anxious to give charities
sufficient time to prepare properly for any changes which might affect them.

The Act received Royal Assent on 8 November 2006, but its implementation 11.02
has been planned to take place throughout 2007 and into 2008. The first changes
which may be expected to have an impact on charity trustees are that the measures
designed to de-regulate smaller charities will be brought into effect. Other deregulatory measures are also expected to be implemented reasonably quickly. A
series of regional events will be held to explain the Act to charities, and further
public consultation on the public benefit test will be undertaken. The Charity
Commission will have a modernized framework in order to carry out its duties and
functions. These changes are expected early in 2007.

Many key measures in the Act require consultation, guidance, or secondary 11.03
legislation before they can be commenced. The example given by the Cabinet
Office of this type of measure is that the new definition of charity and the public
benefit test will not be brought into force until there is an accessible appeal right
through the Charity Tribunal and the consultation on the public benefit test is
completed.

A first commencement order is expected in early 2007 and will bring around 11.04
thirteen sections into force. The provisions concerning the new Charity Commission
and its functions, etc, the relaxation of publicity in relation to schemes, the interim
changes in threshold for small charities, the power to determine membership of a
charity, and the power to enter premises and seize documents will all be included in
this. The ability for charities to purchase indemnity insurance, the changes to the
restrictions on mortgages of charity land, and the power of unincorporated charities
to modify procedures or powers are also all to be within the first commencement
order.

In the second half of 2007 it is anticipated that the provisions on mergers, 11.05
many of the fundraising reforms, and matters such as the auditing and accounting
requirements will be brought into force.

11.06   The third commencement order is expected in early 2008, when the provisions covering the public benefit test, the Charity Tribunal, and the CIO will be brought into force. Some of the items in the third commencement order represent the most radical changes instituted by the Charities Act 2006.

11.07   Although the Charities Act 2006 contains some innovative and fundamental changes to the law, it is essentially a modernization of the existing law. As can be seen from the earlier chapters of this book, the Charities Act 1993 remains as the bedrock of the statutory provisions concerning charities. The system of amending, inserting, and, if necessary, substituting parts of the Charities Act 1993, has the effect of making the Charities Act 2006 difficult to read or understand in isolation from the 1993 Act. Whilst some of the provisions in the 2006 Act are novel, others are designed to address persistent areas of concern for trustees and the Charity Commission. It is expected that a consolidation statute will follow, so that there will be one Act containing the provisions of both the Charities Act 1993 and the Charities Act 2006. In the meantime the Commission intends to publish guides to the Charities Act 2006. This book is offered as a guide to the new provisions, rather than as a review either of the Charities Act 1993, or of the considerable body of charity law remaining unchanged by the Act.

APPENDIX 1

Charities Act 2006

CONTENTS

PART 1
MEANING OF "CHARITY" AND "CHARITABLE PURPOSE"

PART 2
REGULATION OF CHARITIES

CHAPTER 1
THE CHARITY COMMISSION

Establishment of Charity Commission

Commission's objectives, general functions etc.

CHAPTER 2
THE CHARITY TRIBUNAL

CHAPTER 3
REGISTRATION OF CHARITIES

General

CHAPTER 2
FUND-RAISING

CHAPTER 3
FINANCIAL ASSISTANCE

PART 4
MISCELLANEOUS AND GENERAL

79. Commencement
80. Short title and extent

An Act to provide for the establishment and functions of the Charity Commission for England and Wales and the Charity Tribunal; to make other amendments of the law about charities, including provision about charitable incorporated organisations; to make further provision about public charitable collections and other fund-raising carried on in connection with charities and other institutions; to make other provision about the funding of such institutions; and for connected purposes.

[8th November 2006]

BE IT ENACTED by the Queen's most Excellent Majesty, by and with the advice and consent of the Lords Spiritual and Temporal, and Commons, in this present Parliament assembled, and by the authority of the same, as follows:—

PART 1
MEANING OF "CHARITY" AND "CHARITABLE PURPOSE"

1. Meaning of "charity"

(1) For the purposes of the law of England and Wales, "charity" means an institution which—
  (a) is established for charitable purposes only, and
  (b) falls to be subject to the control of the High Court in the exercise of its jurisdiction with respect to charities.
(2) The definition of "charity" in subsection (1) does not apply for the purposes of an enactment if a different definition of that term applies for those purposes by virtue of that or any other enactment.
(3) A reference in any enactment or document to a charity within the meaning of the Charitable Uses Act 1601 (c. 4) or the preamble to it is to be construed as a reference to a charity as defined by subsection (1).[1]

---

[1] Sections 1 and 2 of the Charities Act 2006 are completely new. Unlike much of the Charities Act 2006 these sections are not inserted into the Charities Act 1993. The list of charitable purposes is a

2. Meaning of "charitable purpose"

(1) For the purposes of the law of England and Wales, a charitable purpose is a purpose which—

    (a) falls within subsection (2), and

    (b) is for the public benefit (see section 3).

(2) A purpose falls within this subsection if it falls within any of the following descriptions of purposes—

    (a) the prevention or relief of poverty;

    (b) the advancement of education;

    (c) the advancement of religion;

    (d) the advancement of health or the saving of lives;

    (e) the advancement of citizenship or community development;

    (f) the advancement of the arts, culture, heritage or science;

    (g) the advancement of amateur sport;

    (h) the advancement of human rights, conflict resolution or reconciliation or the promotion of religious or racial harmony or equality and diversity;

    (i) the advancement of environmental protection or improvement;

    (j) the relief of those in need by reason of youth, age, ill-health, disability, financial hardship or other disadvantage;

    (k) the advancement of animal welfare;

    (l) the promotion of the efficiency of the armed forces of the Crown, or of the efficiency of the police, fire and rescue services or ambulance services;

    (m) any other purposes within subsection (4).

(3) In subsection (2)—

    (a) in paragraph (c) "religion" includes—

      (i) a religion which involves belief in more than one god, and

      (ii) a religion which does not involve belief in a god;

    (b) in paragraph (d) "the advancement of health" includes the prevention or relief of sickness, disease or human suffering;

    (c) paragraph (e) includes—

      (i) rural or urban regeneration, and

      (ii) the promotion of civic responsibility, volunteering, the voluntary sector or the effectiveness or efficiency of charities;

    (d) in paragraph (g) "sport" means sports or games which promote health by involving physical or mental skill or exertion;

    (e) paragraph (j) includes relief given by the provision of accommodation or care to the persons mentioned in that paragraph; and

    (f) in paragraph (l) "fire and rescue services" means services provided by fire and rescue authorities under Part 2 of the Fire and Rescue Services Act 2004 (c. 21).

(4) The purposes within this subsection (see subsection (2)(m)) are—

    (a) any purposes not within paragraphs (a) to (l) of subsection (2) but recognised as charitable purposes under existing charity law or by virtue of section 1 of the Recreational Charities Act 1958 (c. 17);

restatement of the existing law in statutory form. See Stephen Lloyd, 'The meaning of Charity', *The Times*, 12 December 2006.

(b) any purposes that may reasonably be regarded as analogous to, or within the spirit of, any purposes falling within any of those paragraphs or paragraph (a) above; and

(c) any purposes that may reasonably be regarded as analogous to, or within the spirit of, any purposes which have been recognised under charity law as falling within paragraph (b) above or this paragraph.

(5) Where any of the terms used in any of paragraphs (a) to (l) of subsection (2), or in subsection (3), has a particular meaning under charity law, the term is to be taken as having the same meaning where it appears in that provision.

(6) Any reference in any enactment or document (in whatever terms)—

(a) to charitable purposes, or

(b) to institutions having purposes that are charitable under charity law,

is to be construed in accordance with subsection (1).

(7) Subsection (6)—

(a) applies whether the enactment or document was passed or made before or after the passing of this Act, but

(b) does not apply where the context otherwise requires.

(8) In this section—

"charity law" means the law relating to charities in England and Wales; and

"existing charity law" means charity law as in force immediately before the day on which this section comes into force.

3. The "public benefit" test

(1) This section applies in connection with the requirement in section 2(1)(b) that a purpose falling within section 2(2) must be for the public benefit if it is to be a charitable purpose.

(2) In determining whether that requirement is satisfied in relation to any such purpose, it is not to be presumed that a purpose of a particular description is for the public benefit.

(3) In this Part any reference to the public benefit is a reference to the public benefit as that term is understood for the purposes of the law relating to charities in England and Wales.

(4) Subsection (3) applies subject to subsection (2).[2]

4. Guidance as to operation of public benefit requirement

(1) The Charity Commission for England and Wales (see section 6 of this Act) must issue guidance in pursuance of its public benefit objective.

(2) That objective is to promote awareness and understanding of the operation of the requirement mentioned in section 3(1) (see section 1B(3) and (4) of the Charities Act 1993 (c. 10), as inserted by section 7 of this Act).

(3) The Commission may from time to time revise any guidance issued under this section.

(4) The Commission must carry out such public and other consultation as it considers appropriate—

(a) before issuing any guidance under this section, or

---

[2] The inclusion of the public benefit test is the most radical change in the law. See Chapter 2.

    (b) (unless it considers that it is unnecessary to do so) before revising any such guidance.

(5) The Commission must publish any guidance issued or revised under this section in such manner as it considers appropriate.

(6) The charity trustees of a charity must have regard to any such guidance when exercising any powers or duties to which the guidance is relevant.[3]

5. Special provisions about recreational charities, sports clubs etc.

(1) The Recreational Charities Act 1958 (c. 17) is amended in accordance with subsections (2) and (3).

(2) In section 1 (certain recreational and similar purposes deemed to be charitable) for subsection (2) substitute—

"(2) The requirement in subsection (1) that the facilities are provided in the interests of social welfare cannot be satisfied if the basic conditions are not met.

(2A) The basic conditions are—
    (a) that the facilities are provided with the object of improving the conditions of life for the persons for whom the facilities are primarily intended; and
    (b) that either—
       (i) those persons have need of the facilities by reason of their youth, age, infirmity or disability, poverty, or social and economic circumstances, or
       (ii) the facilities are to be available to members of the public at large or to male, or to female, members of the public at large."

(3) Section 2 (miners' welfare trusts) is omitted.

(4) A registered sports club established for charitable purposes is to be treated as not being so established, and accordingly cannot be a charity.

(5) In subsection (4) a "registered sports club" means a club for the time being registered under Schedule 18 to the Finance Act 2002 (c. 23) (relief for community amateur sports club).

PART 2
REGULATION OF CHARITIES

CHAPTER 1
THE CHARITY COMMISSION

Establishment of Charity Commission[4]

6. The Charity Commission

(1) After section 1 of the 1993 Act insert—

---

[3] The Charity Commission must provide this guidance. The first guidance was released in October 2006 and appears in this book as Appendix 2.

[4] The new ss 1A–1E are inserted into the previous legislation (Charities Act 1993). Many of the new provisions are inserted into the Charities Act 1993, making the new Act difficult to read. A consolidation statute is expected. Reading the legislation will become much easier if this is done.

"1A The Charity Commission[5]

(1) There shall be a body corporate to be known as the Charity Commission for England and Wales (in this Act referred to as "the Commission").

(2) In Welsh the Commission shall be known as 'Comisiwn Elusennau Cymru a Lloegr'.

(3) The functions of the Commission shall be performed on behalf of the Crown.

(4) In the exercise of its functions the Commission shall not be subject to the direction or control of any Minister of the Crown or other government department.

(5) But subsection (4) above does not affect—

(a) any provision made by or under any enactment;

(b) any administrative controls exercised over the Commission's expenditure by the Treasury.

(6) The provisions of Schedule 1A to this Act shall have effect with respect to the Commission."

(2) Schedule 1 (which inserts the new Schedule 1A into the 1993 Act) has effect.

(3) The office of Charity Commissioner for England and Wales is abolished.

(4) The functions of the Charity Commissioners for England and Wales and their property, rights and liabilities are by virtue of this subsection transferred to the Charity Commission for England and Wales.

(5) Any enactment or document has effect, so far as necessary for the purposes of or in consequence of the transfer effected by subsection (4), as if any reference to the Charity Commissioners for England and Wales or to any Charity Commissioner for England and Wales were a reference to the Charity Commission for England and Wales.

(6) Section 1 of, and Schedule 1 to, the 1993 Act cease to have effect.

(7) Schedule 2 (which contains supplementary provision relating to the establishment of the Charity Commission for England and Wales) has effect.

Commission's objectives, general functions etc

7. The Commission's objectives, general functions and duties

After section 1A of the 1993 Act (inserted by section 6 above) insert—

"1B The Commission's objectives

(1) The Commission has the objectives set out in subsection (2).

(2) The objectives are—

1. The public confidence objective.

2. The public benefit objective.

3. The compliance objective.

4. The charitable resources objective.

5. The accountability objective.

(3) Those objectives are defined as follows—

---

[5] The re-defining of the role of the Charity Commission is one of the most fundamental changes in emphasis in the new provisions. The Charity Commission is given specific functions and duties to carry out. In carrying out these duties the Commission will become accountable to the Charity Tribunal.

1. The public confidence objective is to increase public trust and confidence in charities.
2. The public benefit objective is to promote awareness and understanding of the operation of the public benefit requirement.
3. The compliance objective is to promote compliance by charity trustees with their legal obligations in exercising control and management of the administration of their charities.
4. The charitable resources objective is to promote the effective use of charitable resources.
5. The accountability objective is to enhance the accountability of charities to donors, beneficiaries and the general public.

(4) In this section "the public benefit requirement" means the requirement in section 2(1)(b) of the Charities Act 2006 that a purpose falling within section 2(2) of that Act must be for the public benefit if it is to be a charitable purpose.

1C The Commission's general functions

(1) The Commission has the general functions set out in subsection (2).
(2) The general functions are—
1. Determining whether institutions are or are not charities.
2. Encouraging and facilitating the better administration of charities.
3. Identifying and investigating apparent misconduct or mismanagement in the administration of charities and taking remedial or protective action in connection with misconduct or mismanagement therein.
4. Determining whether public collections certificates should be issued, and remain in force, in respect of public charitable collections.
5. Obtaining, evaluating and disseminating information in connection with the performance of any of the Commission's functions or meeting any of its objectives.
6. Giving information or advice, or making proposals, to any Minister of the Crown on matters relating to any of the Commission's functions or meeting any of its objectives.

(3) The Commission's fifth general function includes (among other things) the maintenance of an accurate and up-to-date register of charities under section 3 below.
(4) The Commission's sixth general function includes (among other things) complying, so far as is reasonably practicable, with any request made by a Minister of the Crown for information or advice on any matter relating to any of its functions.
(5) In this section 'public charitable collection' and 'public collections certificate' have the same meanings as in Chapter 1 of Part 3 of the Charities Act 2006.

1D The Commission's general duties

(1) The Commission has the general duties set out in subsection (2).
(2) The general duties are—
1. So far as is reasonably practicable the Commission must, in performing its functions, act in a way—
   (a) which is compatible with its objectives, and
   (b) which it considers most appropriate for the purpose of meeting those objectives.

2. So far as is reasonably practicable the Commission must, in performing its functions, act in a way which is compatible with the encouragement of—
   (a) all forms of charitable giving, and
   (b) voluntary participation in charity work.
3. In performing its functions the Commission must have regard to the need to use its resources in the most efficient, effective and economic way.
4. In performing its functions the Commission must, so far as relevant, have regard to the principles of best regulatory practice (including the principles under which regulatory activities should be proportionate, accountable, consistent, transparent and targeted only at cases in which action is needed).
5. In performing its functions the Commission must, in appropriate cases, have regard to the desirability of facilitating innovation by or on behalf of charities.
6. In managing its affairs the Commission must have regard to such generally accepted principles of good corporate governance as it is reasonable to regard as applicable to it.

1E The Commission's incidental powers

(1) The Commission has power to do anything which is calculated to facilitate, or is conducive or incidental to, the performance of any of its functions or general duties.
(2) However, nothing in this Act authorises the Commission—
   (a) to exercise functions corresponding to those of a charity trustee in relation to a charity, or
   (b) otherwise to be directly involved in the administration of a charity.
(3) Subsection (2) does not affect the operation of section 19A or 19B below (power of Commission to give directions as to action to be taken or as to application of charity property)."

CHAPTER 2
THE CHARITY TRIBUNAL

8. The Charity Tribunal

(1) After section 2 of the 1993 Act insert—[6]

"PART 1A
THE CHARITY TRIBUNAL

2A The Charity Tribunal

(1) There shall be a tribunal to be known as the Charity Tribunal (in this Act referred to as 'the Tribunal').
(2) In Welsh the Tribunal shall be known as 'Tribiwnlys Elusennau'.

---

[6] The same legislative method of inserting the new provisions into existing legislation is used to establish the Charity Tribunal. This is a completely new Tribunal. See Chapter 6. Procedural rules have not yet been drafted but will follow (see below). Sections 2A–2D are inserted, but also see Sch 4 to this Act.

(3) The provisions of Schedule 1B to this Act shall have effect with respect to the constitution of the Tribunal and other matters relating to it.

(4) The Tribunal shall have jurisdiction to hear and determine—

    (a) such appeals and applications as may be made to the Tribunal in accordance with Schedule 1C to this Act, or any other enactment, in respect of decisions, orders or directions of the Commission, and

    (b) such matters as may be referred to the Tribunal in accordance with Schedule 1D to this Act by the Commission or the Attorney General.

(5) Such appeals, applications and matters shall be heard and determined by the Tribunal in accordance with those Schedules, or any such enactment, taken with section 2B below and rules made under that section.

2B Practice and procedure

(1) The Lord Chancellor may make rules—

    (a) regulating the exercise of rights to appeal or to apply to the Tribunal and matters relating to the making of references to it;

    (b) about the practice and procedure to be followed in relation to proceedings before the Tribunal.

(2) Rules under subsection (1)(a) above may, in particular, make provision—

    (a) specifying steps which must be taken before appeals, applications or references are made to the Tribunal (and the period within which any such steps must be taken);

    (b) specifying the period following the Commission's final decision, direction or order within which such appeals or applications may be made;

    (c) requiring the Commission to inform persons of their right to appeal or apply to the Tribunal following a final decision, direction or order of the Commission;

    (d) specifying the manner in which appeals, applications or references to the Tribunal are to be made.

(3) Rules under subsection (1)(b) above may, in particular, make provision—

    (a) for the President or a legal member of the Tribunal (see paragraph 1(2)(b) of Schedule 1B to this Act) to determine preliminary, interlocutory or ancillary matters;

    (b) for matters to be determined without an oral hearing in specified circumstances;

    (c) for the Tribunal to deal with urgent cases expeditiously;

    (d) about the disclosure of documents;

    (e) about evidence;

    (f) about the admission of members of the public to proceedings;

    (g) about the representation of parties to proceedings;

    (h) about the withdrawal of appeals, applications or references;

    (i) about the recording and promulgation of decisions;

    (j) about the award of costs.

(4) Rules under subsection (1)(a) or (b) above may confer a discretion on—

    (a) the Tribunal,

    (b) a member of the Tribunal, or

    (c) any other person.

(5) The Tribunal may award costs only in accordance with subsections (6) and (7) below.

(6) If the Tribunal considers that any party to proceedings before it has acted vexatiously, frivolously or unreasonably, the Tribunal may order that party to pay to any other

party to the proceedings the whole or part of the costs incurred by that other party in connection with the proceedings.

(7) If the Tribunal considers that a decision, direction or order of the Commission which is the subject of proceedings before it was unreasonable, the Tribunal may order the Commission to pay to any other party to the proceedings the whole or part of the costs incurred by that other party in connection with the proceedings.

(8) Rules of the Lord Chancellor under this section—

    (a) shall be made by statutory instrument, and

    (b) shall be subject to annulment in pursuance of a resolution of either House of Parliament.

(9) Section 86(3) below applies in relation to rules of the Lord Chancellor under this section as it applies in relation to regulations and orders of the Minister under this Act.

2C Appeal from Tribunal

(1) A party to proceedings before the Tribunal may appeal to the High Court against a decision of the Tribunal.

(2) Subject to subsection (3) below, an appeal may be brought under this section against a decision of the Tribunal only on a point of law.

(3) In the case of an appeal under this section against a decision of the Tribunal which determines a question referred to it by the Commission or the Attorney General, the High Court—

    (a) shall consider afresh the question referred to the Tribunal, and

    (b) may take into account evidence which was not available to the Tribunal.

(4) An appeal under this section may be brought only with the permission of—

    (a) the Tribunal, or

    (b) if the Tribunal refuses permission, the High Court.

(5) For the purposes of subsection (1) above—

    (a) the Commission and the Attorney General are to be treated as parties to all proceedings before the Tribunal, and

    (b) rules under section 2B(1) above may include provision as to who else is to be treated as being (or not being) a party to proceedings before the Tribunal.

2D Intervention by Attorney General

(1) This section applies to any proceedings—

    (a) before the Tribunal, or

    (b) on an appeal from the Tribunal,

to which the Attorney General is not a party.

(2) The Tribunal or, in the case of an appeal from the Tribunal, the court may at any stage of the proceedings direct that all the necessary papers in the proceedings be sent to the Attorney General.

(3) A direction under subsection (2) may be made by the Tribunal or court—

    (a) of its own motion, or

    (b) on the application of any party to the proceedings.

(4) The Attorney General may—

    (a) intervene in the proceedings in such manner as he thinks necessary or expedient, and

    (b) argue before the Tribunal or court any question in relation to the proceedings which the Tribunal or court considers it necessary to have fully argued.

(5) Subsection (4) applies whether or not the Tribunal or court has given a direction under subsection (2)."

(2) Schedule 3 (which inserts the new Schedule 1B into the 1993 Act) has effect.

(3) Schedule 4 (which inserts the new Schedules 1C and 1D into the 1993 Act) has effect.

CHAPTER 3
REGISTRATION OF CHARITIES

General

9. Registration of charities

For section 3 of the 1993 Act substitute[7]—

"3   Register of charities

(1) There shall continue to be a register of charities, which shall be kept by the Commission.

(2) The register shall be kept by the Commission in such manner as it thinks fit.

(3) The register shall contain—

    (a) the name of every charity registered in accordance with section 3A below (registration), and

    (b) such other particulars of, and such other information relating to, every such charity as the Commission thinks fit.

(4) The Commission shall remove from the register—

    (a) any institution which it no longer considers is a charity, and

    (b) any charity which has ceased to exist or does not operate.

(5) If the removal of an institution under subsection (4)(a) above is due to any change in its trusts, the removal shall take effect from the date of that change.

(6) A charity which is for the time being registered under section 3A(6) below (voluntary registration) shall be removed from the register if it so requests.

(7) The register (including the entries cancelled when institutions are removed from the register) shall be open to public inspection at all reasonable times.

(8) Where any information contained in the register is not in documentary form, subsection (7) above shall be construed as requiring the information to be available for public inspection in legible form at all reasonable times.

(9) If the Commission so determines, subsection (7) shall not apply to any particular information contained in the register that is specified in the determination.

(10) Copies (or particulars) of the trusts of any registered charity as supplied to the Commission under section 3B below (applications for registration etc.) shall, so long as the charity remains on the register—

    (a) be kept by the Commission, and

    (b) be open to public inspection at all reasonable times.

---

[7] This section completely replaces the existing s 3 of the Charities Act 1993.

3A Registration of charities

(1) Every charity must be registered in the register of charities unless subsection (2) below applies to it.

(2) The following are not required to be registered—

    (a) any exempt charity (see Schedule 2 to this Act);

    (b) any charity which for the time being—

        (i) is permanently or temporarily excepted by order of the Commission, and

        (ii) complies with any conditions of the exception,

    and whose gross income does not exceed £100,000;[8]

    (c) any charity which for the time being—

        (i) is, or is of a description, permanently or temporarily excepted by regulations made by the Secretary of State, and

        (ii) complies with any conditions of the exception,

    and whose gross income does not exceed £100,000; and

    (d) any charity whose gross income does not exceed £5,000.

(3) For the purposes of subsection (2)(b) above—

    (a) any order made or having effect as if made under section 3(5)(b) of this Act (as originally enacted) and in force immediately before the appointed day has effect as from that day as if made under subsection (2)(b) (and may be varied or revoked accordingly); and

    (b) no order may be made under subsection (2)(b) so as to except on or after the appointed day any charity that was not excepted immediately before that day.

(4) For the purposes of subsection (2)(c) above—

    (a) any regulations made or having effect as if made under section 3(5)(b) of this Act (as originally enacted) and in force immediately before the appointed day have effect as from that day as if made under subsection (2)(c) (and may be varied or revoked accordingly);

    (b) such regulations shall be made under subsection (2)(c) as are necessary to secure that all of the formerly specified institutions are excepted under that provision (subject to compliance with any conditions of the exception and the financial limit mentioned in that provision); but

    (c) otherwise no regulations may be made under subsection (2)(c) so as to except on or after the appointed day any description of charities that was not excepted immediately before that day.

(5) In subsection (4)(b) above 'formerly specified institutions' means—

    (a) any institution falling within section 3(5B)(a) or (b) of this Act as in force immediately before the appointed day (certain educational institutions); or

    (b) any institution ceasing to be an exempt charity by virtue of section 11 of the Charities Act 2006 or any order made under that section.

(6) A charity within—

    (a) subsection (2)(b) or (c) above, or

    (b) subsection (2)(d) above,

    must, if it so requests, be registered in the register of charities.

(7) The Minister may by order amend—

    (a) subsection (2)(b) and (c) above, or

---

[8] The thresholds which trigger the requirement to register have changed. Small charities are not registrable.

(b) subsection (2)(d) above,

by substituting a different sum for the sum for the time being specified there.

(8) The Minister may only make an order under subsection (7) above—

    (a) so far as it amends subsection (2)(b) and (c), if he considers it expedient to so with a view to reducing the scope of the exception provided by those provisions;

    (b) so far as it amends subsection (2)(d), if he considers it expedient to do so in consequence of changes in the value of money or with a view to extending the scope of the exception provided by that provision,

and no order may be made by him under subsection (7)(a) unless a copy of a report under section 73 of the Charities Act 2006 (report on operation of that Act) has been laid before Parliament in accordance with that section.

(9) In this section 'the appointed day' means the day on which subsections (1) to (5) above come into force by virtue of an order under section 79 of the Charities Act 2006 relating to section 9 of that Act (registration of charities).

(10) In this section any reference to a charity's 'gross income' shall be construed, in relation to a particular tim—

    (a) as a reference to the charity's gross income in its financial year immediately preceding that time, or

    (b) if the Commission so determines, as a reference to the amount which the Commission estimates to be the likely amount of the charity's gross income in such financial year of the charity as is specified in the determination.

(11) The following provisions of this section—

    (a) subsection (2)(b) and (c),

    (b) subsections (3) to (5), and

    (c) subsections (6)(a), (7)(a), (8)(a) and (9),

shall cease to have effect on such day as the Minister may by order appoint for the purposes of this subsection.

3B Duties of trustees in connection with registration

(1) Where a charity required to be registered by virtue of section 3A(1) above is not registered, it is the duty of the charity trustees—

    (a) to apply to the Commission for the charity to be registered, and

    (b) to supply the Commission with the required documents and information.

(2) The 'required documents and information' are—

    (a) copies of the charity's trusts or (if they are not set out in any extant document) particulars of them,

    (b) such other documents or information as may be prescribed by regulations made by the Minister, and

    (c) such other documents or information as the Commission may require for the purposes of the application.

(3) Where an institution is for the time being registered, it is the duty of the charity trustees (or the last charity trustees)—

    (a) to notify the Commission if the institution ceases to exist, or if there is any change in its trusts or in the particulars of it entered in the register, and

    (b) (so far as appropriate), to supply the Commission with particulars of any such change and copies of any new trusts or alterations of the trusts.

(4) Nothing in subsection (3) above requires a person—

(a) to supply the Commission with copies of schemes for the administration of a charity made otherwise than by the court,

(b) to notify the Commission of any change made with respect to a registered charity by such a scheme, or

(c) if he refers the Commission to a document or copy already in the possession of the Commission, to supply a further copy of the document.

(5) Where a copy of a document relating to a registered charity—

(a) is not required to be supplied to the Commission as the result of subsection (4) above, but

(b) is in the possession of the Commission,

a copy of the document shall be open to inspection under section 3(10) above as if supplied to the Commission under this section."

10. Interim changes in threshold for registration of small charities

(1) At any time before the appointed day, the Minister may by order amend section 3 of the 1993 Act (the register of charities) so as to—

(a) replace section 3(5)(c) (threshold for registration of small charities) with a provision referring to a charity whose gross income does not exceed such sum as is prescribed in the order, and

(b) define "gross income" for the purposes of that provision.

(2) Subsection (1) does not affect the existing power under section 3(12) of that Act to increase the financial limit specified in section 3(5)(c).

(3) This section ceases to have effect on the appointed day.

(4) In this section "the appointed day" means the day on which section 3A(1) to (5) of the 1993 Act (as substituted by section 9 of this Act) come into force by virtue of an order under section 79 of this Act.

Exempt charities: registration and regulation

11. Changes in exempt charities

(1) Schedule 2 to the 1993 Act[9] (exempt charities) is amended as follows.

(2) In paragraph (a) (general exemption by reference to law existing prior to Charities Act 1960 (c. 58)) after "1855" insert "*(but see Note 1)*".

(3) In paragraph (b) (certain specified universities, colleges and schools)—

(a) before "Queen Mary and Westfield College" insert "and"; and

(b) omit "and the colleges of Winchester and Eton".

(4) Before paragraph (i) insert—

"(h) a higher education corporation;".

(5) After paragraph (i) insert—

"(j) a further education corporation;".

(6) In paragraph (w) (exemption for institutions administered by or on behalf of institutions exempted under preceding provisions) after "last-mentioned institution" insert "*(but see Note 2)*".

(7) Omit paragraph (x) (Church Commissioners and institutions administered by them).

---

[9] The detailed list of exempt charities in the Charities Act 1993 is amended by this section. The provisions are quite detailed and consolidation of the provisions would be particularly welcome at this level of detail.

(8) In paragraph (y) (industrial and provident societies etc.) for the words from "and any" onwards substitute "and which is also registered in the register of social landlords under Part 1 of the Housing Act 1996;".

(9) At the end insert—

"*Notes*

1. Paragraph (a) above does not include—

(a) any Investment Fund or Deposit Fund within the meaning of the Church Funds Investment Measure 1958,

(b) any investment fund or deposit fund within the meaning of the Methodist Church Funds Act 1960, or

(c) the representative body of the Welsh Church or property administered by it.

2. Paragraph (w) above does not include any students' union."

(10) In section 24 of the 1993 Act (schemes to establish common investment funds), in subsection (8) (fund is to be a charity and, if the scheme admits only exempt charities, an exempt charity) omit the words from "; and if the scheme" onwards.

(11) The Minister may by order make such further amendments of Schedule 2 to the 1993 Act as he considers appropriate for securing—

(a) that (so far as they are charities) institutions of a particular description become or (as the case may be) cease to be exempt charities, or

(b) that (so far as it is a charity) a particular institution becomes or (as the case may be) ceases to be an exempt charity,

or for removing from that Schedule an institution that has ceased to exist.

(12) An order under subsection (11) may only be made for the purpose mentioned in paragraph (a) or (b) of that subsection if the Minister is satisfied that the order is desirable in the interests of ensuring appropriate or effective regulation of the charities or charity concerned in connection with compliance by the charity trustees of the charities or charity with their legal obligations in exercising control and management of the administration of the charities or charity.

(13) The Minister may by order make such amendments or other modifications of any enactment as he considers appropriate in connection with—

(a) charities of a particular description becoming, or ceasing to be, exempt charities, or

(b) a particular charity becoming, or ceasing to be, an exempt charity,

by virtue of any provision made by or under this section.

(14) In this section "exempt charity" has the same meaning as in the 1993 Act.

12. Increased regulation of exempt charities under 1993 Act[10]

(1) The 1993 Act is amended in accordance with Schedule 5 (which has effect for increasing the extent to which exempt charities are subject to regulation under that Act).

13. General duty of principal regulator in relation to exempt charity

(1) This section applies to any body or Minister of the Crown who is the principal regulator in relation to an exempt charity.

(2) The body or Minister must do all that it or he reasonably can to meet the compliance objective in relation to the charity.

---

[10] This is a radical change extending the Charity Commission's power to regulate such charities.

(3) The compliance objective is to promote compliance by the charity trustees with their legal obligations in exercising control and management of the administration of the charity.

(4) In this section—

(a) "exempt charity" has the same meaning as in the 1993 Act; and

(b) "principal regulator", in relation to an exempt charity, means such body or Minister of the Crown as is prescribed as its principal regulator by regulations made by the Minister.

(5) Regulations under subsection (4)(b) may make such amendments or other modifications of any enactment as the Minister considers appropriate for the purpose of facilitating, or otherwise in connection with, the discharge by a principal regulator of the duty under subsection (2).

14. Commission to consult principal regulator before exercising powers in relation to exempt charity[11]

After section 86 of the 1993 Act insert—

"86A Consultation by Commission before exercising powers in relation to exempt charity

Before exercising in relation to an exempt charity any specific power exercisable by it in relation to the charity, the Commission must consult the charity's principal regulator."

CHAPTER 4
APPLICATION OF PROPERTY CY-PRÈS

Cy-près occasions

15. Application cy-près by reference to current circumstances

(1) Section 13 of the 1993 Act (occasions for applying property cy-près) is amended[12] as follows.

(2) In subsection (1)(c), (d) and (e)(iii), for "the spirit of the gift" substitute "the appropriate considerations".

(3) After subsection (1) insert—

"(1A) In subsection (1) above "the appropriate considerations" means—

(a) (on the one hand) the spirit of the gift concerned, and

(b) (on the other) the social and economic circumstances prevailing at the time of the proposed alteration of the original purposes."

16. Application cy-près of gifts by donors unknown or disclaiming[13]

(1) Section 14 of the 1993 Act (application cy-près of gifts of donors unknown or disclaiming) is amended as follows.

(2) In subsection (4) (power of court to direct that property is to be treated as belonging to donors who cannot be identified) after "court", in both places, insert "or the Commission".

---

[11] This provision amends the Charities Act 1993.
[12] The existing provision (s 13) in the Charities Act 1993 is amended and modernized.
[13] This section amends s 14 of the Charities Act 1993.

17. **Application cy-près of gifts made in response to certain solicitations**

After section 14 of the 1993 Act insert[14]—

"**14A Application cy-près of gifts made in response to certain solicitations**

(1) This section applies to property given—
   (a) for specific charitable purposes, and
   (b) in response to a solicitation within subsection (2) below.

(2) A solicitation is within this subsection if—
   (a) it is made for specific charitable purposes, and
   (b) it is accompanied by a statement to the effect that property given in response to it will, in the event of those purposes failing, be applicable cy-près as if given for charitable purposes generally, unless the donor makes a relevant declaration at the time of making the gift.

(3) A "relevant declaration" is a declaration in writing by the donor to the effect that, in the event of the specific charitable purposes failing, he wishes the trustees holding the property to give him the opportunity to request the return of the property in question (or a sum equal to its value at the time of the making of the gift).

(4) Subsections (5) and (6) below apply if—
   (a) a person has given property as mentioned in subsection (1) above,
   (b) the specific charitable purposes fail, and
   (c) the donor has made a relevant declaration.

(5) The trustees holding the property must take the prescribed steps for the purpose of—
   (a) informing the donor of the failure of the purposes,
   (b) enquiring whether he wishes to request the return of the property (or a sum equal to its value), and
   (c) if within the prescribed period he makes such a request, returning the property (or such a sum) to him.

(6) If those trustees have taken all appropriate prescribed steps but—
   (a) they have failed to find the donor, or
   (b) the donor does not within the prescribed period request the return of the property (or a sum equal to its value),
   section 14(1) above shall apply to the property as if it belonged to a donor within paragraph (b) of that subsection (application of property where donor has disclaimed right to return of property).

(7) If—
   (a) a person has given property as mentioned in subsection (1) above,
   (b) the specific charitable purposes fail, and
   (c) the donor has not made a relevant declaration,
   section 14(1) above shall similarly apply to the property as if it belonged to a donor within paragraph (b) of that subsection.

(8) For the purposes of this section—
   (a) 'solicitation' means a solicitation made in any manner and however communicated to the persons to whom it is addressed,
   (b) it is irrelevant whether any consideration is or is to be given in return for the property in question, and

---

[14] This is a completely new section inserted into the Charities Act 1993.

(c) where any appeal consists of both solicitations that are accompanied by statements within subsection (2)(b) and solicitations that are not so accompanied, a
person giving property as a result of the appeal is to be taken to have responded
to the former solicitations and not the latter, unless he proves otherwise.

(9) In this section 'prescribed' means prescribed by regulations made by the Commission, and any such regulations shall be published by the Commission in such
manner as it thinks fit.

(10) Subsections (7) and (10) of section 14 shall apply for the purposes of this section
as they apply for the purposes of section 14."

Schemes

18. Cy-près schemes[15]

After section 14A of the 1993 Act (inserted by section 17 above) insert—

"14B Cy-près schemes

(1) The power of the court or the Commission to make schemes for the application
of property cy-près shall be exercised in accordance with this section.

(2) Where any property given for charitable purposes is applicable cy-près, the court or
the Commission may make a scheme providing for the property to be applied—
    (a) for such charitable purposes, and
    (b) (if the scheme provides for the property to be transferred to another charity)
        by or on trust for such other charity,
    as it considers appropriate, having regard to the matters set out in subsection (3).

(3) The matters are—
    (a) the spirit of the original gift,
    (b) the desirability of securing that the property is applied for charitable purposes
        which are close to the original purposes, and
    (c) the need for the relevant charity to have purposes which are suitable and
        effective in the light of current social and economic circumstances.
    The "relevant charity" means the charity by or on behalf of which the property is
    to be applied under the scheme.

(4) If a scheme provides for the property to be transferred to another charity, the scheme
may impose on the charity trustees of that charity a duty to secure that the property is
applied for purposes which are, so far as is reasonably practicable, similar in character
to the original purposes.

(5) In this section references to property given include the property for the time being
representing the property originally given or property derived from it.

(6) In this section references to the transfer of property to a charity are references to its
transfer—
    (a) to the charity, or
    (b) to the charity trustees, or
    (c) to any trustee for the charity, or
    (d) to a person nominated by the charity trustees to hold it in trust for the charity,
    as the scheme may provide."

---

[15] See Chapter 10. Both s 14A and s 14B are inserted into the existing Charities Act 1993.

CHAPTER 5
ASSISTANCE AND SUPERVISION OF CHARITIES BY COURT
AND COMMISSION

Suspension or removal of trustees etc. from membership

19. Power to suspend or remove trustees etc. from membership of charity[16]

After section 18 of the 1993 Act insert—

"**18A Power to suspend or remove trustees etc. from membership of charity**

(1) This section applies where the Commission makes—
  (a) an order under section 18(1) above suspending from his office or employment any trustee, charity trustee, officer, agent or employee of a charity, or
  (b) an order under section 18(2) above removing from his office or employment any officer, agent or employee of a charity,
and the trustee, charity trustee, officer, agent or employee (as the case may be) is a member of the charity.

(2) If the order suspends the person in question from his office or employment, the Commission may also make an order suspending his membership of the charity for the period for which he is suspended from his office or employment.

(3) If the order removes the person in question from his office or employment, the Commission may also make an order—
  (a) terminating his membership of the charity, and
  (b) prohibiting him from resuming his membership of the charity without the Commission's consent.

(4) If an application for the Commission's consent under subsection (3)(b) above is made five years or more after the order was made, the Commission must grant the application unless satisfied that, by reason of any special circumstances, it should be refused."

Directions by Commission

20. Power to give specific directions for protection of charity[17]

After section 19 of the 1993 Act insert—

"**19A Power to give specific directions for protection of charity**

(1) This section applies where, at any time after the Commission has instituted an inquiry under section 8 above with respect to any charity, it is satisfied as mentioned in section 18(1)(a) or (b) above.

(2) The Commission may by order direct—
  (a) the charity trustees,
  (b) any trustee for the charity,
  (c) any officer or employee of the charity, or
  (d) (if a body corporate) the charity itself,
to take any action specified in the order which the Commission considers to be expedient in the interests of the charity.

---

[16] The power to remove a person from membership of a charity is new. Again the legislative scheme is by the insertion of the new provisions into the Charities Act 1993.
[17] This section supplements existing powers and is inserted into the Charities Act 1993. Sections 19A and 19B are new.

(3) An order under this section—

    (a) may require action to be taken whether or not it would otherwise be within the powers exercisable by the person or persons concerned, or by the charity, in relation to the administration of the charity or to its property, but

    (b) may not require any action to be taken which is prohibited by any Act of Parliament or expressly prohibited by the trusts of the charity or is inconsistent with its purposes.

(4) Anything done by a person or body under the authority of an order under this section shall be deemed to be properly done in the exercise of the powers mentioned in subsection (3)(a) above.

(5) Subsection (4) does not affect any contractual or other rights arising in connection with anything which has been done under the authority of such an order."

21. Power to direct application of charity property

After section 19A of the 1993 Act (inserted by section 20 above) insert—

"19B Power to direct application of charity property

(1) This section applies where the Commission is satisfied—

    (a) that a person or persons in possession or control of any property held by or on trust for a charity is or are unwilling to apply it properly for the purposes of the charity, and

    (b) that it is necessary or desirable to make an order under this section for the purpose of securing a proper application of that property for the purposes of the charity.

(2) The Commission may by order direct the person or persons concerned to apply the property in such manner as is specified in the order.

(3) An order under this section—

    (a) may require action to be taken whether or not it would otherwise be within the powers exercisable by the person or persons concerned in relation to the property, but

    (b) may not require any action to be taken which is prohibited by any Act of Parliament or expressly prohibited by the trusts of the charity.

(4) Anything done by a person under the authority of an order under this section shall be deemed to be properly done in the exercise of the powers mentioned in subsection (3)(a) above.

(5) Subsection (4) does not affect any contractual or other rights arising in connection with anything which has been done under the authority of such an order."

Publicity relating to schemes

22. Relaxation of publicity requirements relating to schemes[18] etc.

For section 20 of the 1993 Act substitute—

"20 Publicity relating to schemes

(1) The Commission may not—

    (a) make any order under this Act to establish a scheme for the administration of a charity, or

---

[18] Instead of the insertion of a new supplementary provision, this section substitutes a new section for the corresponding provision in the Charities Act 1993.

(b) submit such a scheme to the court or the Minister for an order giving it effect, unless, before doing so, the Commission has complied with the publicity requirements in subsection (2) below.

This is subject to any disapplication of those requirements under subsection (4) below.

(2) The publicity requirements are—
   (a) that the Commission must give public notice of its proposals, inviting representations to be made to it within a period specified in the notice; and
   (b) that, in the case of a scheme relating to a local charity (other than an ecclesiastical charity) in a parish or in a community in Wales, the Commission must communicate a draft of the scheme to the parish or community council (or, where a parish has no council, to the chairman of the parish meeting).

(3) The time when any such notice is given or any such communication takes place is to be decided by the Commission.

(4) The Commission may determine that either or both of the publicity requirements is or are not to apply in relation to a particular scheme if it is satisfied that—
   (a) by reason of the nature of the scheme, or
   (b) for any other reason, compliance with the requirement or requirements is unnecessary.

(5) Where the Commission gives public notice of any proposals under this section, the Commission—
   (a) must take into account any representations made to it within the period specified in the notice, and
   (b) may (without further notice) proceed with the proposals either without modifications or with such modifications as it thinks desirable.

(6) Where the Commission makes an order under this Act to establish a scheme for the administration of a charity, a copy of the order must be available, for at least a month after the order is published, for public inspection at all reasonable times—
   (a) at the Commission's office, and
   (b) if the charity is a local charity, at some convenient place in the area of the charity.

Paragraph (b) does not apply if the Commission is satisfied that for any reason it is unnecessary for a copy of the scheme to be available locally.

(7) Any public notice of any proposals which is to be given under this section—
   (a) is to contain such particulars of the proposals, or such directions for obtaining information about them, as the Commission thinks sufficient and appropriate, and
   (b) is to be given in such manner as the Commission thinks sufficient and appropriate.

20A Publicity for orders relating to trustees or other individuals

(1) The Commission may not make any order under this Act to appoint, discharge or remove a charity trustee or trustee for a charity, other than—
   (a) an order relating to the official custodian, or
   (b) an order under section 18(1)(ii) above,
   unless, before doing so, the Commission has complied with the publicity requirement in subsection (2) below.

   This is subject to any disapplication of that requirement under subsection (4) below.

(2) The publicity requirement is that the Commission must give public notice of its proposals, inviting representations to be made to it within a period specified in the notice.

(3) The time when any such notice is given is to be decided by the Commission.

(4) The Commission may determine that the publicity requirement is not to apply in relation to a particular order if it is satisfied that for any reason compliance with the requirement is unnecessary.

(5) Before the Commission makes an order under this Act to remove without his consent—

(a) a charity trustee or trustee for a charity, or

(b) an officer, agent or employee of a charity,

the Commission must give him not less than one month's notice of its proposals, inviting representations to be made to it within a period specified in the notice.

This does not apply if the person cannot be found or has no known address in the United Kingdom.

(6) Where the Commission gives notice of any proposals under this section, the Commission—

(a) must take into account any representations made to it within the period specified in the notice, and

(b) may (without further notice) proceed with the proposals either without modifications or with such modifications as it thinks desirable.

(7) Any notice of any proposals which is to be given under this section—

(a) is to contain such particulars of the proposals, or such directions for obtaining information about them, as the Commission thinks sufficient and appropriate, and

(b) (in the case of a public notice) is to be given in such manner as the Commission thinks sufficient and appropriate.

(8) Any notice to be given under subsection (5)—

(a) may be given by post, and

(b) if given by post, may be addressed to the recipient's last known address in the United Kingdom."

Common investment schemes

23. Participation of Scottish and Northern Irish charities in common investment schemes etc.

(1) After section 24(3) of the 1993 Act (common investment schemes) insert—

"(3A) A common investment scheme may provide for appropriate bodies to be admitted to participate in the scheme (in addition to the participating charities) to such extent as the trustees appointed to manage the fund may determine.

(3B) In this section 'appropriate body' means—

(a) a Scottish recognised body, or

(b) a Northern Ireland charity,

and, in the application of the relevant provisions in relation to a scheme which contains provisions authorised by subsection (3A) above, 'charity' includes an appropriate body.

'The relevant provisions' are subsections (1) and (4) to (6) and (in relation only to a charity within paragraph (b)) subsection (7)."

(2) In section 25(2) of that Act (application of provisions of section 24 to common deposit funds) for "subsections (2) to (4)" substitute "subsections (2), (3) and (4)".

(3) At the end of section 25 add—

"(4) A common deposit scheme may provide for appropriate bodies to be admitted to participate in the scheme (in addition to the participating charities) to such extent as the trustees appointed to manage the fund may determine.

(5) In this section 'appropriate body' means—

    (a) a Scottish recognised body, or

    (b) a Northern Ireland charity,

and, in the application of the relevant provisions in relation to a scheme which contains provisions authorised by subsection (4) above, 'charity' includes an appropriate body.

(6) 'The relevant provisions' are—

    (a) subsection (1) above, and

    (b) subsections (4) and (6) of section 24 above, as they apply in accordance with subsections (2) and (3) above, and

    (c) (in relation only to a charity within subsection (5)(b) above) subsection (7) of that section, as it so applies."

(4) After section 25 insert—

"25A Meaning of "Scottish recognised body" and "Northern Ireland charity" in sections 24 and 25

(1) In sections 24 and 25 above 'Scottish recognised body' means a body—

    (a) established under the law of Scotland, or

    (b) managed or controlled wholly or mainly in or from Scotland,

to which the Commissioners for Her Majesty's Revenue and Customs have given intimation, which has not subsequently been withdrawn, that relief is due under section 505 of the Income and Corporation Taxes Act 1988 in respect of income of the body which is applicable and applied to charitable purposes only.

(2) In those sections 'Northern Ireland charity' means an institution—

    (a) which is a charity under the law of Northern Ireland, and

    (b) to which the Commissioners for Her Majesty's Revenue and Customs have given intimation, which has not subsequently been withdrawn, that relief is due under section 505 of the Income and Corporation Taxes Act 1988 in respect of income of the institution which is applicable and applied to charitable purposes only."

(5) In section 100(4) of the 1993 Act (provisions extending to Northern Ireland) for "extends" substitute "and sections 24 to 25A extend".

Advice or other assistance

24. Power to give advice and guidance[19]

For section 29 of the 1993 Act substitute—

"29 Power to give advice and guidance

(1) The Commission may, on the written application of any charity trustee or trustee for a charity, give that person its opinion or advice in relation to any matter—

---

[19] This is a very important section in practice. It has been redrafted and the new s 29 substitutes the Charities Act 1993 provision.

(a) relating to the performance of any duties of his, as such a trustee, in relation to the charity concerned, or

(b) otherwise relating to the proper administration of the charity.

(2) A charity trustee or trustee for a charity who acts in accordance with any opinion or advice given by the Commission under subsection (1) above (whether to him or to another trustee) is to be taken, as regards his responsibility for so acting, to have acted in accordance with his trust.

(3) But subsection (2) above does not apply to a person if, when so acting, either—

(a) he knows or has reasonable cause to suspect that the opinion or advice was given in ignorance of material facts, or

(b) a decision of the court or the Tribunal has been obtained on the matter or proceedings are pending to obtain one.

(4) The Commission may, in connection with its second general function mentioned in section 1C(2) above, give such advice or guidance with respect to the administration of charities as it considers appropriate.

(5) Any advice or guidance so given may relate to—

(a) charities generally,

(b) any class of charities, or

(c) any particular charity,

and may take such form, and be given in such manner, as the Commission considers appropriate."

25. Power to determine membership of charity[20]

After section 29 of the 1993 Act (as substituted by section 24 of this Act) insert—

"29A Power to determine membership of charity

(1) The Commission may—

(a) on the application of a charity, or

(b) at any time after the institution of an inquiry under section 8 above with respect to a charity,

determine who are the members of the charity.

(2) The Commission's power under subsection (1) may also be exercised by a person appointed by the Commission for the purpose.

(3) In a case within subsection (1)(b) the Commission may, if it thinks fit, so appoint the person appointed to conduct the inquiry."

Powers of entry etc.

26. Power to enter premises and seize documents etc.[21]

(1) After section 31 of the 1993 Act insert—

"31A Power to enter premises

(1) A justice of the peace may issue a warrant under this section if satisfied, on information given on oath by a member of the Commission's staff, that there are reasonable grounds for believing that each of the conditions in subsection (2) below is satisfied.

---

[20] This is an extension to the s 29 power of the Charity Commission. Section 29A is inserted into the Charities Act 1993.

[21] This power existed elsewhere in legislation, and its inclusion is a welcome consolidation and achieved by way of amendment to the Charities Act 1993.

(2) The conditions are—
    (a) that an inquiry has been instituted under section 8 above;
    (b) that there is on the premises to be specified in the warrant any document or information relevant to that inquiry which the Commission could require to be produced or furnished under section 9(1) above; and
    (c) that, if the Commission were to make an order requiring the document or information to be so produced or furnished—
        (i) the order would not be complied with, or
        (ii) the document or information would be removed, tampered with, concealed or destroyed.

(3) A warrant under this section is a warrant authorising the member of the Commission's staff who is named in it—
    (a) to enter and search the premises specified in it;
    (b) to take such other persons with him as the Commission considers are needed to assist him in doing anything that he is authorised to do under the warrant;
    (c) to take possession of any documents which appear to fall within subsection (2)(b) above, or to take any other steps which appear to be necessary for preserving, or preventing interference with, any such documents;
    (d) to take possession of any computer disk or other electronic storage device which appears to contain information falling within subsection (2)(b), or information contained in a document so falling, or to take any other steps which appear to be necessary for preserving, or preventing interference with, any such information;
    (e) to take copies of, or extracts from, any documents or information falling within paragraph (c) or (d);
    (f) to require any person on the premises to provide an explanation of any such document or information or to state where any such documents or information may be found;
    (g) to require any such person to give him such assistance as he may reasonably require for the taking of copies or extracts as mentioned in paragraph (e) above.

(4) Entry and search under such a warrant must be at a reasonable hour and within one month of the date of its issue.

(5) The member of the Commission's staff who is authorised under such a warrant ('the authorised person') must, if required to do so, produce—
    (a) the warrant, and
    (b) documentary evidence that he is a member of the Commission's staff,
    for inspection by the occupier of the premises or anyone acting on his behalf.

(6) The authorised person must make a written record of—
    (a) the date and time of his entry on the premises;
    (b) the number of persons (if any) who accompanied him onto the premises, and the names of any such persons;
    (c) the period for which he (and any such persons) remained on the premises;
    (d) what he (and any such persons) did while on the premises; and
    (e) any document or device of which he took possession while there.

(7) If required to do so, the authorised person must give a copy of the record to the occupier of the premises or someone acting on his behalf.

(8) Unless it is not reasonably practicable to do so, the authorised person must comply with the following requirements before leaving the premises, namely—

  (a) the requirements of subsection (6), and

  (b) any requirement made under subsection (7) before he leaves the premises.

  (9) Where possession of any document or device is taken under this section—

  (a) the document may be retained for so long as the Commission considers that it is necessary to retain it (rather than a copy of it) for the purposes of the relevant inquiry under section 8 above, or

  (b) the device may be retained for so long as the Commission considers that it is necessary to retain it for the purposes of that inquiry,

   as the case may be.

  (10) Once it appears to the Commission that the retention of any document or device has ceased to be so necessary, it shall arrange for the document or device to be returned as soon as is reasonably practicable—

  (a) to the person from whose possession it was taken, or

  (b) to any of the charity trustees of the charity to which it belonged or related.

  (11) A person who intentionally obstructs the exercise of any rights conferred by a warrant under this section is guilty of an offence and liable on summary conviction—

  (a) to imprisonment for a term not exceeding 51 weeks, or

  (b) to a fine not exceeding level 5 on the standard scale,

   or to both."

(2) In Part 1 of Schedule 1 to the Criminal Justice and Police Act 2001 (c. 16) (powers of seizure to which section 50 applies), after paragraph 56 insert—

"56A Charities Act 1993 (c. 10)

The power of seizure conferred by section 31A(3) of the Charities Act 1993 (seizure of material for the purposes of an inquiry under section 8 of that Act)."

Mortgages of charity land

27. Restrictions on mortgaging[22]

  (1) Section 38 of the 1993 Act (restrictions on mortgaging) is amended as follows.

  (2) For subsections (2) and (3) substitute—

  "(2) Subsection (1) above shall not apply to a mortgage of any such land if the charity trustees have, before executing the mortgage, obtained and considered proper advice, given to them in writing, on the relevant matters or matter mentioned in subsection (3) or (3A) below (as the case may be).

  (3) In the case of a mortgage to secure the repayment of a proposed loan or grant, the relevant matters are—

  (a) whether the loan or grant is necessary in order for the charity trustees to be able to pursue the particular course of action in connection with which they are seeking the loan or grant;

  (b) whether the terms of the loan or grant are reasonable having regard to the status of the charity as the prospective recipient of the loan or grant; and

  (c) the ability of the charity to repay on those terms the sum proposed to be paid by way of loan or grant.

---

[22] This provision is an amendment to the Charities Act 1993 rather than a substitution.

(3A) In the case of a mortgage to secure the discharge of any other proposed obligation, the relevant matter is whether it is reasonable for the charity trustees to undertake to discharge the obligation, having regard to the charity's purposes.

(3B) Subsection (3) or (as the case may be) subsection (3A) above applies in relation to such a mortgage as is mentioned in that subsection whether the mortgage—

(a) would only have effect to secure the repayment of the proposed loan or grant or the discharge of the proposed obligation, or

(b) would also have effect to secure the repayment of sums paid by way of loan or grant, or the discharge of other obligations undertaken, after the date of its execution.

(3C) Subsection (3D) below applies where—

(a) the charity trustees of a charity have executed a mortgage of land held by or in trust for a charity in accordance with subsection (2) above, and

(b) the mortgage has effect to secure the repayment of sums paid by way of loan or grant, or the discharge of other obligations undertaken, after the date of its execution.

(3D) In such a case, the charity trustees must not after that date enter into any transaction involving—

(a) the payment of any such sums, or

(b) the undertaking of any such obligations,

unless they have, before entering into the transaction, obtained and considered proper advice, given to them in writing, on the matters or matter mentioned in subsection (3)(a) to (c) or (3A) above (as the case may be)."

(3) In subsection (4) (meaning of "proper advice")—

(a) for "subsection (2) above" substitute "this section"; and

(b) for "the making of the loan in question" substitute "relation to the loan, grant or other transaction in connection with which his advice is given".

CHAPTER 6
AUDIT OR EXAMINATION OF ACCOUNTS WHERE CHARITY IS NOT A COMPANY

28. Annual audit or examination of accounts of charities which are not companies[23]

(1) Section 43 of the 1993 Act (annual audit or examination of accounts of charities which are not companies) is amended as follows.

(2) For subsection (1) substitute—

"(1) Subsection (2) below applies to a financial year of a charity if—

(a) the charity's gross income in that year exceeds £500,000; or

(b) the charity's gross income in that year exceeds the accounts threshold and at the end of the year the aggregate value of its assets (before deduction of liabilities) exceeds £2.8 million.

---

[23] Many of the accounting provisions have been amended. For accounts generally, see the SORP relevant to charity accounts. The latest version is from 2005, but it is contemplated that periodic reviews of SORP will be undertaken.

'The accounts threshold' means £100,000 or such other sum as is for the time being specified in section 42(3) above."

(3) In subsection (2) (accounts required to be audited) for paragraph (a) substitute—

"(a) would be eligible for appointment as auditor of theb charity under Part 2 of the Companies Act 1989 if the charity were a company, or".

(4) In subsection (3) (independent examinations instead of audits)—

(a) for the words from "and its gross income" to "subsection (4) below)" substitute "but its gross income in that year exceeds £10,000,"; and

(b) at the end insert—

"This is subject to the requirements of subsection (3A) below where the gross income exceeds £250,000, and to any order under subsection (4) below."

(5) After subsection (3) insert—

"(3A) If subsection (3) above applies to the accounts of a charity for a year and the charity's gross income in that year exceeds £250,000, a person qualifies as an independent examiner for the purposes of paragraph (a) of that subsection if (and only if) he is an independent person who is—

(a) a member of a body for the time being specified in section 249D(3) of the Companies Act 1985 (reporting accountants);

(b) a member of the Chartered Institute of Public Finance and Accountancy; or

(c) a Fellow of the Association of Charity Independent Examiners."

(6) For subsection (8) substitute—

"(8) The Minister may by order—

(a) amend subsection (1)(a) or (b), (3) or (3A) above by substituting a different sum for any sum for the time being specified there;

(b) amend subsection (3A) by adding or removing a description of person to or from the list in that subsection or by varying any entry for the time being included in that list."

29. Duty of auditor etc. of charity which is not a company to report matters to Commission[24]

(1) After section 44 of the 1993 Act insert—

"44A Duty of auditors etc. to report matters to Commission

(1) This section applies to—

(a) a person acting as an auditor or independent examiner appointed by or in relation to a charity under section 43 above,

(b) a person acting as an auditor or examiner appointed under section 43A(2) or (3) above, and

(c) the Auditor General for Wales acting under section 43B(2) or (3) above.

(2) If, in the course of acting in the capacity mentioned in subsection (1) above, a person to whom this section applies becomes aware of a matter—

---

[24] There is an extension to the duty of auditors or independent examiners of a charity's accounts to act as 'whistleblowers' concerning matters in charity accounts.

(a) which relates to the activities or affairs of the charity or of any connected institution or body, and

(b) which he has reasonable cause to believe is likely to be of material significance for the purposes of the exercise by the Commission of its functions under section 8 or 18 above,

he must immediately make a written report on the matter to the Commission.

(3) If, in the course of acting in the capacity mentioned in subsection (1) above, a person to whom this section applies becomes aware of any matter—

(a) which does not appear to him to be one that he is required to report under subsection (2) above, but

(b) which he has reasonable cause to believe is likely to be relevant for the purposes of the exercise by the Commission of any of its functions,

he may make a report on the matter to the Commission.

(4) Where the duty or power under subsection (2) or (3) above has arisen in relation to a person acting in the capacity mentioned in subsection (1), the duty or power is not affected by his subsequently ceasing to act in that capacity.

(5) Where a person makes a report as required or authorised by subsection (2) or (3), no duty to which he is subject is to be regarded as contravened merely because of any information or opinion contained in the report.

(6) In this section "connected institution or body", in relation to a charity, means—

(a) an institution which is controlled by, or

(b) a body corporate in which a substantial interest is held by,

the charity or any one or more of the charity trustees acting in his or their capacity as such.

(7) Paragraphs 3 and 4 of Schedule 5 to this Act apply for the purposes of subsection (6) above as they apply for the purposes of provisions of that Schedule."

(2) In section 46 of the 1993 Act (special provisions as respects accounts and annual reports of exempt and excepted charities)—

(a) in subsection (1) for "sections 41 to 45" substitute "sections 41 to 44 or section 45"; and

(b) after subsection (2) insert—

"(2A) Section 44A(2) to (7) above shall apply in relation to a person appointed to audit, or report on, the accounts of an exempt charity which is not a company as they apply in relation to a person such as is mentioned in section 44A(1).

(2B) But section 44A(2) to (7) so apply with the following modifications—

(a) any reference to a person acting in the capacity mentioned in section 44A(1) is to be read as a reference to his acting as a person appointed as mentioned in subsection (2A) above; and

(b) any reference to the Commission or to any of its functions is to be read as a reference to the charity's principal regulator or to any of that person's functions in relation to the charity as such."

30. Group accounts[25]

(1) After section 49 of the 1993 Act insert—

"49A Group accounts

The provisions of Schedule 5A to this Act shall have effect with respect to—

(a) the preparation and auditing of accounts in respect of groups consisting of parent charities and their subsidiary undertakings (within the meaning of that Schedule), and

(b) other matters relating to such groups."

(2) Schedule 6 (which inserts the new Schedule 5A into the 1993 Act) has effect.

CHAPTER 7
CHARITABLE COMPANIES

31. Relaxation of restriction on altering memorandum etc. of charitable company

(1) Section 64 of the 1993 Act (alteration of objects clause etc.) is amended as follows.

(2) For subsection (2) substitute—

"(2) Where a charity is a company, any regulated alteration by the company—

(a) requires the prior written consent of the Commission, and

(b) is ineffective if such consent has not been obtained.

(2A) The following are 'regulated alterations'—

(a) any alteration of the objects clause in the company's memorandum of association,

(b) any alteration of any provision of its memorandum or articles of association directing the application of property of the company on its dissolution, and

(c) any alteration of any provision of its memorandum or articles of association where the alteration would provide authorisation for any benefit to be obtained by directors or members of the company or persons connected with them.

(2B) For the purposes of subsection (2A) above—

(a) 'benefit' means a direct or indirect benefit of any nature, except that it does not include any remuneration (within the meaning of section 73A below) whose receipt may be authorised under that section; and

(b) the same rules apply for determining whether a person is connected with a director or member of the company as apply, in accordance with section 73B(5) and (6) below, for determining whether a person is connected with a charity trustee for the purposes of section 73A."

(3) In subsection (3) (documents required to be delivered to registrar of companies), for "any such alteration" substitute "a regulated alteration".

32. Annual audit or examination of accounts of charitable companies

(1) In section 249A(4) of the Companies Act 1985 (c. 6) (circumstances in which charitable company's accounts may be subject to an accountant's report instead of an audit)—

---

[25] The legislative scheme is again by either amendment to the Charities Act 1993 provisions, or by substitution. The requirement to prepare group accounts is new and inserted into the existing Charities Act 1993 provisions.

(a) in paragraph (b) (gross income between £90,000 and £250,000) for "£250,000" substitute "£500,000"; and

(b) in paragraph (c) (balance sheet total not more than £1.4 million) for "£1.4 million" substitute "£2.8 million".

(2) In section 249B(1C) of that Act (circumstances in which parent company or subsidiary not disqualified for exemption from auditing requirement), in paragraph (b) (group's aggregate turnover not more than £350,000 net or £420,000 gross in case of charity), for "£350,000 net (or £420,000 gross)" substitute "£700,000 net (or £840,000 gross)".

33. Duty of auditor etc. of charitable company to report matters to Commission

After section 68 of the 1993 Act insert—

"68A Duty of charity's auditors etc. to report matters to Commission

(1) Section 44A(2) to (7) above shall apply in relation to a person acting as—

(a) an auditor of a charitable company appointed under Chapter 5 of Part 11 of the Companies Act 1985 (auditors), or

(b) a reporting accountant appointed by a charitable company for the purposes of section 249C of that Act (report required instead of audit),

as they apply in relation to a person such as is mentioned in section 44A(1).

(2) For this purpose any reference in section 44A to a person acting in the capacity mentioned in section 44A(1) is to be read as a reference to his acting in the capacity mentioned in subsection (1) of this section.

(3) In this section 'charitable company' means a charity which is a company."

CHAPTER 8
CHARITABLE INCORPORATED ORGANISATIONS

34. Charitable incorporated organisations[26]

Schedule 7, which makes provision about charitable incorporated organisations, has effect.

CHAPTER 9
CHARITY TRUSTEES ETC.

Waiver of disqualification

35. Waiver of trustee's disqualification

In section 72 of the 1993 Act (disqualification for being trustee of a charity) after subsection (4) insert—

"(4A) If—

(a) a person disqualified under subsection (1)(d) or (e) makes an application under subsection (4) above five years or more after the date on which his disqualification took effect, and

---

[26] Section 34 of the Charities Act 2006 introduces a new corporate form for charities, the details of which are contained in Sch 7 to the 2006 Act.

      (b) the Commission is not prevented from granting the application by virtue of paragraphs (a) and (b) of subsection (4),
      the Commission must grant the application unless satisfied that, by reason of any special circumstances, it should be refused."

Remuneration of trustees etc.

36. Remuneration of trustees etc. providing services to charity[27]

After section 73 of the 1993 Act insert—

"73A Remuneration of trustees etc. providing services to charity

(1)   This section applies to remuneration for services provided by a person to or on behalf of a charity where—
    (a) he is a charity trustee or trustee for the charity, or
    (b) he is connected with a charity trustee or trustee for the charity and the remuneration might result in that trustee obtaining any benefit.
    This is subject to subsection (7) below.

(2)   If conditions A to D are met in relation to remuneration within subsection (1), the person providing the services ('the relevant person') is entitled to receive the remuneration out of the funds of the charity.

(3)   Condition A is that the amount or maximum amount of the remuneration—
    (a) is set out in an agreement in writing between—
      (i) the charity or its charity trustees (as the case may be), and
      (ii) the relevant person,
      under which the relevant person is to provide the services in question to or on behalf of the charity, and
    (b) does not exceed what is reasonable in the circumstances for the provision by that person of the services in question.

(4)   Condition B is that, before entering into that agreement, the charity trustees decided that they were satisfied that it would be in the best interests of the charity for the services to be provided by the relevant person to or on behalf of the charity for the amount or maximum amount of remuneration set out in the agreement.

(5)   Condition C is that if immediately after the agreement is entered into there is, in the case of the charity, more than one person who is a charity trustee and is—
    (a) a person in respect of whom an agreement within subsection (3) above is in force, or
    (b) a person who is entitled to receive remuneration out of the funds of the charity otherwise than by virtue of such an agreement, or
    (c) a person connected with a person falling within paragraph (a) or (b) above,
    the total number of them constitute a minority of the persons for the time being holding office as charity trustees of the charity.

(6)   Condition D is that the trusts of the charity do not contain any express provision that prohibits the relevant person from receiving the remuneration.

(7)   Nothing in this section applies to—

---

[27] Inserted into the Charities Act 1993. There will now be a s 73A, s 73B, and s 73C in the Charities Act 1993.

(a) any remuneration for services provided by a person in his capacity as a charity trustee or trustee for a charity or under a contract of employment, or

(b) any remuneration not within paragraph (a) which a person is entitled to receive out of the funds of a charity by virtue of any provision or order within subsection (8).

(8) The provisions or orders within this subsection are—

(a) any provision contained in the trusts of the charity,

(b) any order of the court or the Commission,

(c) any statutory provision contained in or having effect under an Act of Parliament other than this section.

(9) Section 73B below applies for the purposes of this section.

73B Supplementary provisions for purposes of section 73A

(1) Before entering into an agreement within section 73A(3) the charity trustees must have regard to any guidance given by the Commission concerning the making of such agreements.

(2) The duty of care in section 1(1) of the Trustee Act 2000 applies to a charity trustee when making such a decision as is mentioned in section 73A(4).

(3) For the purposes of section 73A(5) an agreement within section 73A(3) is in force so long as any obligations under the agreement have not been fully discharged by a party to it.

(4) In section 73A—

'benefit' means a direct or indirect benefit of any nature;

'maximum amount', in relation to remuneration, means the maximum amount of the remuneration whether specified in or ascertainable under the terms of the agreement in question;

'remuneration' includes any benefit in kind (and 'amount' accordingly includes monetary value);

'services', in the context of remuneration for services, includes goods that are supplied in connection with the provision of services.

(5) For the purposes of section 73A the following persons are 'connected' with a charity trustee or trustee for a charity—

(a) a child, parent, grandchild, grandparent, brother or sister of the trustee;

(b) the spouse or civil partner of the trustee or of any person falling within paragraph (a);

(c) a person carrying on business in partnership with the trustee or with any person falling within paragraph (a) or (b);

(d) an institution which is controlled—

(i) by the trustee or by any person falling within paragraph (a), (b) or (c), or

(ii) by two or more persons falling within sub-paragraph (i), when taken together;

(e) a body corporate in which—

(i) the trustee or any connected person falling within any of paragraphs (a) to (c) has a substantial interest, or

(ii) two or more persons falling within sub-paragraph (i), when taken together, have a substantial interest.

(6) Paragraphs 2 to 4 of Schedule 5 to this Act apply for the purposes of subsection (5) above as they apply for the purposes of provisions of that Schedule."

37. Disqualification of trustee receiving remuneration by virtue of section 36

After section 73B of the 1993 Act (inserted by section 36 above) insert—

"73C Disqualification of trustee receiving remuneration under section 73A

(1) This section applies to any charity trustee or trustee for a charity—

    (a) who is or would be entitled to remuneration under an agreement or proposed agreement within section 73A(3) above, or

    (b) who is connected with a person who is or would be so entitled.

(2) The charity trustee or trustee for a charity is disqualified from acting as such in relation to any decision or other matter connected with the agreement.

(3) But any act done by such a person which he is disqualified from doing by virtue of subsection (2) above shall not be invalid by reason only of that disqualification.

(4) Where the Commission is satisfied—

    (a) that a person ('the disqualified trustee') has done any act which he was disqualified from doing by virtue of subsection (2) above, and

    (b) that the disqualified trustee or a person connected with him has received or is to receive from the charity any remuneration under the agreement in question,

it may make an order under subsection (5) or (6) below (as appropriate).

(5) An order under this subsection is one requiring the disqualified trustee—

    (a) to reimburse to the charity the whole or part of the remuneration received as mentioned in subsection (4)(b) above;

    (b) to the extent that the remuneration consists of a benefit in kind, to reimburse to the charity the whole or part of the monetary value (as determined by the Commission) of the benefit in kind.

(6) An order under this subsection is one directing that the disqualified trustee or (as the case may be) connected person is not to be paid the whole or part of the remuneration mentioned in subsection (4)(b) above.

(7) If the Commission makes an order under subsection (5) or (6) above, the disqualified trustee or (as the case may be) connected person accordingly ceases to have any entitlement under the agreement to so much of the remuneration (or its monetary value) as the order requires him to reimburse to the charity or (as the case may be) as it directs is not to be paid to him.

(8) Subsections (4) to (6) of section 73B above apply for the purposes of this section as they apply for the purposes of section 73A above."

Liability of trustees etc.

38. Power of Commission to relieve trustees, auditors etc. from liability for breach of trust or duty[28]

After section 73C of the 1993 Act (inserted by section 37 above) insert—

"73D Power to relieve trustees, auditors etc. from liability for breach of trust or duty

(1) This section applies to a person who is or has been—

    (a) a charity trustee or trustee for a charity,

---

[28] This provision (and the following sections) is innovative. The Charity Commission may, in certain circumstances, relieve a person from personal liability for acts done in relation to a charity.

(b) a person appointed to audit a charity's accounts (whether appointed under an enactment or otherwise), or

(c) an independent examiner, reporting accountant or other person appointed to examine or report on a charity's accounts (whether appointed under an enactment or otherwise).

(2) If the Commission considers—

(a) that a person to whom this section applies is or may be personally liable for a breach of trust or breach of duty committed in his capacity as a person within paragraph (a), (b) or (c) of subsection (1) above, but

(b) that he has acted honestly and reasonably and ought fairly to be excused for the breach of trust or duty,

the Commission may make an order relieving him wholly or partly from any such liability.

(3) An order under subsection (2) above may grant the relief on such terms as the Commission thinks fit.

(4) Subsection (2) does not apply in relation to any personal contractual liability of a charity trustee or trustee for a charity.

(5) For the purposes of this section and section 73E below—

(a) subsection (1)(b) above is to be read as including a reference to the Auditor General for Wales acting as auditor under section 43B above, and

(b) subsection (1)(c) above is to be read as including a reference to the Auditor General for Wales acting as examiner under that section;

and in subsection (1)(b) and (c) any reference to a charity's accounts is to be read as including any group accounts prepared by the charity trustees of a charity.

(6) This section does not affect the operation of—

(a) section 61 of the Trustee Act 1925 (power of court to grant relief to trustees),

(b) section 727 of the Companies Act 1985 (power of court to grant relief to officers or auditors of companies), or

(c) section 73E below (which extends section 727 to auditors etc. of charities which are not companies).

73E Court's power to grant relief to apply to all auditors etc. of charities which are not companies

(1) Section 727 of the Companies Act 1985 (power of court to grant relief to officers or auditors of companies) shall have effect in relation to a person to whom this section applies as it has effect in relation to a person employed as an auditor by a company.

(2) This section applies to—

(a) a person acting in a capacity within section 73D(1)(b) or (c) above in a case where, apart from this section, section 727 would not apply in relation to him as a person so acting, and

(b) a charity trustee of a CIO."

39. Trustees' indemnity insurance

After section 73E of the 1993 Act (inserted by section 38 above) insert—

"73F Trustees' indemnity insurance

(1) The charity trustees of a charity may arrange for the purchase, out of the funds of the charity, of insurance designed to indemnify the charity trustees or any trustees for the charity against any personal liability in respect of—

(a) any breach of trust or breach of duty committed by them in their capacity as charity trustees or trustees for the charity, or

(b) any negligence, default, breach of duty or breach of trust committed by them in their capacity as directors or officers of the charity (if it is a body corporate) or of any body corporate carrying on any activities on behalf of the charity.

(2) The terms of such insurance must, however, be so framed as to exclude the provision of any indemnity for a person in respect of—

(a) any liability incurred by him to pay—

(i) a fine imposed in criminal proceedings, or

(ii) a sum payable to a regulatory authority by way of a penalty in respect of non-compliance with any requirement of a regulatory nature (however arising);

(b) any liability incurred by him in defending any criminal proceedings in which he is convicted of an offence arising out of any fraud or dishonesty, or wilful or reckless misconduct, by him; or

(c) any liability incurred by him to the charity that arises out of any conduct which he knew (or must reasonably be assumed to have known) was not in the interests of the charity or in the case of which he did not care whether it was in the best interests of the charity or not.

(3) For the purposes of subsection (2)(b) above—

(a) the reference to any such conviction is a reference to one that has become final;

(b) a conviction becomes final—

(i) if not appealed against, at the end of the period for bringing an appeal, or

(ii) if appealed against, at the time when the appeal (or any further appeal) is disposed of; and

(c) an appeal is disposed of—

(i) if it is determined and the period for bringing any further appeal has ended, or

(ii) if it is abandoned or otherwise ceases to have effect.

(4) The charity trustees of a charity may not purchase insurance under this section unless they decide that they are satisfied that it is in the best interests of the charity for them to do so.

(5) The duty of care in section 1(1) of the Trustee Act 2000 applies to a charity trustee when making such a decision.

(6) The Minister may by order make such amendments of subsections (2) and (3) above as he considers appropriate.

(7) No order may be made under subsection (6) above unless a draft of the order has been laid before and approved by a resolution of each House of Parliament.

(8) This section—

(a) does not authorise the purchase of any insurance whose purchase is expressly prohibited by the trusts of the charity, but

(b) has effect despite any provision prohibiting the charity trustees or trustees for the charity receiving any personal benefit out of the funds of the charity."

CHAPTER 10
POWERS OF UNINCORPORATED CHARITIES

40. Power to transfer all property[29]

For section 74 of the 1993 Act substitute—

"74 Power to transfer all property of unincorporated charity

(1) This section applies to a charity if—
   (a) its gross income in its last financial year did not exceed £10,000,
   (b) it does not hold any designated land, and
   (c) it is not a company or other body corporate.
   'Designated land' means land held on trusts which stipulate that it is to be used for the purposes, or any particular purposes, of the charity.

(2) The charity trustees of such a charity may resolve for the purposes of this section—
   (a) that all the property of the charity should be transferred to another charity specified in the resolution, or
   (b) that all the property of the charity should be transferred to two or more charities specified in the resolution in accordance with such division of the property between them as is so specified.

(3) Any charity so specified may be either a registered charity or a charity which is not required to be registered.

(4) But the charity trustees of a charity ('the transferor charity') do not have power to pass a resolution under subsection (2) above unless they are satisfied—
   (a) that it is expedient in the interests of furthering the purposes for which the property is held by the transferor charity for the property to be transferred in accordance with the resolution, and
   (b) that the purposes (or any of the purposes) of any charity to which property is to be transferred under the resolution are substantially similar to the purposes (or any of the purposes) of the transferor charity.

(5) Any resolution under subsection (2) above must be passed by a majority of not less than two-thirds of the charity trustees who vote on the resolution.

(6) Where charity trustees have passed a resolution under subsection (2), they must send a copy of it to the Commission, together with a statement of their reasons for passing it.

(7) Having received the copy of the resolution, the Commission—
   (a) may direct the charity trustees to give public notice of the resolution in such manner as is specified in the direction, and
   (b) if it gives such a direction, must take into account any representations made to it by persons appearing to it to be interested in the charity, where those representations are made to it within the period of 28 days beginning with the date when public notice of the resolution is given by the charity trustees.

(8) The Commission may also direct the charity trustees to provide the Commission with additional information or explanations relating to—

---

[29] The existing s 74 of the Charities Act 1993 is replaced. The following sections are inserted into the Charities Act 1993, further expanding the provisions on transfers from one charity to another and the consequences of such a transfer.

(a) the circumstances in and by reference to which they have decided to act under this section, or

(b) their compliance with any obligation imposed on them by or under this section in connection with the resolution.

(9) Subject to the provisions of section 74A below, a resolution under subsection (2) above takes effect at the end of the period of 60 days beginning with the date on which the copy of it was received by the Commission.

(10) Where such a resolution has taken effect, the charity trustees must arrange for all the property of the transferor charity to be transferred in accordance with the resolution, and on terms that any property so transferred—

(a) is to be held by the charity to which it is transferred ('the transferee charity') in accordance with subsection (11) below, but

(b) when so held is nevertheless to be subject to any restrictions on expenditure to which it was subject as property of the transferor charity;

and the charity trustees must arrange for the property to be so transferred by such date after the resolution takes effect as they agree with the charity trustees of the transferee charity or charities concerned.

(11) The charity trustees of any charity to which property is transferred under this section must secure, so far as is reasonably practicable, that the property is applied for such of its purposes as are substantially similar to those of the transferor charity.

But this requirement does not apply if those charity trustees consider that complying with it would not result in a suitable and effective method of applying the property.

(12) For the purpose of enabling any property to be transferred to a charity under this section, the Commission may, at the request of the charity trustees of that charity, make orders vesting any property of the transferor charity—

(a) in the transferee charity, in its charity trustees or in any trustee for that charity, or

(b) in any other person nominated by those charity trustees to hold property in trust for that charity.

(13) The Minister may by order amend subsection (1) above by substituting a different sum for the sum for the time being specified there.

(14) In this section references to the transfer of property to a charity are references to its transfer—

(a) to the charity, or

(b) to the charity trustees, or

(c) to any trustee for the charity, or

(d) to a person nominated by the charity trustees to hold it in trust for the charity, as the charity trustees may determine.

(15) Where a charity has a permanent endowment, this section has effect in accordance with section 74B.

74A Resolution not to take effect or to take effect at later date

(1) This section deals with circumstances in which a resolution under section 74(2) above either—

(a) does not take effect under section 74(9) above, or

(b) takes effect at a time later than that mentioned in section 74(9).

(2) A resolution does not take effect under section 74(9) above if before the end of—

(a) the period of 60 days mentioned in section 74(9) ('the 60-day period'), or

(b) that period as modified by subsection (3) or (4) below,

the Commission notifies the charity trustees in writing that it objects to the resolution, either on procedural grounds or on the merits of the proposals contained in the resolution.

'On procedural grounds' means on the grounds that any obligation imposed on the charity trustees by or under section 74 above has not been complied with in connection with the resolution.

(3) If under section 74(7) above the Commission directs the charity trustees to give public notice of a resolution, the running of the 60-day period is suspended by virtue of this subsection—

(a) as from the date on which the direction is given to the charity trustees, and

(b) until the end of the period of 42 days beginning with the date on which public notice of the resolution is given by the charity trustees.

(4) If under section 74(8) above the Commission directs the charity trustees to provide any information or explanations, the running of the 60-day period is suspended by virtue of this subsection—

(a) as from the date on which the direction is given to the charity trustees, and

(b) until the date on which the information or explanations is or are provided to the Commission.

(5) Subsection (6) below applies once the period of time, or the total period of time, during which the 60-day period is suspended by virtue of either or both of subsections (3) and (4) above exceeds 120 days.

(6) At that point the resolution (if not previously objected to by the Commission) is to be treated as if it had never been passed.

74B Transfer where charity has permanent endowment

(1) This section provides for the operation of section 74 above where a charity within section 74(1) has a permanent endowment (whether or not the charity's trusts contain provision for the termination of the charity).

(2) In such a case section 74 applies as follows—

(a) if the charity has both a permanent endowment and other property ('unrestricted property')—

(i) a resolution under section 74(2) must relate to both its permanent endowment and its unrestricted property, and

(ii) that section applies in relation to its unrestricted property in accordance with subsection (3) below and in relation to its permanent endowment in accordance with subsections (4) to (11) below;

(b) if all of the property of the charity is comprised in its permanent endowment, that section applies in relation to its permanent endowment in accordance with subsections (4) to (11) below.

(3) Section 74 applies in relation to unrestricted property of the charity as if references in that section to all or any of the property of the charity were references to all or any of its unrestricted property.

(4) Section 74 applies in relation to the permanent endowment of the charity with the following modifications.

(5) References in that section to all or any of the property of the charity are references to all or any of the property comprised in its permanent endowment.

(6) If the property comprised in its permanent endowment is to be transferred to a single charity, the charity trustees must (instead of being satisfied as mentioned in section 74(4)(b)) be satisfied that the proposed transferee charity has purposes which are substantially similar to all of the purposes of the transferor charity.

(7) If the property comprised in its permanent endowment is to be transferred to two or more charities, the charity trustees must (instead of being satisfied as mentioned in section 74(4)(b)) be satisfied—

(a) that the proposed transferee charities, taken together, have purposes which are substantially similar to all of the purposes of the transferor charity, and

(b) that each of the proposed transferee charities has purposes which are substantially similar to one or more of the purposes of the transferor charity.

(8) In the case of a transfer to which subsection (7) above applies, the resolution under section 74(2) must provide for the property comprised in the permanent endowment of the charity to be divided between the transferee charities in such a way as to take account of such guidance as may be given by the Commission for the purposes of this section.

(9) The requirement in section 74(11) shall apply in the case of every such transfer, and in complying with that requirement the charity trustees of a transferee charity must secure that the application of property transferred to the charity takes account of any such guidance.

(10) Any guidance given by the Commission for the purposes of this section may take such form and be given in such manner as the Commission considers appropriate.

(11) For the purposes of sections 74 and 74A above, any reference to any obligation imposed on the charity trustees by or under section 74 includes a reference to any obligation imposed on them by virtue of any of subsections (6) to (8) above.

(12) Section 74(14) applies for the purposes of this section as it applies for the purposes of section 74."

41. **Power to replace purposes**[30]

After section 74B of the 1993 Act (inserted by section 40 above) insert—

"74C Power to replace purposes of unincorporated charity

(1) This section applies to a charity if—

(a) its gross income in its last financial year did not exceed £ 10,000,

(b) it does not hold any designated land, and

(c) it is not a company or other body corporate.

'Designated land' means land held on trusts which stipulate that it is to be used for the purposes, or any particular purposes, of the charity.

(2) The charity trustees of such a charity may resolve for the purposes of this section that the trusts of the charity should be modified by replacing all or any of the purposes of the charity with other purposes specified in the resolution.

(3) The other purposes so specified must be charitable purposes.

(4) But the charity trustees of a charity do not have power to pass a resolution under subsection (2) above unless they are satisfied—

---

[30] Many of the new provisions are inserted into the existing Charities Act 1993, as is this one.

(a) that it is expedient in the interests of the charity for the purposes in question to be replaced, and

(b) that, so far as is reasonably practicable, the new purposes consist of or include purposes that are similar in character to those that are to be replaced.

(5) Any resolution under subsection (2) above must be passed by a majority of not less than two-thirds of the charity trustees who vote on the resolution.

(6) Where charity trustees have passed a resolution under subsection (2), they must send a copy of it to the Commission, together with a statement of their reasons for passing it.

(7) Having received the copy of the resolution, the Commission—

(a) may direct the charity trustees to give public notice of the resolution in such manner as is specified in the direction, and

(b) if it gives such a direction, must take into account any representations made to it by persons appearing to it to be interested in the charity, where those representations are made to it within the period of 28 days beginning with the date when public notice of the resolution is given by the charity trustees.

(8) The Commission may also direct the charity trustees to provide the Commission with additional information or explanations relating to—

(a) the circumstances in and by reference to which they have decided to act under this section, or

(b) their compliance with any obligation imposed on them by or under this section in connection with the resolution.

(9) Subject to the provisions of section 74A above (as they apply in accordance with subsection (10) below), a resolution under subsection (2) above takes effect at the end of the period of 60 days beginning with the date on which the copy of it was received by the Commission.

(10) Section 74A above applies to a resolution under subsection (2) of this section as it applies to a resolution under subsection (2) of section 74 above, except that any reference to section 74(7), (8) or (9) is to be read as a reference to subsection (7), (8) or (9) above.

(11) As from the time when a resolution takes effect under subsection (9) above, the trusts of the charity concerned are to be taken to have been modified in accordance with the terms of the resolution.

(12) The Minister may by order amend subsection (1) above by substituting a different sum for the sum for the time being specified there."

42. **Power to modify powers or procedures**

After section 74C of the 1993 Act (inserted by section 41 above) insert—

"**74D Power to modify powers or procedures of unincorporated charity**

(1) This section applies to any charity which is not a company or other body corporate.

(2) The charity trustees of such a charity may resolve for the purposes of this section that any provision of the trusts of the charity—

(a) relating to any of the powers exercisable by the charity trustees in the administration of the charity, or

(b) regulating the procedure to be followed in any respect in connection with its administration,

should be modified in such manner as is specified in the resolution.

(3)   Subsection (4) applies if the charity is an unincorporated association with a body of members distinct from the charity trustees.

(4)   Any resolution of the charity trustees under subsection (2) must be approved by a further resolution which is passed at a general meeting of the body either—
  (a) by a majority of not less than two-thirds of the members entitled to attend and vote at the meeting who vote on the resolution, or
  (b) by a decision taken without a vote and without any expression of dissent in response to the question put to the meeting.

(5)   Where—
  (a) the charity trustees have passed a resolution under subsection (2), and
  (b) (if subsection (4) applies) a further resolution has been passed under that subsection,

  the trusts of the charity are to be taken to have been modified in accordance with the terms of the resolution.

(6)   The trusts are to be taken to have been so modified as from such date as is specified for this purpose in the resolution under subsection (2), or (if later) the date when any such further resolution was passed under subsection (4)."

CHAPTER 11
POWERS TO SPEND CAPITAL AND MERGERS

Spending of capital

43. Power to spend capital[31]
For section 75 of the 1993 Act substitute—

"75 Power of unincorporated charities to spend capital: general

(1)   This section applies to any available endowment fund of a charity which is not a company or other body corporate.

(2)   But this section does not apply to a fund if section 75A below (power of larger charities to spend capital given for particular purpose) applies to it.

(3)   Where the condition in subsection (4) below is met in relation to the charity, the charity trustees may resolve for the purposes of this section that the fund, or a portion of it, ought to be freed from the restrictions with respect to expenditure of capital that apply to it.

(4)   The condition in this subsection is that the charity trustees are satisfied that the purposes set out in the trusts to which the fund is subject could be carried out more effectively if the capital of the fund, or the relevant portion of the capital, could be expended as well as income accruing to it, rather than just such income.

(5)   Once the charity trustees have passed a resolution under subsection (3) above, the fund or portion may by virtue of this section be expended in carrying out the purposes set out in the trusts to which the fund is subject without regard to the restrictions mentioned in that subsection.

---

[31] Section 75 of the Charities Act 1993 is rewritten and a new s 75 inserted into that Act by s 43 of the Charities Act 2006.

(6) The fund or portion may be so expended as from such date as is specified for this purpose in the resolution.

(7) In this section 'available endowment fund', in relation to a charity, means—
    (a) the whole of the charity's permanent endowment if it is all subject to the same trusts, or
    (b) any part of its permanent endowment which is subject to any particular trusts that are different from those to which any other part is subject.

75A Power of larger unincorporated charities to spend capital given for particular purpose

(1) This section applies to any available endowment fund of a charity which is not a company or other body corporate if—
    (a) the capital of the fund consists entirely of property given—
        (i) by a particular individual,
        (ii) by a particular institution (by way of grant or otherwise), or
        (iii) by two or more individuals or institutions in pursuit of a common purpose, and
    (b) the financial condition in subsection (2) below is met.

(2) The financial condition in this subsection is met if—
    (a) the relevant charity's gross income in its last financial year exceeded £1,000, and
    (b) the market value of the endowment fund exceeds £10,000.

(3) Where the condition in subsection (4) below is met in relation to the charity, the charity trustees may resolve for the purposes of this section that the fund, or a portion of it, ought to be freed from the restrictions with respect to expenditure of capital that apply to it.

(4) The condition in this subsection is that the charity trustees are satisfied that the purposes set out in the trusts to which the fund is subject could be carried out more effectively if the capital of the fund, or the relevant portion of the capital, could be expended as well as income accruing to it, rather than just such income.

(5) The charity trustees—
    (a) must send a copy of any resolution under subsection (3) above to the Commission, together with a statement of their reasons for passing it, and
    (b) may not implement the resolution except in accordance with the following provisions of this section.

(6) Having received the copy of the resolution the Commission may—
    (a) direct the charity trustees to give public notice of the resolution in such manner as is specified in the direction, and
    (b) if it gives such a direction, must take into account any representations made to it by persons appearing to it to be interested in the charity, where those representations are made to it within the period of 28 days beginning with the date when public notice of the resolution is given by the charity trustees.

(7) The Commission may also direct the charity trustees to provide the Commission with additional information or explanations relating to—
    (a) the circumstances in and by reference to which they have decided to act under this section, or
    (b) their compliance with any obligation imposed on them by or under this section in connection with the resolution.

(8) When considering whether to concur with the resolution the Commission must take into account—

    (a) any evidence available to it as to the wishes of the donor or donors mentioned in subsection (1)(a) above, and

    (b) any changes in the circumstances relating to the charity since the making of the gift or gifts (including, in particular, its financial position, the needs of its beneficiaries, and the social, economic and legal environment in which it operates).

(9) The Commission must not concur with the resolution unless it is satisfied—

    (a) that its implementation would accord with the spirit of the gift or gifts mentioned in subsection (1)(a) above (even though it would be inconsistent with the restrictions mentioned in subsection (3) above), and

    (b) that the charity trustees have complied with the obligations imposed on them by or under this section in connection with the resolution.

(10) Before the end of the period of three months beginning with the relevant date, the Commission must notify the charity trustees in writing either—

    (a) that the Commission concurs with the resolution, or

    (b) that it does not concur with it.

(11) In subsection (10) 'the relevant date' means—

    (a) in a case where the Commission directs the charity trustees under subsection (6) above to give public notice of the resolution, the date when that notice is given, and

    (b) in any other case, the date on which the Commission receives the copy of the resolution in accordance with subsection (5) above.

(12) Where—

    (a) the charity trustees are notified by the Commission that it concurs with the resolution, or

    (b) the period of three months mentioned in subsection (10) above has elapsed without the Commission notifying them that it does not concur with the resolution,

the fund or portion may, by virtue of this section, be expended in carrying out the purposes set out in the trusts to which the fund is subject without regard to the restrictions mentioned in subsection (3).

(13) The Minister may by order amend subsection (2) above by substituting a different sum for any sum specified there.

(14) In this section—

    (a) 'available endowment fund' has the same meaning as in section 75 above,

    (b) 'market value', in relation to an endowment fund, means—

        (i) the market value of the fund as recorded in the accounts for the last financial year of the relevant charity, or

        (ii) if no such value was so recorded, the current market value of the fund as determined on a valuation carried out for the purpose, and

    (c) the reference in subsection (1) to the giving of property by an individual includes his giving it under his will.

75B Power to spend capital subject to special trusts

(1) This section applies to any available endowment fund of a special trust which, as the result of a direction under section 96(5) below, is to be treated as a separate charity ('the relevant charity') for the purposes of this section.

(2) Where the condition in subsection (3) below is met in relation to the relevant charity, the charity trustees may resolve for the purposes of this section that the fund, or a portion of it, ought to be freed from the restrictions with respect to expenditure of capital that apply to it.

(3) The condition in this subsection is that the charity trustees are satisfied that the purposes set out in the trusts to which the fund is subject could be carried out more effectively if the capital of the fund, or the relevant portion of the capital, could be expended as well as income accruing to it, rather than just such income.

(4) Where the market value of the fund exceeds £10,000 and the capital of the fund consists entirely of property given—
(a) by a particular individual,
(b) by a particular institution (by way of grant or otherwise), or
(c) by two or more individuals or institutions in pursuit of a common purpose,

subsections (5) to (11) of section 75A above apply in relation to the resolution and that gift or gifts as they apply in relation to a resolution under section 75A(3) and the gift or gifts mentioned in section 75A(1)(a).

(5) Where—
(a) the charity trustees have passed a resolution under subsection (2) above, and
(b) (in a case where section 75A(5) to (11) above apply in accordance with subsection (4) above) either—
(i) the charity trustees are notified by the Commission that it concurs with the resolution, or
(ii) the period of three months mentioned in section 75A(10) has elapsed without the Commission notifying them that it does not concur with the resolution,
the fund or portion may, by virtue of this section, be expended in carrying out the purposes set out in the trusts to which the fund is subject without regard to the restrictions mentioned in subsection (2).

(6) The fund or portion may be so expended as from such date as is specified for this purpose in the resolution.

(7) The Minister may by order amend subsection (4) above by substituting a different sum for the sum specified there.

(8) In this section—
(a) 'available endowment fund' has the same meaning as in section 75 above,
(b) 'market value' has the same meaning as in section 75A above, and
(c) the reference in subsection (4) to the giving of property by an individual includes his giving it under his will."

Mergers

44. Merger of charities[32]
After section 75B of the 1993 Act (inserted by section 43 above) insert—

---

[32] This is a new section, inserted into the Charities Act 1993, allowing charities to merge together to create a new charity which may be registered with the Charity Commission. See below.

"Mergers

75C Register of charity mergers

(1) The Commission shall establish and maintain a register of charity mergers.

(2) The register shall be kept by the Commission in such manner as it thinks fit.

(3) The register shall contain an entry in respect of every relevant charity merger which is notified to the Commission in accordance with subsections (6) to (9) and such procedures as it may determine.

(4) In this section 'relevant charity merger' means—

(a) a merger of two or more charities in connection with which one of them ('the transferee') has transferred to it all the property of the other or others, each of which (a 'transferor') ceases to exist, or is to cease to exist, on or after the transfer of its property to the transferee, or

(b) a merger of two or more charities ('transferors') in connection with which both or all of them cease to exist, or are to cease to exist, on or after the transfer of all of their property to a new charity ('the transferee').

(5) In the case of a merger involving the transfer of property of any charity which has both a permanent endowment and other property ('unrestricted property') and whose trusts do not contain provision for the termination of the charity, subsection (4)(a) or (b) applies in relation to any such charity as if—

(a) the reference to all of its property were a reference to all of its unrestricted property, and

(b) any reference to its ceasing to exist were omitted.

(6) A notification under subsection (3) above may be given in respect of a relevant charity merger at any time after—

(a) the transfer of property involved in the merger has taken place, or

(b) (if more than one transfer of property is so involved) the last of those transfers has taken place.

(7) If a vesting declaration is made in connection with a relevant charity merger, a notification under subsection (3) above must be given in respect of the merger once the transfer, or the last of the transfers, mentioned in subsection (6) above has taken place.

(8) A notification under subsection (3) is to be given by the charity trustees of the transferee and must—

(a) specify the transfer or transfers of property involved in the merger and the date or dates on which it or they took place;

(b) include a statement that appropriate arrangements have been made with respect to the discharge of any liabilities of the transferor charity or charities; and

(c) in the case of a notification required by subsection (7), set out the matters mentioned in subsection (9).

(9) The matters are—

(a) the fact that the vesting declaration in question has been made;

(b) the date when the declaration was made; and

(c) the date on which the vesting of title under the declaration took place by virtue of section 75E(2) below.

(10) In this section and section 75D—

(a) any reference to a transfer of property includes a transfer effected by a vesting declaration; and

(b) 'vesting declaration' means a declaration to which section 75E(2) below applies.

(11) Nothing in this section or section 75E or 75F applies in a case where section 69K (amalgamation of CIOs) or 69M (transfer of CIO's undertaking) applies.

75D Register of charity mergers: supplementary

(1) Subsection (2) applies to the entry to be made in the register in respect of a relevant charity merger, as required by section 75C(3) above.

(2) The entry must—
(a) specify the date when the transfer or transfers of property involved in the merger took place,
(b) if a vesting declaration was made in connection with the merger, set out the matters mentioned in section 75C(9) above, and
(c) contain such other particulars of the merger as the Commission thinks fit.

(3) The register shall be open to public inspection at all reasonable times.

(4) Where any information contained in the register is not in documentary form, subsection (3) above shall be construed as requiring the information to be available for public inspection in legible form at all reasonable times.

(5) In this section—

'the register' means the register of charity mergers;

'relevant charity merger' has the same meaning as in section 75C.

75E Pre-merger vesting declarations

(1) Subsection (2) below applies to a declaration which—
(a) is made by deed for the purposes of this section by the charity trustees of the transferor,
(b) is made in connection with a relevant charity merger, and
(c) is to the effect that (subject to subsections (3) and (4)) all of the transferor's property is to vest in the transferee on such date as is specified in the declaration ('the specified date').

(2) The declaration operates on the specified date to vest the legal title to all of the transferor's property in the transferee, without the need for any further document transferring it.

This is subject to subsections (3) and (4).

(3) Subsection (2) does not apply to—
(a) any land held by the transferor as security for money subject to the trusts of the transferor (other than land held on trust for securing debentures or debenture stock);
(b) any land held by the transferor under a lease or agreement which contains any covenant (however described) against assignment of the transferor's interest without the consent of some other person, unless that consent has been obtained before the specified date; or
(c) any shares, stock, annuity or other property which is only transferable in books kept by a company or other body or in a manner directed by or under any enactment.

(4) In its application to registered land within the meaning of the Land Registration Act 2002, subsection (2) has effect subject to section 27 of that Act (dispositions required to be registered).

(5)   In this section 'relevant charity merger' has the same meaning as in section 75C.

(6)   In this section—

(a)   any reference to the transferor, in relation to a relevant charity merger, is a reference to the transferor (or one of the transferors) within the meaning of section 75C above, and

(b)   any reference to all of the transferor's property, where the transferor is a charity within section 75C(5), is a reference to all of the transferor's unrestricted property (within the meaning of that provision).

(7)   In this section any reference to the transferee, in relation to a relevant charity merger, is a reference to—

(a)   the transferee (within the meaning of section 75C above), if it is a company or other body corporate, and

(b)   otherwise, to the charity trustees of the transferee (within the meaning of that section).

75F   Effect of registering charity merger on gifts to transferor[33]

(1)   This section applies where a relevant charity merger is registered in the register of charity mergers.

(2)   Any gift which—

(a)   is expressed as a gift to the transferor, and

(b)   takes effect on or after the date of registration of the merger,

takes effect as a gift to the transferee, unless it is an excluded gift.

(3)   A gift is an 'excluded gift' if—

(a)   the transferor is a charity within section 75C(5), and

(b)   the gift is intended to be held subject to the trusts on which the whole or part of the charity's permanent endowment is held.

(4)   In this section—

'relevant charity merger' has the same meaning as in section 75C; and

'transferor' and 'transferee' have the same meanings as in section 75E."

PART 3
FUNDING FOR CHARITABLE, BENEVOLENT OR PHILANTHROPIC INSTITUTIONS

CHAPTER 1
PUBLIC CHARITABLE COLLECTIONS

Preliminary

45. Regulation of public charitable collections[34]

(1) This Chapter regulates public charitable collections, which are of the following two types—

(a) collections in a public place; and

(b) door to door collections.

---

[33] This section allows gifts to be transferred into a newly merged charity.

[34] This section and the ones following it establish a new two-step procedure to regulate fundraising by charities. These are not inserted into the Charities Act 1993 but are part of the Charities Act 2006. Detailed regulations are expected.

(2) For the purposes of this Chapter—

    (a) "public charitable collection" means (subject to section 46) a charitable appeal which is—

        (i) in any public place, or

        (ii) by means of visits to houses or business premises (or both);

    (b) "charitable appeal" means an appeal to members of the public which is—

        (i) an appeal to them to give money or other property, or

        (ii) an appeal falling within subsection (4),

        (or both) and which is made in association with a representation that the whole or any part of its proceeds is to be applied for charitable, benevolent or philanthropic purposes;

    (c) a "collection in a public place" is a public charitable collection that is made in a public place, as mentioned in paragraph (a)(i);

    (d) a "door to door collection" is a public charitable collection that is made by means of visits to houses or business premises (or both), as mentioned in paragraph (a)(ii).

(3) For the purposes of subsection (2)(b)—

    (a) the reference to the giving of money is to doing so by whatever means; and

    (b) it does not matter whether the giving of money or other property is for consideration or otherwise.

(4) An appeal falls within this subsection if it consists in or includes—

    (a) the making of an offer to sell goods or to supply services, or

    (b) the exposing of goods for sale,

to members of the public.

(5) In this section—

"business premises" means any premises used for business or other commercial purposes;

"house" includes any part of a building constituting a separate dwelling;

"public place" means—

    (a) any highway, and

    (b) (subject to subsection (6)) any other place to which, at any time when the appeal is made, members of the public have or are permitted to have access and which either—

        (i) is not within a building, or

        (ii) if within a building, is a public area within any station, airport or shopping precinct or any other similar public area.

(6) In subsection (5), paragraph (b) of the definition of "public place" does not include—

    (a) any place to which members of the public are permitted to have access only if any payment or ticket required as a condition of access has been made or purchased; or

    (b) any place to which members of the public are permitted to have access only by virtue of permission given for the purposes of the appeal in question.

46. Charitable appeals that are not public charitable collections

(1) A charitable appeal is not a public charitable collection if the appeal—

    (a) is made in the course of a public meeting; or

    (b) is made—

        (i) on land within a churchyard or burial ground contiguous or adjacent to a place of public worship, or

        (ii) on other land occupied for the purposes of a place of public worship and contiguous or adjacent to it,

    where the land is enclosed or substantially enclosed (whether by any wall or building or otherwise); or

    (c) is made on land to which members of the public have access only—

        (i) by virtue of the express or implied permission of the occupier of the land, or

        (ii) by virtue of any enactment,

    and the occupier is the promoter of the collection; or

    (d) is an appeal to members of the public to give money or other property by placing it in an unattended receptacle.

(2) For the purposes of subsection (1)(c) "the occupier", in relation to unoccupied land, means the person entitled to occupy it.

(3) For the purposes of subsection (1)(d) a receptacle is unattended if it is not in the possession or custody of a person acting as a collector.

47. Other definitions for purposes of this Chapter

(1) In this Chapter—

"charitable, benevolent or philanthropic institution" means—

(a) a charity, or

(b) an institution (other than a charity) which is established for charitable, benevolent, or philanthropic purposes;

"collector", in relation to a public charitable collection, means any person by whom the appeal in question is made (whether made by him alone or with others and whether made by him for remuneration or otherwise);

"local authority" means a unitary authority, the council of a district so far as it is not a unitary authority, the council of a London borough or of a Welsh county or county borough, the Common Council of the City of London or the Council of the Isles of Scilly;

"prescribed" means prescribed by regulations under section 63;

"proceeds", in relation to a public charitable collection, means all money or other property given (whether for consideration or otherwise) in response to the charitable appeal in question;

"promoter", in relation to a public charitable collection, means—

(a) a person who (whether alone or with others and whether for remuneration or otherwise) organises or controls the conduct of the charitable appeal in question, or

(b) where there is no person acting as mentioned in paragraph (a), any person who acts as a collector in respect of the collection,

and associated expressions are to be construed accordingly;

"public collections certificate" means a certificate issued by the Commission under section 52.

(2) In subsection (1) "unitary authority" means—

(a) the council of a county so far as it is the council for an area for which there are no district councils;

(b) the council of any district comprised in an area for which there is no county council.

(3) The functions exercisable under this Chapter by a local authority are to be exercisable-

(a) as respects the Inner Temple, by its Sub-Treasurer, and

(b) as respects the Middle Temple, by its Under Treasurer;

and references in this Chapter to a local authority or to the area of a local authority are to be construed accordingly.

Restrictions on conducting collections

48. Restrictions on conducting collections in a public place

(1) A collection in a public place must not be conducted unless—

(a) the promoters of the collection hold a public collections certificate in force under section 52 in respect of the collection, and

(b) the collection is conducted in accordance with a permit issued under section 59 by the local authority in whose area it is conducted.

(2) Subsection (1) does not apply to a public charitable collection which is an exempt collection by virtue of section 50 (local, short-term collections).

(3) Where—

(a) a collection in a public place is conducted in contravention of subsection (1), and

(b) the circumstances of the case do not fall within section 50(6),

every promoter of the collection is guilty of an offence and liable on summary conviction to a fine not exceeding level 5 on the standard scale.

49. Restrictions on conducting door to door collections

(1) A door to door collection must not be conducted unless the promoters of the collection—

(a) hold a public collections certificate in force under section 52 in respect of the collection, and

(b) have within the prescribed period falling before the day (or the first of the days) on which the collection takes place—

(i) notified the local authority in whose area the collection is to be conducted of the matters mentioned in subsection (3), and

(ii) provided that authority with a copy of the certificate mentioned in paragraph (a).

(2) Subsection (1) does not apply to a door to door collection which is an exempt collection by virtue of section 50 (local, short-term collections).

(3) The matters referred to in subsection (1)(b)(i) are—

(a) the purpose for which the proceeds of the appeal are to be applied;

(b) the prescribed particulars of when the collection is to be conducted;

(c) the locality within which the collection is to be conducted; and

(d) such other matters as may be prescribed.

(4) Where—
    (a) a door to door collection is conducted in contravention of subsection (1), and
    (b) the circumstances of the case do not fall within section 50(6),
every promoter of the collection is guilty of an offence and liable on summary conviction to a fine not exceeding level 5 on the standard scale.
This is subject to subsection (5).

(5) Where—
    (a) a door to door collection is conducted in contravention of subsection (1),
    (b) the appeal is for goods only, and
    (c) the circumstances of the case do not fall within section 50(6),
every promoter of the collection is guilty of an offence and liable on summary conviction to a fine not exceeding level 3 on the standard scale.

(6) In subsection (5) "goods" includes all personal chattels other than things in action and money.

50. Exemption for local, short-term collections

(1) A public charitable collection is an exempt collection if—
    (a) it is a local, short-term collection (see subsection (2)), and
    (b) the promoters notify the local authority in whose area it is to be conducted of the matters mentioned in subsection (3) within the prescribed period falling before the day (or the first of the days) on which the collection takes place,
unless, within the prescribed period beginning with the date when they are so notified, the local authority serve a notice under subsection (4) on the promoters.

(2) A public charitable collection is a local, short term collection if—
    (a) the appeal is local in character; and
    (b) the duration of the appeal does not exceed the prescribed period of time.

(3) The matters referred to in subsection (1)(b) are—
    (a) the purpose for which the proceeds of the appeal are to be applied;
    (b) the date or dates on which the collection is to be conducted;
    (c) the place at which, or the locality within which, the collection is to be conducted; and
    (d) such other matters as may be prescribed.

(4) Where it appears to the local authority—
    (a) that the collection is not a local, short-term collection, or
    (b) that the promoters or any of them have or has on any occasion—
        (i) breached any provision of regulations made under section 63, or
        (ii) been convicted of an offence within section 53(2)(a)(i) to (v),
they must serve on the promoters written notice of their decision to that effect and the reasons for their decision.

(5) That notice must also state the right of appeal conferred by section 62(1) and the time within which such an appeal must be brought.

(6) Where—
    (a) a collection in a public place is conducted otherwise than in accordance with section 48(1) or a door to door collection is conducted otherwise than in accordance with section 49(1), and
    (b) the collection is a local, short term collection but the promoters do not notify the local authority as mentioned in subsection (1)(b),

every promoter of the collection is guilty of an offence and liable on summary conviction to a fine not exceeding level 3 on the standard scale.

Public collections certificates

51. Applications for certificates

(1) A person or persons proposing to promote public charitable collections (other than exempt collections) may apply to the Charity Commission for a public collections certificate in respect of those collections.

(2) The application must be made—

(a) within the specified period falling before the first of the collections is to commence, or

(b) before such later date as the Commission may allow in the case of that application.

(3) The application must—

(a) be made in such form as may be specified,

(b) specify the period for which the certificate is sought (which must be no more than 5 years), and

(c) contain such other information as may be specified.

(4) An application under this section may be made for a public collections certificate in respect of a single collection; and the references in this Chapter, in the context of such certificates, to public charitable collections are to be read accordingly.

(5) In subsections (2) and (3) "specified" means specified in regulations made by the Commission after consulting such persons or bodies of persons as it considers appropriate.

(6) Regulations under subsection (5)—

(a) must be published in such manner as the Commission considers appropriate,

(b) may make different provision for different cases or descriptions of case, and

(c) may make such incidental, supplementary, consequential or transitional provision as the Commission considers appropriate.

(7) In this section "exempt collection" means a public charitable collection which is an exempt collection by virtue of section 50.

52. Determination of applications and issue of certificates

(1) On receiving an application for a public collections certificate made in accordance with section 51, the Commission may make such inquiries (whether under section 54 or otherwise) as it thinks fit.

(2) The Commission must, after making any such inquiries, determine the application by either—

(a) issuing a public collections certificate in respect of the collections, or

(b) refusing the application on one or more of the grounds specified in section 53(1).

(3) A public collections certificate—

(a) must specify such matters as may be prescribed, and

(b) shall (subject to section 56) be in force for—

(i) the period specified in the application in accordance with section 51(3)(b), or

(ii) such shorter period as the Commission thinks fit.

(4) The Commission may, at the time of issuing a public collections certificate, attach to it such conditions as it thinks fit.

(5) Conditions attached under subsection (4) may include conditions prescribed for the purposes of that subsection.

(6) The Commission must secure that the terms of any conditions attached under subsection (4) are consistent with the provisions of any regulations under section 63 (whether or not prescribing conditions for the purposes of that subsection).

(7) Where the Commission—

(a) refuses to issue a certificate, or

(b) attaches any condition to it,

it must serve on the applicant written notice of its decision and the reasons for its decision.

(8) That notice must also state the right of appeal conferred by section 57(1) and the time within which such an appeal must be brought.

53. Grounds for refusing to issue a certificate

(1) The grounds on which the Commission may refuse an application for a public collections certificate are—

(a) that the applicant has been convicted of a relevant offence;

(b) where the applicant is a person other than a charitable, benevolent or philanthropic institution for whose benefit the collections are proposed to be conducted, that the Commission is not satisfied that the applicant is authorised (whether by any such institution or by any person acting on behalf of any such institution) to promote the collections;

(c) that it appears to the Commission that the applicant, in promoting any other collection authorised under this Chapter or under section 119 of the 1982 Act, failed to exercise the required due diligence;

(d) that the Commission is not satisfied that the applicant will exercise the required due diligence in promoting the proposed collections;

(e) that it appears to the Commission that the amount likely to be applied for charitable, benevolent or philanthropic purposes in consequence of the proposed collections would be inadequate, having regard to the likely amount of the proceeds of the collections;

(f) that it appears to the Commission that the applicant or any other person would be likely to receive an amount by way of remuneration in connection with the collections that would be excessive, having regard to all the circumstances;

(g) that the applicant has failed to provide information—

(i) required for the purposes of the application for the certificate or a previous application, or

(ii) in response to a request under section 54(1);

(h) that it appears to the Commission that information so provided to it by the applicant is false or misleading in a material particular;

(i) that it appears to the Commission that the applicant or any person authorised by him—

(i) has breached any conditions attached to a previous public collections certificate, or

(ii) has persistently breached any conditions attached to a permit issued under section 59;

(j) that it appears to the Commission that the applicant or any person authorised by him has on any occasion breached any provision of regulations made under section 63(1)(b).

(2) For the purposes of subsection (1)—
  (a) a "relevant offence" is—
    (i) an offence under section 5 of the 1916 Act;
    (ii) an offence under the 1939 Act;
    (iii) an offence under section 119 of the 1982 Act or regulations made under it;
    (iv) an offence under this Chapter;
    (v) an offence involving dishonesty; or
    (vi) an offence of a kind the commission of which would, in the opinion of the Commission, be likely to be facilitated by the issuing to the applicant of a public collections certificate; and
  (b) the "required due diligence" is due diligence—
    (i) to secure that persons authorised by the applicant to act as collectors for the purposes of the collection were (or will be) fit and proper persons;
    (ii) to secure that such persons complied (or will comply) with the provisions of regulations under section 63(1)(b) of this Act or (as the case may be) section 119 of the 1982 Act; or
    (iii) to prevent badges or certificates of authority being obtained by persons other than those the applicant had so authorised.

(3) Where an application for a certificate is made by more than one person, any reference to the applicant in subsection (1) or (2) is to be construed as a reference to any of the applicants.

(4) Subject to subsections (5) and (6), the reference in subsection (2)(b)(iii) to badges or certificates of authority is a reference to badges or certificates of authority in a form prescribed by regulations under section 63(1)(b) of this Act or (as the case may be) under section 119 of the 1982 Act.

(5) Subsection (2)(b) applies to the conduct of the applicant (or any of the applicants) in relation to any public charitable collection authorised—
  (a) under regulations made under section 5 of the 1916 Act (collection of money or sale of articles in a street or other public place), or
  (b) under the 1939 Act (collection of money or other property by means of visits from house to house),
as it applies to his conduct in relation to a collection authorised under this Chapter, but subject to the modifications set out in subsection (6).

(6) The modifications are—
  (a) in the case of a collection authorised under regulations made under the 1916 Act—
    (i) the reference in subsection (2)(b)(ii) to regulations under section 63(1)(b) of this Act is to be construed as a reference to the regulations under which the collection in question was authorised, and
    (ii) the reference in subsection (2)(b)(iii) to badges or certificates of authority is to be construed as a reference to any written authority provided to a collector pursuant to those regulations; and
  (b) in the case of a collection authorised under the 1939 Act—

        (i) the reference in subsection (2)(b)(ii) to regulations under section 63(1)(b) of this Act is to be construed as a reference to regulations under section 4 of that Act, and

       (ii) the reference in subsection (2)(b)(iii) to badges or certificates of authority is to be construed as a reference to badges or certificates of authority in a form prescribed by such regulations.

(7) In subsections (1)(c) and (5) a reference to a collection authorised under this Chapter is a reference to a public charitable collection that—

    (a) is conducted in accordance with section 48 or section 49 (as the case may be), or

    (b) is an exempt collection by virtue of section 50.

(8) In this section—

"the 1916 Act" means the Police, Factories, &c. (Miscellaneous Provisions) Act 1916 (c. 31);

"the 1939 Act" means the House to House Collections Act 1939 (c. 44); and

"the 1982 Act" means the Civic Government (Scotland) Act 1982 (c. 45).

54. Power to call for information and documents

(1) The Commission may request—

    (a) any applicant for a public collections certificate, or

    (b) any person to whom such a certificate has been issued,

to provide it with any information in his possession, or document in his custody or under this control, which is relevant to the exercise of any of its functions under this Chapter.

(2) Nothing in this section affects the power conferred on the Commission by section 9 of the 1993 Act.

55. Transfer of certificate between trustees of unincorporated charity

(1) One or more individuals to whom a public collections certificate has been issued ("the holders") may apply to the Commission for a direction that the certificate be transferred to one or more other individuals ("the recipients").

(2) An application under subsection (1) must—

    (a) be in such form as may be specified, and

    (b) contain such information as may be specified.

(3) The Commission may direct that the certificate be transferred if it is satisfied that—

    (a) each of the holders is or was a trustee of a charity which is not a body corporate;

    (b) each of the recipients is a trustee of that charity and consents to the transfer; and

    (c) the charity trustees consent to the transfer.

(4) Where the Commission refuses to direct that a certificate be transferred, it must serve on the holders written notice of—

    (a) its decision, and

    (b) the reasons for its decision.

(5) That notice must also state the right of appeal conferred by section 57(2) and the time within which such an appeal must be brought.

(6) Subsections (5) and (6) of section 51 apply for the purposes of subsection (2) of this section as they apply for the purposes of subsection (3) of that section.

(7) Except as provided by this section, a public collections certificate is not transferable.

56. Withdrawal or variation etc. of certificates

    (1)   Where subsection (2), (3) or (4) applies, the Commission may—

        (a) withdraw a public collections certificate,

        (b) suspend such a certificate,

        (c) attach any condition (or further condition) to such a certificate, or

        (d) vary any existing condition of such a certificate.

    (2)   This subsection applies where the Commission—

        (a) has reason to believe there has been a change in the circumstances which prevailed at the time when it issued the certificate, and

        (b) is of the opinion that, if the application for the certificate had been made in the new circumstances, it would not have issued the certificate or would have issued it subject to different or additional conditions.

    (3)   This subsection applies where—

        (a) the holder of a certificate has unreasonably refused to provide any information or document in response to a request under section 54(1), or

        (b) the Commission has reason to believe that information provided to it by the holder of a certificate (or, where there is more than one holder, by any of them) for the purposes of the application for the certificate, or in response to such a request, was false or misleading in a material particular.

    (4)   This subsection applies where the Commission has reason to believe that there has been or is likely to be a breach of any condition of a certificate, or that a breach of such a condition is continuing.

    (5)   Any condition imposed at any time by the Commission under subsection (1) (whether by attaching a new condition to the certificate or by varying an existing condition) must be one that it would be appropriate for the Commission to attach to the certificate under section 52(4) if the holder was applying for it in the circumstances prevailing at that time.

    (6)   The exercise by the Commission of the power conferred by paragraph (b), (c) or (d) of subsection (1) on one occasion does not prevent it from exercising any of the powers conferred by that subsection on a subsequent occasion; and on any subsequent occasion the reference in subsection (2)(a) to the time when the Commission issued the certificate is a reference to the time when it last exercised any of those powers.

    (7)   Where the Commission—

        (a) withdraws or suspends a certificate,

        (b) attaches a condition to a certificate, or

        (c) varies an existing condition of a certificate,

        it must serve on the holder written notice of its decision and the reasons for its decision.

    (8)   That notice must also state the right of appeal conferred by section 57(3) and the time within which such an appeal must be brought.

    (9)   If the Commission—

        (a) considers that the interests of the public require a decision by it under this section to have immediate effect, and

        (b) includes a statement to that effect and the reasons for it in the notice served under subsection (7),

        the decision takes effect when that notice is served on the holder.

(10) In any other case the certificate shall continue to have effect as if it had not been withdrawn or suspended or (as the case may be) as if the condition had not been attached or varied—

   (a) until the time for bringing an appeal under section 57(3) has expired, or

   (b) if such an appeal is duly brought, until the determination or abandonment of the appeal.

(11) A certificate suspended under this section shall (subject to any appeal and any withdrawal of the certificate) remain suspended until—

   (a) such time as the Commission may by notice direct that the certificate is again in force, or

   (b) the end of the period of six months beginning with the date on which the suspension takes effect,

whichever is the sooner.

57. Appeals against decisions of the Commission

(1) A person who has duly applied to the Commission for a public collections certificate may appeal to the Charity Tribunal ("the Tribunal") against a decision of the Commission under section 52—

   (a) to refuse to issue the certificate, or

   (b) to attach any condition to it.

(2) A person to whom a public collections certificate has been issued may appeal to the Tribunal against a decision of the Commission not to direct that the certificate be transferred under section 55.

(3) A person to whom a public collections certificate has been issued may appeal to the Tribunal against a decision of the Commission under section 56—

   (a) to withdraw or suspend the certificate,

   (b) to attach a condition to the certificate, or

   (c) to vary an existing condition of the certificate.

(4) The Attorney General may appeal to the Tribunal against a decision of the Commission—

   (a) to issue, or to refuse to issue, a certificate,

   (b) to attach, or not to attach, any condition to a certificate (whether under section 52 or section 56),

   (c) to direct, or not to direct, that a certificate be transferred under section 55,

   (d) to withdraw or suspend, or not to withdraw or suspend, a certificate, or

   (e) to vary, or not to vary, an existing condition of a certificate.

(5) In determining an appeal under this section, the Tribunal—

   (a) must consider afresh the decision appealed against, and

   (b) may take into account evidence which was not available to the Commission.

(6) On an appeal under this section, the Tribunal may—

   (a) dismiss the appeal,

   (b) quash the decision, or

   (c) substitute for the decision another decision of a kind that the Commission could have made;

and in any case the Tribunal may give such directions as it thinks fit, having regard to the provisions of this Chapter and of regulations under section 63.

(7) If the Tribunal quashes the decision, it may remit the matter to the Commission (either generally or for determination in accordance with a finding made or direction given by the Tribunal).

58. Applications for permits to conduct collections in public places

(1) A person or persons proposing to promote a collection in a public place (other than an exempt collection) in the area of a local authority may apply to the authority for a permit to conduct that collection.

(2) The application must be made within the prescribed period falling before the day (or the first of the days) on which the collection is to take place, except as provided in subsection (4).

(3) The application must—

    (a) specify the date or dates in respect of which it is desired that the permit, if issued, should have effect (which, in the case of two or more dates, must not span a period of more than 12 months);

    (b) be accompanied by a copy of the public collections certificate in force under section 52 in respect of the proposed collection; and

    (c) contain such information as may be prescribed.

(4) Where an application ("the certificate application") has been made in accordance with section 51 for a public collections certificate in respect of the collection and either—

    (a) the certificate application has not been determined by the end of the period mentioned in subsection (2) above, or

    (b) the certificate application has been determined by the issue of such a certificate but at a time when there is insufficient time remaining for the application mentioned in subsection (2) ("the permit application") to be made by the end of that period,

the permit application must be made as early as practicable before the day (or the first of the days) on which the collection is to take place.

(5) In this section "exempt collection" means a collection in a public place which is an exempt collection by virtue of section 50.

59. Determination of applications and issue of permits

(1) On receiving an application made in accordance with section 58 for a permit in respect of a collection in a public place, a local authority must determine the application within the prescribed period by either—

    (a) issuing a permit in respect of the collection, or

    (b) refusing the application on the ground specified in section 60(1).

(2) Where a local authority issue such a permit, it shall (subject to section 61) have effect in respect of the date or dates specified in the application in accordance with section 58(3)(a).

(3) At the time of issuing a permit under this section, a local authority may attach to it such conditions within paragraphs (a) to (d) below as they think fit, having regard to the local circumstances of the collection—

(a) conditions specifying the day of the week, date, time or frequency of the collection;

(b) conditions specifying the locality or localities within their area in which the collection may be conducted;

(c) conditions regulating the manner in which the collection is to be conducted;

(d) such other conditions as may be prescribed for the purposes of this subsection.

(4) A local authority must secure that the terms of any conditions attached under subsection (3) are consistent with the provisions of any regulations under section 63 (whether or not prescribing conditions for the purposes of that subsection).

(5) Where a local authority—

(a) refuse to issue a permit, or

(b) attach any condition to it,

they must serve on the applicant written notice of their decision and the reasons for their decision.

(6) That notice must also state the right of appeal conferred by section 62(2) and the time within which such an appeal must be brought.

60. Refusal of permits

(1) The only ground on which a local authority may refuse an application for a permit to conduct a collection in a public place is that it appears to them that the collection would cause undue inconvenience to members of the public by reason of—

(a) the day or the week or date on or in which,

(b) the time at which,

(c) the frequency with which, or

(d) the locality or localities in which,

it is proposed to be conducted.

(2) In making a decision under subsection (1), a local authority may have regard to the fact (where it is the case) that the collection is proposed to be conducted—

(a) wholly or partly in a locality in which another collection in a public place is already authorised to be conducted under this Chapter, and

(b) on a day on which that other collection is already so authorised, or on the day falling immediately before, or immediately after, any such day.

(3) A local authority must not, however, have regard to the matters mentioned in subsection (2) if it appears to them—

(a) that the proposed collection would be conducted only in one location, which is on land to which members of the public would have access only-

(i) by virtue of the express or implied permission of the occupier of the land, or

(ii) by virtue of any enactment, and

(b) that the occupier of the land consents to that collection being conducted there;

and for this purpose "the occupier", in relation to unoccupied land, means the person entitled to occupy it.

(4) In this section a reference to a collection in a public place authorised under this Chapter is a reference to a collection in a public place that—

(a) is conducted in accordance with section 48, or

(b) is an exempt collection by virtue of section 50.

61. Withdrawal or variation etc. of permits

(1) Where subsection (2), (3) or (4) applies, a local authority who have issued a permit under section 59 may—

(a) withdraw the permit,

(b) attach any condition (or further condition) to the permit, or

(c) vary any existing condition of the permit.

(2) This subsection applies where the local authority—

(a) have reason to believe that there has been a change in the circumstances which prevailed at the time when they issued the permit, and

(b) are of the opinion that, if the application for the permit had been made in the new circumstances, they would not have issued the permit or would have issued it subject to different or additional conditions.

(3) This subsection applies where the local authority have reason to believe that any information provided to them by the holder of a permit (or, where there is more than one holder, by any of them) for the purposes of the application for the permit was false or misleading in a material particular.

(4) This subsection applies where the local authority have reason to believe that there has been or is likely to be a breach of any condition of a permit issued by them, or that a breach of such a condition is continuing.

(5) Any condition imposed at any time by a local authority under subsection (1) (whether by attaching a new condition to the permit or by varying an existing condition) must be one that it would be appropriate for the authority to attach to the permit under section 59(3) if the holder was applying for it in the circumstances prevailing at that time.

(6) The exercise by a local authority of the power conferred by paragraph (b) or (c) of subsection (1) on one occasion does not prevent them from exercising any of the powers conferred by that subsection on a subsequent occasion; and on any subsequent occasion the reference in subsection (2)(a) to the time when the local authority issued the permit is a reference to the time when they last exercised any of those powers.

(7) Where under this section a local authority—

(a) withdraw a permit,

(b) attach a condition to a permit, or

(c) vary an existing condition of a permit,

they must serve on the holder written notice of their decision and the reasons for their decision.

(8) That notice must also state the right of appeal conferred by section 62(3) and the time within which such an appeal must be brought.

(9) Where a local authority withdraw a permit under this section, they must send a copy of their decision and the reasons for it to the Commission.

(10) Where a local authority under this section withdraw a permit, attach any condition to a permit, or vary an existing condition of a permit, the permit shall continue to have effect as if it had not been withdrawn or (as the case may be) as if the condition had not been attached or varied—

(a) until the time for bringing an appeal under section 62(3) has expired, or

(b) if such an appeal is duly brought, until the determination or abandonment of the appeal.

62. Appeals against decisions of local authority

(1) A person who, in relation to a public charitable collection, has duly notified a local authority of the matters mentioned in section 50(3) may appeal to a magistrates' court against a decision of the local authority under section 50(4)—

   (a) that the collection is not a local, short-term collection, or

   (b) that the promoters or any of them has breached any such provision, or been convicted of any such offence, as is mentioned in paragraph (b) of that subsection.

(2) A person who has duly applied to a local authority for a permit to conduct a collection in a public place in the authority's area may appeal to a magistrates' court against a decision of the authority under section 59—

   (a) to refuse to issue a permit, or

   (b) to attach any condition to it.

(3) A person to whom a permit has been issued may appeal to a magistrates' court against a decision of the local authority under section 61—

   (a) to withdraw the permit,

   (b) to attach a condition to the permit, or

   (c) to vary an existing condition of the permit.

(4) An appeal under subsection (1), (2) or (3) shall be by way of complaint for an order, and the Magistrates' Courts Act 1980 (c. 43) shall apply to the proceedings.

(5) Any such appeal shall be brought within 14 days of the date of service on the person in question of the relevant notice under section 50(4), section 59(5) or (as the case may be) section 61(7); and for the purposes of this section an appeal shall be taken to be brought when the complaint is made.

(6) An appeal against the decision of a magistrates' court on an appeal under subsection (1), (2) or (3) may be brought to the Crown Court.

(7) On an appeal to a magistrates' court or the Crown Court under this section, the court may confirm, vary or reverse the local authority's decision and generally give such directions as it thinks fit, having regard to the provisions of this Chapter and of any regulations under section 63.

(8) On an appeal against a decision of a local authority under section 50(4), directions under subsection (7) may include a direction that the collection may be conducted—

   (a) on the date or dates notified in accordance with section 50(3)(b), or

   (b) on such other date or dates as may be specified in the direction;

and if so conducted the collection is to be regarded as one that is an exempt collection by virtue of section 50.

(9) It shall be the duty of the local authority to comply with any directions given by the court under subsection (7); but the authority need not comply with any directions given by a magistrates' court-

   (a) until the time for bringing an appeal under subsection (6) has expired, or

   (b) if such an appeal is duly brought, until the determination or abandonment of the appeal.

Supplementary

63. Regulations

(1) The Minister may make regulations—

    (a) prescribing the matters which a local authority are to take into account in determining whether a collection is local in character for the purposes of section 50(2)(a);

    (b) for the purpose of regulating the conduct of public charitable collections;

    (c) prescribing anything falling to be prescribed by virtue of any provision of this Chapter.

(2) The matters which may be prescribed by regulations under subsection (1)(a) include—

    (a) the extent of the area within which the appeal is to be conducted;

    (b) whether the appeal forms part of a series of appeals;

    (c) the number of collectors making the appeal and whether they are acting for remuneration or otherwise;

    (d) the financial resources (of any description) of any charitable, benevolent or philanthropic institution for whose benefit the appeal is to be conducted;

    (e) where the promoters live or have any place of business.

(3) Regulations under subsection (1)(b) may make provision—

    (a) about the keeping and publication of accounts;

    (b) for the prevention of annoyance to members of the public;

    (c) with respect to the use by collectors of badges and certificates of authority, or badges incorporating such certificates, including, in particular, provision—

        (i) prescribing the form of such badges and certificates;

        (ii) requiring a collector, on request, to permit his badge, or any certificate of authority held by him of the purposes of the collection, to be inspected by a constable or a duly authorised officer of a local authority, or by an occupier of any premises visited by him in the course of the collection;

    (d) for prohibiting persons under a prescribed age from acting as collectors, and prohibiting others from causing them so to act.

(4) Nothing in subsection (2) or (3) prejudices the generality of subsection (1)(a) or (b).

(5) Regulations under this section may provide that any failure to comply with a specified provision of the regulations is to be an offence punishable on summary conviction by a fine not exceeding level 2 on the standard scale.

(6) Before making regulations under this section the Minister must consult such persons or bodies of persons as he considers appropriate.

64. Offences

(1) A person commits an offence if, in connection with any charitable appeal, he displays or uses—

    (a) a prescribed badge or prescribed certificate of authority which is not for the time being held by him for the purposes of the appeal pursuant to regulations under section 63, or

(b) any badge or article, or any certificate or other document, so nearly resembling a prescribed badge or (as the case may be) a prescribed certificate of authority as to be likely to deceive a member of the public.

(2) A person commits an offence if—

(a) for the purposes of an application made under section 51 or section 58, or

(b) for the purposes of section 49 or section 50,

he knowingly or recklessly furnishes any information which is false or misleading in a material particular.

(3) A person guilty of an offence under this section is liable on summary conviction to a fine not exceeding level 5 on the standard scale.

(4) In subsection (1) "prescribed badge" and "prescribed certificate of authority" mean respectively a badge and a certificate of authority in such form as may be prescribed.

65. Offences by bodies corporate

(1) Where any offence under this Chapter or any regulations made under it—

(a) is committed by a body corporate, and

(b) is proved to have been committed with the consent or connivance of, or to be attributable to any neglect on the part of, any director, manager, secretary or other similar officer of the body corporate, or any person who was purporting to act in any such capacity,

he as well as the body corporate shall be guilty of that offence and shall be liable to be proceeded against and punished accordingly.

(2) In subsection (1) "director", in relation to a body corporate whose affairs are managed by its members, means a member of the body corporate.

66. Service of documents

(1) This section applies to any notice required to be served under this Chapter.

(2) A notice to which this section applies may be served on a person (other than a body corporate)—

(a) by delivering it to that person;

(b) by leaving it at his last known address in the United Kingdom; or

(c) by sending it by post to him at that address.

(3) A notice to which this section applies may be served on a body corporate by delivering it or sending it by post—

(a) to the registered or principal office of the body in the United Kingdom, or

(b) if it has no such office in the United Kingdom, to any place in the United Kingdom where it carries on business or conducts its activities (as the case may be).

(4) A notice to which this section applies may also be served on a person (including a body corporate) by sending it by post to that person at an address notified by that person for the purposes of this subsection to the person or persons by whom it is required to be served.

CHAPTER 2
FUND-RAISING

67. Statements indicating benefits for charitable institutions and fund-raisers[35]

(1) Section 60 of the Charities Act 1992 (c. 41) (fund-raisers required to indicate institutions benefiting and arrangements for remuneration) is amended as follows.

(2) In subsection (1) (statements by professional fund-raisers raising money for particular charitable institutions), for paragraph (c) substitute—

"(c) the method by which the fund-raiser's remuneration in connection with the appeal is to be determined and the notifiable amount of that remuneration."

(3) In subsection (2) (statements by professional fund-raisers raising money for charitable purposes etc.), for paragraph (c) substitute—

"(c) the method by which his remuneration in connection with the appeal is to be determined and the notifiable amount of that remuneration."

(4) In subsection (3) (statements by commercial participators raising money for particular charitable institutions), for paragraph (c) substitute—

"(c) the notifiable amount of whichever of the following sums is applicable in the circumstances—

(i) the sum representing so much of the consideration given for goods or services sold or supplied by him as is to be given to or applied for the benefit of the institution or institutions concerned,

(ii) the sum representing so much of any other proceeds of a promotional venture undertaken by him as is to be so given or applied, or

(iii) the sum of the donations by him in connection with the sale or supply of any such goods or services which are to be so given or supplied."

(5) After subsection (3) insert—

"(3A) In subsections (1) to (3) a reference to the 'notifiable amount' of any remuneration or other sum is a reference—

(a) to the actual amount of the remuneration or sum, if that is known at the time when the statement is made; and

(b) otherwise to the estimated amount of the remuneration or sum, calculated as accurately as is reasonably possible in the circumstances."

68. Statements indicating benefits for charitable institutions and collectors

After section 60 of the 1992 Act insert—

"60A Other persons making appeals required to indicate institutions benefiting and arrangements for remuneration

(1) Subsections (1) and (2) of section 60 apply to a person acting for reward as a collector in respect of a public charitable collection as they apply to a professional fund-raiser.

(2) But those subsections do not so apply to a person excluded by virtue of—

(a) subsection (3) below, or

(b) section 60B(1) (exclusion of lower-paid collectors).

---

[35] Fundraising is regulated in the Charities Act 1992, which is amended by the following sections which are inserted into the Charities Act 1992.

(3) Those subsections do not so apply to a person if—

    (a) section 60(1) or (2) applies apart from subsection (1) (by virtue of the exception in section 58(2)(c) for persons treated as promoters), or

    (b) subsection (4) or (5) applies,

in relation to his acting for reward as a collector in respect of the collection mentioned in subsection (1) above.

(4) Where a person within subsection (6) solicits money or other property for the benefit of one or more particular charitable institutions, the solicitation shall be accompanied by a statement clearly indicating—

    (a) the name or names of the institution or institutions for whose benefit the solicitation is being made;

    (b) if there is more than one such institution, the proportions in which the institutions are respectively to benefit;

    (c) the fact that he is an officer, employee or trustee of the institution or company mentioned in subsection (6); and

    (d) the fact that he is receiving remuneration as an officer, employee or trustee or (as the case may be) for acting as a collector.

(5) Where a person within subsection (6) solicits money or other property for charitable, benevolent or philanthropic purposes of any description (rather than for the benefit of one or more particular charitable institutions), the solicitation shall be accompanied by a statement clearly indicating—

    (a) the fact that he is soliciting money or other property for those purposes and not for the benefit of any particular charitable institution or institutions;

    (b) the method by which it is to be determined how the proceeds of the appeal are to be distributed between different charitable institutions;

    (c) the fact that he is an officer, employee or trustee of the institution or company mentioned in subsection (6); and

    (d) the fact that he is receiving remuneration as an officer, employee or trustee or (as the case may be) for acting as a collector.

(6) A person is within this subsection if—

    (a) he is an officer or employee of a charitable institution or a company connected with any such institution, or a trustee of any such institution,

    (b) he is acting as a collector in that capacity, and

    (c) he receives remuneration either in his capacity as officer, employee or trustee or for acting as a collector.

(7) But a person is not within subsection (6) if he is excluded by virtue of section 60B(4).

(8) Where any requirement of—

    (a) subsection (1) or (2) of section 60, as it applies by virtue of subsection (1) above, or

    (b) subsection (4) or (5) above,

is not complied with in relation to any solicitation, the collector concerned shall be guilty of an offence and liable on summary conviction to a fine not exceeding level 5 on the standard scale.

(9) Section 60(8) and (9) apply in relation to an offence under subsection (8) above as they apply in relation to an offence under section 60(7).

(10) In this section—

'the appeal', in relation to any solicitation by a collector, means the campaign or other fund-raising venture in the course of which the solicitation is made;

'collector' has the meaning given by section 47(1) of the Charities Act 2006;

'public charitable collection' has the meaning given by section 45 of that Act.

60B Exclusion of lower-paid collectors from provisions of section 60A

(1) Section 60(1) and (2) do not apply (by virtue of section 60A(1)) to a person who is under the earnings limit in subsection (2) below.

(2) A person is under the earnings limit in this subsection if he does not receive—

    (a) more than—

        (i) £5 per day, or

        (ii) £500 per year,

    by way of remuneration for acting as a collector in relation to relevant collections, or

    (b) more than £500 by way of remuneration for acting as a collector in relation to the collection mentioned in section 60A(1).

(3) In subsection (2) 'relevant collections' means public charitable collections conducted for the benefit of—

    (a) the charitable institution or institutions, or

    (b) the charitable, benevolent or philanthropic purposes,

for whose benefit the collection mentioned in section 60A(1) is conducted.

(4) A person is not within section 60A(6) if he is under the earnings limit in subsection (5) below.

(5) A person is under the earnings limit in this subsection if the remuneration received by him as mentioned in section 60A(6)(c)—

    (a) is not more than—

        (i) £5 per day, or

        (ii) £500 per year, or

    (b) if a lump sum, is not more than £500.

(6) The Minister may by order amend subsections (2) and (5) by substituting a different sum for any sum for the time being specified there."

69. Reserve power to control fund-raising by charitable institutions

After section 64 of the 1992 Act insert—

"64A   Reserve power to control fund-raising by charitable institutions

(1) The Minister may make such regulations as appear to him to be necessary or desirable for or in connection with regulating charity fund-raising.

(2) In this section 'charity fund-raising' means activities which are carried on by—

    (a) charitable institutions,

    (b) persons managing charitable institutions, or

    (c) persons or companies connected with such institutions,

and involve soliciting or otherwise procuring funds for the benefit of such institutions or companies connected with them, or for general charitable, benevolent or philanthropic purposes.

But 'activities' does not include primary purpose trading.

(3) Regulations under this section may, in particular, impose a good practice requirement on the persons managing charitable institutions in circumstances where—
(a) those institutions,
(b) the persons managing them, or
(c) persons or companies connected with such institutions,

are engaged in charity fund-raising.

(4) A 'good practice requirement' is a requirement to take all reasonable steps to ensure that the fund-raising is carried out in such a way that—
(a) it does not unreasonably intrude on the privacy of those from whom funds are being solicited or procured;
(b) it does not involve the making of unreasonably persistent approaches to persons to donate funds;
(c) it does not result in undue pressure being placed on persons to donate funds;
(d) it does not involve the making of any false or misleading representation about any of the matters mentioned in subsection (5).

(5) The matters are—
(a) the extent or urgency of any need for funds on the part of any charitable institution or company connected with such an institution;
(b) any use to which funds donated in response to the fund-raising are to be put by such an institution or company;
(c) the activities, achievements or finances of such an institution or company.

(6) Regulations under this section may provide that a person who persistently fails, without reasonable excuse, to comply with any specified requirement of the regulations is to be guilty of an offence and liable on summary conviction to a fine not exceeding level 2 on the standard scale.

(7) For the purposes of this section—
(a) 'funds' means money or other property;
(b) 'general charitable, benevolent or philanthropic purposes' means charitable, benevolent or philanthropic purposes other than those associated with one or more particular institutions;
(c) the persons 'managing' a charitable institution are the charity trustees or other persons having the general control and management of the administration of the institution; and
(d) a person is 'connected' with a charitable institution if he is an employee or agent of—
(i) the institution,
(ii) the persons managing it, or
(iii) a company connected with it,

or he is a volunteer acting on behalf of the institution or such a company.

(8) In this section 'primary purpose trading', in relation to a charitable institution, means any trade carried on by the institution or a company connected with it where—
(a) the trade is carried on in the course of the actual carrying out of a primary purpose of the institution; or
(b) the work in connection with the trade is mainly carried out by beneficiaries of the institution."

CHAPTER 3
FINANCIAL ASSISTANCE

70. Power of relevant Minister to give financial assistance to charitable, benevolent or philanthropic institutions

(1) A relevant Minister may give financial assistance to any charitable, benevolent or philanthropic institution in respect of any of the institution's activities which directly or indirectly benefit the whole or any part of England (whether or not they also benefit any other area).

(2) Financial assistance under subsection (1) may be given in any form and, in particular, may be given by way of—

(a) grants,

(b) loans,

(c) guarantees, or

(d) incurring expenditure for the benefit of the person assisted.

(3) Financial assistance under subsection (1) may be given on such terms and conditions as the relevant Minister considers appropriate.

(4) Those terms and conditions may, in particular, include provision as to—

(a) the purposes for which the assistance may be used;

(b) circumstances in which the assistance is to be repaid, or otherwise made good, to the relevant Minister, and the manner in which that is to be done;

(c) the making of reports to the relevant Minister regarding the uses to which the assistance has been put;

(d) the keeping, and making available for inspection, of accounts and other records;

(e) the carrying out of examinations by the Comptroller and Auditor General into the economy, efficiency and effectiveness with which the assistance has been used;

(f) the giving by the institution of financial assistance in any form to other persons on such terms and conditions as the institution or the relevant Minister considers appropriate.

(5) A person receiving assistance under this section must comply with the terms and conditions on which it is given, and compliance may be enforced by the relevant Minister.

(6) A relevant Minister may make arrangements for—

(a) assistance under subsection (1) to be given, or

(b) any other of his functions under this section to be exercised,

by some other person.

(7) Arrangements under subsection (6) may make provision for the functions concerned to be so exercised—

(a) either wholly or to such extent as may be specified in the arrangements, and

(b) either generally or in such cases or circumstances as may be so specified,

but do not prevent the functions concerned from being exercised by a relevant Minister.

(8) As soon as possible after 31st March in each year, a relevant Minister must make a report on any exercise by him of any powers under this section during the period of 12 months ending on that day.

(9) The relevant Minister must lay a copy of the report before each House of Parliament.

(10) In this section "charitable, benevolent or philanthropic institution" means—
    (a) a charity, or
    (b) an institution (other than a charity) which is established for charitable, benevolent or philanthropic purposes.

(11) In this section "relevant Minister" means the Secretary of State or the Minister for the Cabinet Office.

71. Power of National Assembly for Wales to give financial assistance to charitable, benevolent or philanthropic institutions

(1) The National Assembly for Wales may give financial assistance to any charitable, benevolent or philanthropic institution in respect of any of the institution's activities which directly or indirectly benefit the whole or any part of Wales (whether or not they also benefit any other area).

(2) Financial assistance under subsection (1) may be given in any form and, in particular, may be given by way of—
    (a) grants,
    (b) loans,
    (c) guarantees, or
    (d) incurring expenditure for the benefit of the person assisted.

(3) Financial assistance under subsection (1) may be given on such terms and conditions as the Assembly considers appropriate.

(4) Those terms and conditions may, in particular, include provision as to—
    (a) the purposes for which the assistance may be used;
    (b) circumstances in which the assistance is to be repaid, or otherwise made good, to the Assembly, and the manner in which that is to be done;
    (c) the making of reports to the Assembly regarding the uses to which the assistance has been put;
    (d) the keeping, and making available for inspection, of accounts and other records;
    (e) the carrying out of examinations by the Auditor General for Wales into the economy, efficiency and effectiveness with which the assistance has been used;
    (f) the giving by the institution of financial assistance in any form to other persons on such terms and conditions as the institution or the Assembly considers appropriate.

(5) A person receiving assistance under this section must comply with the terms and conditions on which it is given, and compliance may be enforced by the Assembly.

(6) The Assembly may make arrangements for—
    (a) assistance under subsection (1) to be given, or
    (b) any other of its functions under this section to be exercised,
    by some other person.

(7) Arrangements under subsection (6) may make provision for the functions concerned to be so exercised—
    (a) either wholly or to such extent as may be specified in the arrangements, and
    (b) either generally or in such cases or circumstances as may be so specified,
    but do not prevent the functions concerned from being exercised by the Assembly.

(8) After 31st March in each year, the Assembly must publish a report on the exercise of powers under this section during the period of 12 months ending on that day.

(9) In this section "charitable, benevolent or philanthropic institution" means—

(a) a charity, or

(b) an institution (other than a charity) which is established for charitable, benevolent or philanthropic purposes.

PART 4
MISCELLANEOUS AND GENERAL

Miscellaneous

72. Disclosure of information to and by Northern Ireland regulator

(1) This section applies if a body (referred to in this section as "the Northern Ireland regulator") is established to exercise functions in Northern Ireland which are similar in nature to the functions exercised in England and Wales by the Charity Commission.

(2) The Minister may by regulations authorise relevant public authorities to disclose information to the Northern Ireland regulator for the purpose of enabling or assisting the Northern Ireland regulator to discharge any of its functions.

(3) If the regulations authorise the disclosure of Revenue and Customs information, they must contain provision in relation to that disclosure which corresponds to the provision made in relation to the disclosure of such information by section 10(2) to (4) of the 1993 Act (as substituted by paragraph 104 of Schedule 8 to this Act).

(4) In the case of information disclosed to the Northern Ireland regulator pursuant to regulations made under this section, any power of the Northern Ireland regulator to disclose the information is exercisable subject to any express restriction subject to which the information was disclosed to the Northern Ireland regulator.

(5) Subsection (4) does not apply in relation to Revenue and Customs information disclosed to the Northern Ireland regulator pursuant to regulations made under this section; but any such information may not be further disclosed except with the consent of the Commissioners for Her Majesty's Revenue and Customs.

(6) Any person specified, or of a description specified, in regulations made under this section who discloses information in contravention of subsection (5) is guilty of an offence and liable-

(a) on summary conviction, to imprisonment for a term not exceeding 12 months or to a fine not exceeding the statutory maximum, or both;

(b) on conviction on indictment, to imprisonment for a term not exceeding two years or to a fine, or both.

(7) It is a defence for a person charged with an offence under subsection (5) of disclosing information to prove that he reasonably believed—

(a) that the disclosure was lawful, or

(b) that the information had already and lawfully been made available to the public.

(8) In the application of this section to Scotland or Northern Ireland, the reference to 12 months in subsection (6) is to be read as a reference to 6 months.

(9) In this section—

"relevant public authority" means—

(a) any government department (other than a Northern Ireland department),

(b) any local authority in England, Wales or Scotland,

(c) any person who is a constable in England and Wales or Scotland,

(d) any other body or person discharging functions of a public nature (including a body or person discharging regulatory functions in relation to any description of activities), except a body or person whose functions are exercisable only or mainly in or as regards Northern Ireland and relate only or mainly to transferred matters;

"Revenue and Customs information" means information held as mentioned in section 18(1) of the Commissioners for Revenue and Customs Act 2005 (c. 11);

"transferred matter" has the same meaning as in the Northern Ireland Act 1998 (c. 47).

73. Report on operation of this Act

(1) The Minister must, before the end of the period of five years beginning with the day on which this Act is passed, appoint a person to review generally the operation of this Act.

(2) The review must address, in particular, the following matters—
    (a) the effect of the Act on—
        (i)   excepted charities,
        (ii) public confidence in charities,
        (iii) the level of charitable donations, and
        (iv) the willingness of individuals to volunteer,
    (b) the status of the Charity Commission as a government department, and
    (c) any other matters the Minister considers appropriate.

(3) After the person appointed under subsection (1) has completed his review, he must compile a report of his conclusions.

(4) The Minister must lay before Parliament a copy of the report mentioned in subsection (3).

(5) For the purposes of this section a charity is an excepted charity if—
    (a) it falls within paragraph (b) or (c) of section 3A(2) of the 1993 Act (as amended by section 9 of this Act), or
    (b) it does not fall within either of those paragraphs but, immediately before the appointed day (within the meaning of section 10 of this Act), it fell within section 3(5)(b) or (5B)(b) of the 1993 Act.

General

74. Orders and regulations

(1) Any power of a relevant Minister to make an order or regulations under this Act is exercisable by statutory instrument.

(2) Any such power—
    (a) may be exercised so as to make different provision for different cases or descriptions of case or different purposes or areas, and
    (b) includes power to make such incidental, supplementary, consequential, transitory, transitional or saving provision as the relevant Minister considers appropriate.

(3) Subject to subsection (4), orders or regulations made by a relevant Minister under this Act are to be subject to annulment in pursuance of a resolution of either House of Parliament.

(4) Subsection (3) does not apply to—

    (a) any order under section 11,

    (b) any regulations under section 13(4)(b) which amend any provision of an Act,

    (c) any regulations under section 72,

    (d) any order under section 75(4) which amends or repeals any provision of an Act or an Act of the Scottish Parliament,

    (e) any order under section 76 or 77, or

    (f) any order under section 79(2).

(5) No order or regulations within subsection (4)(a), (b), (c), (d) or (e) may be made by a relevant Minister (whether alone or with other provisions) unless a draft of the order or regulations has been laid before, and approved by resolution of, each House of Parliament.

(6) If a draft of an instrument containing an order under section 11 would, apart from this subsection, be treated for the purposes of the Standing Orders of either House of Parliament as a hybrid instrument, it is to proceed in that House as if it were not such an instrument.

(7) In this section "relevant Minister" means the Secretary of State or the Minister for the Cabinet Office.

75. Amendments, repeals, revocations and transitional provisions

(1) Schedule 8 contains minor and consequential amendments.

(2) Schedule 9 makes provision for the repeal and revocation of enactments (including enactments which are spent).

(3) Schedule 10 contains transitional provisions and savings.

(4) A relevant Minister may by order make—

    (a) such supplementary, incidental or consequential provision, or

    (b) such transitory, transitional or saving provision,

as he considers appropriate for the general purposes, or any particular purposes, of this Act or in consequence of, or for giving full effect to, any provision made by this Act.

(5) An order under subsection (4) may amend, repeal, revoke or otherwise modify any enactment (including an enactment restating, with or without modifications, an enactment amended by this Act).

(6) In this section "relevant Minister" means the Secretary of State or the Minister for the Cabinet Office.

76. Pre-consolidation amendments[37]

(1) The Minister may by order make such amendments of the enactments relating to charities as in his opinion facilitate, or are otherwise desirable in connection with, the consolidation of the whole or part of those enactments.

(2) An order under this section shall not come into force unless—

    (a) a single Act, or

    (b) a group of two or more Acts,

---

[36] It is not clear when a consolidated Act is expected, but the current complexity of the legislative scheme makes consolidation extremely important if the aims of modernization and access to the law by the public are to be achieved.

is passed consolidating the whole or part of the enactments relating to charities (with or without any other enactments).

(3) If such an Act or group of Acts is passed, the order shall (by virtue of this subsection) come into force immediately before the Act or group of Acts comes into force.

(4) Once an order under this section has come into force, no further order may be made under this section.

(5) In this section—

"amendments" includes repeals, revocations and modifications, and

"the enactments relating to charities" means—

(a) the Charities Act 1992 (c. 41), the Charities Act 1993 (c. 10) and this Act,

(b) any other enactment relating to institutions which fall within section 1(1) of this Act, and

(c) any other enactment, so far as forming part of the law of England and Wales, which makes provision relating to bodies or other institutions which are charities under the law of Scotland or Northern Ireland,

and section 78(2)(a) (definition of "charity") does not apply for the purposes of this section.

77. Amendments reflecting changes in company law audit provisions

(1) The Minister may by order make such amendments of the 1993 Act or this Act as he considers appropriate—

(a) in consequence of, or in connection with, any changes made or to be made by any enactment to the provisions of company law relating to the accounts of charitable companies or to the auditing of, or preparation of reports in respect of, such accounts;

(b) for the purposes of, or in connection with, applying provisions of Schedule 5A to the 1993 Act (group accounts) to charitable companies that are not required to produce group accounts under company law.

(2) In this section—

"accounts" includes group accounts;

"amendments" includes repeals and modifications;

"charitable companies" means companies which are charities;

"company law" means the enactments relating to companies.

78. Interpretation

(1) In this Act—

"the 1992 Act" means the Charities Act 1992 (c. 41);

"the 1993 Act" means the Charities Act 1993 (c. 10).

(2) In this Act—

(a) "charity" has the meaning given by section 1(1);

(b) "charitable purposes" has (in accordance with section 2(6)) the meaning given by section 2(1); and

(c) "charity trustees" has the same meaning as in the 1993 Act;

but (subject to subsection (3) below) the exclusions contained in section 96(2) of the 1993 Act (ecclesiastical corporations etc.) have effect in relation to references to a charity in this Act as they have effect in relation to such references in that Act.

(3) Those exclusions do not have effect in relation to references in section 1 or any reference to the law relating to charities in England and Wales.

(4) In this Act "enactment" includes—

    (a) any provision of subordinate legislation (within the meaning of the Interpretation Act 1978 (c. 30)),

    (b) a provision of a Measure of the Church Assembly or of the General Synod of the Church of England, and

    (c) (in the context of section 6(5) or 75(5)) any provision made by or under an Act of the Scottish Parliament or Northern Ireland legislation,

and references to enactments include enactments passed or made after the passing of this Act.

(5) In this Act "institution" means an institution whether incorporated or not, and includes a trust or undertaking.

(6) In this Act "the Minister" means the Minister for the Cabinet Office.

(7) Subsections (2) to (5) apply except where the context otherwise requires.

79. Commencement

(1) The following provisions come into force on the day on which this Act is passed—

    (a) section 13(4) and (5),

    (b) section 74,

    (c) section 75(4) and (5),

    (d) section 78,

    (e) section 77,

    (f) this section and section 80, and

    (g) the following provisions of Schedule 8—

        paragraph 90(2),

        paragraph 104 so far as it confers power to make regulations, and

        paragraph 174(d),and section 75(1) so far as relating to those provisions.

(2) Otherwise, this Act comes into force on such day as the Minister may by order appoint.

(3) An order under subsection (2)—

    (a) may appoint different days for different purposes or different areas;

    (b) make such provision as the Minister considers necessary or expedient for transitory, transitional or saving purposes in connection with the coming into force of any provision of this Act.

80. Short title and extent

(1) This Act may be cited as the Charities Act 2006.

(2) Subject to subsections (3) to (7), this Act extends to England and Wales only.

(3) The following provisions extend also to Scotland—

    (a) sections 1 to 3 and 5,

    (b) section 6(5),

    (c) sections 72 and 74,

    (d) section 75(2) and (3) and Schedules 9 and 10 so far as relating to the Recreational Charities Act 1958 (c. 17), and

    (e) section 75(4) and (5), sections 76 to 79 and this section.

(4) But the provisions referred to in subsection (3)(a) and (d) affect the law of Scotland only so far as they affect the construction of references to charities or charitable purposes in enactments which relate to matters falling within Section A1 of Part 2 of Schedule 5 to the Scotland Act 1998 (c. 46) (reserved matters: fiscal policy etc.); and so far as they so affect the law of Scotland—

    (a) references in sections 1(1) and 2(1) to the law of England and Wales are to be read as references to the law of Scotland, and

    (b) the reference in section 1(1) to the High Court is to be read as a reference to the Court of Session.

(5) The following provisions extend also to Northern Ireland—

    (a) sections 1 to 3 and 5,

    (b) section 6(5),

    (c) section 23,

    (d) sections 72 and 74,

    (e) section 75(2) and (3) and Schedules 9 and 10 so far as relating to the Recreational Charities Act 1958 (c. 17), and

    (f) section 75(4) and (5), sections 76 to 79 and this section.

(6) But the provisions referred to in subsection (5)(a) and (e) affect the law of Northern Ireland only so far as they affect the construction of references to charities or charitable purposes in enactments which relate to matters falling within paragraph 9 of Schedule 2 to the Northern Ireland Act 1998 (c. 47) (excepted matters: taxes and duties); and so far as they so affect the law of Northern Ireland—

    (a) references in sections 1(1) and 2(1) to the law of England and Wales are to be read as references to the law of Northern Ireland, and

    (b) the reference in section 1(1) to the High Court is to be read as a reference to the High Court in Northern Ireland.

(7) Any amendment, repeal or revocation made by this Act has the same extent as the enactment to which it relates.

(8) But subsection (7) does not apply to any amendment or repeal made in the Recreational Charities Act 1958 by a provision referred to in subsection (3) or (5).

(9) Subsection (7) also does not apply to—

    (a) the amendments made by section 32 in the Companies Act 1985 (c. 6), or

    (b) those made by Schedule 8 in the Police, Factories, &c. (Miscellaneous Provisions) Act 1916 (c. 31), or

    (c) the repeal made in that Act by Schedule 9,

which extend to England and Wales only.

SCHEDULES

SCHEDULE 1

THE CHARITY COMMISSION

1. After Schedule 1 to the 1993 Act insert—

Section 1A "SCHEDULE 1A

THE CHARITY COMMISSION

Membership

1. (1) The Commission shall consist of a chairman and at least four, but not more than eight, other members.

(2) The members shall be appointed by the Minister.

(3) The Minister shall exercise the power in sub-paragraph (2) so as to secure that—

(a) the knowledge and experience of the members of the Commission (taken together) includes knowledge and experience of the matters mentioned in sub-paragraph (4),

(b) at least two members have a seven year general qualification within the meaning of section 71 of the Courts and Legal Services Act 1990, and

(c) at least one member knows about conditions in Wales and has been appointed following consultation with the National Assembly for Wales.

(4) The matters mentioned in this sub-paragraph are—

(a) the law relating to charities,

(b) charity accounts and the financing of charities, and

(c) the operation and regulation of charities of different sizes and descriptions.

(5) In sub-paragraph (3)(c) 'member' does not include the chairman of the Commission.

Terms of appointment and remuneration

2. The members of the Commission shall hold and vacate office as such in accordance with the terms of their respective appointments.

3. (1) An appointment of a person to hold office as a member of the Commission shall be for a term not exceeding three years.

(2) A person holding office as a member of the Commission—

(a) may resign that office by giving notice in writing to the Minister, and

(b) may be removed from office by the Minister on the ground of incapacity or misbehaviour.

(3) Before removing a member of the Commission the Minister shall consult—

(a) the Commission, and

(b) if the member was appointed following consultation with the National Assembly for Wales, the Assembly.

(4) No person may hold office as a member of the Commission for more than ten years in total.

(5) For the purposes of sub-paragraph (4), time spent holding office as a Charity Commissioner for England and Wales shall be counted as time spent holding office as a member of the Commission.

4. (1) The Commission shall pay to its members such remuneration, and such other allowances, as may be determined by the Minister.

(2) The Commission shall, if required to do so by the Minister—

    (a) pay such pension, allowances or gratuities as may be determined by the Minister to or in respect of a person who is or has been a member of the Commission, or

    (b) make such payments as may be so determined towards provision for the payment of a pension, allowances or gratuities to or in respect of such a person.

(3) If the Minister determines that there are special circumstances which make it right for a person ceasing to hold office as a member of the Commission to receive compensation, the Commission shall pay to him a sum by way of compensation of such amount as may be determined by the Minister.

Staff

5. (1) The Commission—

    (a) shall appoint a chief executive, and

    (b) may appoint such other staff as it may determine.

(2) The terms and conditions of service of persons appointed under sub-paragraph (1) are to be such as the Commission may determine with the approval of the Minister for the Civil Service.

Committees

6. (1) The Commission may establish committees and any committee of the Commission may establish sub-committees.

(2) The members of a committee of the Commission may include persons who are not members of the Commission (and the members of a sub-committee may include persons who are not members of the committee or of the Commission).

Procedure etc.

7. (1) The Commission may regulate its own procedure (including quorum).

(2) The validity of anything done by the Commission is not affected by a vacancy among its members or by a defect in the appointment of a member.

Performance of functions

8. Anything authorised or required to be done by the Commission may be done by—

    (a) any member or member of staff of the Commission who is authorised for that purpose by the Commission, whether generally or specially;

    (b) any committee of the Commission which has been so authorised.

Evidence

9. The Documentary Evidence Act 1868 shall have effect as if—

    (a) the Commission were mentioned in the first column of the Schedule to that Act,

    (b) any member or member of staff of the Commission authorised to act on behalf of the Commission were specified in the second column of that Schedule in connection with the Commission, and

(c) the regulations referred to in that Act included any document issued by or under the authority of the Commission.

Execution of documents

10. (1) A document is executed by the Commission by the fixing of its common seal to the document.

(2) But the fixing of that seal to a document must be authenticated by the signature of—

(a) any member of the Commission, or

(b) any member of its staff,

who is authorised for the purpose by the Commission.

(3) A document which is expressed (in whatever form of words) to be executed by the Commission and is signed by—

(a) any member of the Commission, or

(b) any member of its staff,

who is authorised for the purpose by the Commission has the same effect as if executed in accordance with sub-paragraphs (1) and (2).

(4) A document executed by the Commission which makes it clear on its face that it is intended to be a deed has effect, upon delivery, as a deed; and it is to be presumed (unless a contrary intention is proved) to be delivered upon its being executed.

(5) In favour of a purchaser a document is to be deemed to have been duly executed by the Commission if it purports to be signed on its behalf by—

(a) any member of the Commission, or

(b) any member of its staff;

and, where it makes it clear on its face that it is intended to be a deed, it is to be deemed to have been delivered upon its being executed.

(6) For the purposes of this paragraph—

'authorised' means authorised whether generally or specially; and

'purchaser' means a purchaser in good faith for valuable consideration and includes a lessee, mortgagee or other person who for valuable consideration acquired an interest in property.

Annual report

11. (1) As soon as practicable after the end of each financial year the Commission shall publish a report on—

(a) the discharge of its functions,

(b) the extent to which, in its opinion, its objectives (see section 1B of this Act) have been met,

(c) the performance of its general duties (see section 1D of this Act), and

(d) the management of its affairs,

during that year.

(2) The Commission shall lay a copy of each such report before Parliament.

(3) In sub-paragraph (1) above, 'financial year' means—

(a) the period beginning with the date on which the Commission is established and ending with the next 31st March following that date, and

(b) each successive period of 12 months ending with 31st March.

Annual public meeting

12. (1) The Commission shall hold a public meeting ('the annual meeting') for the purpose of enabling a report under paragraph 11 above to be considered.

(2) The annual meeting shall be held within the period of three months beginning with the day on which the report is published.

(3) The Commission shall organise the annual meeting so as to allow—

(a) a general discussion of the contents of the report which is being considered, and

(b) a reasonable opportunity for those attending the meeting to put questions to the Commission about matters to which the report relates.

(4) But subject to sub-paragraph (3) above the annual meeting is to be organised and conducted in such a way as the Commission considers appropriate.

(5) The Commission shall—

(a) take such steps as are reasonable in the circumstances to ensure that notice of the annual meeting is given to every registered charity, and

(b) publish notice of the annual meeting in the way appearing to it to be best calculated to bring it to the attention of members of the public.

(6) Each such notice shall—

(a) give details of the time and place at which the meeting is to be held,

(b) set out the proposed agenda for the meeting,

(c) indicate the proposed duration of the meeting, and

(d) give details of the Commission's arrangements for enabling persons to attend.

(7) If the Commission proposes to alter any of the arrangements which have been included in notices given or published under sub-paragraph (5) above it shall—

(a) give reasonable notice of the alteration, and

(b) publish the notice in the way appearing to it to be best calculated to bring it to the attention of registered charities and members of the public."

House of Commons Disqualification Act 1975 (c. 24)

2. In Part 2 of Schedule 1 to the House of Commons Disqualification Act 1975 (bodies of which all members are disqualified) insert at the appropriate place—
"The Charity Commission."

Northern Ireland Assembly Disqualification Act 1975 (c. 25)

3. In Part 2 of Schedule 1 to the Northern Ireland Assembly Disqualification Act 1975 (bodies of which all members are disqualified) insert at the appropriate place—
"The Charity Commission."

Section 6   SCHEDULE 2

ESTABLISHMENT OF THE CHARITY COMMISSION: SUPPLEMENTARY

1. In this Schedule—

"commencement" means the coming into force of section 6, and
"the Commission" means the Charity Commission.

Appointments to Commission

2. (1) The person who immediately before commencement was the Chief Charity Commissioner for England and Wales is on commencement to become the chairman of
the Commission as if duly appointed under paragraph 1 of Schedule 1A to the 1993
Act.

(2) Any other person who immediately before commencement was a Charity Commissioner for England and Wales is on commencement to become a member of the
Commission as if duly appointed under that paragraph.

(3) While a person holds office as a member of the Commission by virtue of this paragraph
he shall—
 (a) continue to be deemed to be employed in the civil service of the Crown, and
 (b) hold that office on the terms on which he held office as a Charity Commissioner
 for England and Wales immediately before commencement.

(4) Sub-paragraph (3)(b) is subject to—
 (a) sub-paragraph (5),
 (b) paragraph 3(4) and (5) of Schedule 1A to the 1993 Act, and
 (c) any necessary modifications to the terms in question.

(5) No person may hold office as a member of the Commission by virtue of this paragraph
for a term exceeding three years from commencement.

(6) Paragraphs 2 and 3(1) to (3) of Schedule 1A to the 1993 Act, and paragraphs
2 and 3 of Schedule 1 to this Act, shall not apply in relation to a person
while he holds office as a member of the Commission by virtue of this paragraph.

Effect of transfers under section 6

3. (1) Anything which—
 (a) has been done (or has effect as if done) by or in relation to the Commissioners, and
 (b) is in effect immediately before commencement,
 is to be treated as if done by or in relation to the Commission.

(2) Anything (including legal proceedings) which—
 (a) relates to anything transferred by section 6(4), and
 (b) is in the process of being done by or in relation to the Commissioners,
 may be continued by or in relation to the Commission.

(3) But nothing in section 6 or this paragraph affects the validity of anything done by or
in relation to the Commissioners.

(4) In this paragraph "the Commissioners" means the Charity Commissioners for England
and Wales (and includes any person acting for them by virtue of paragraph 3(3) of
Schedule 1 to the 1993 Act).

First annual report of Commission

4. (1) This paragraph applies if there is a period of one or more days which—

    (a) began on the day after the end of the last year for which the Charity Commissioners for England and Wales made a report under section 1(5) of the 1993 Act, and

    (b) ended on the day before commencement.

  (2) The first report published by the Commission under paragraph 11 of Schedule 1A to the 1993 Act shall also be a report on the operations of the Charity Commissioners for England and Wales during the period mentioned in sub-paragraph (1).

Resource accounts of Commission

5. (1) The new Commission and the old Commission shall be treated as being the same government department for the purposes of section 5 of the Government Resources and Accounts Act 2000 (c. 20).

  (2) Resource accounts sent to the Comptroller and Auditor General by the new Commission in respect of any period before commencement shall be resource accounts in the name of the new Commission.

  (3) In this paragraph—

"the new Commission" means the Charity Commission established by section 6, and "the old Commission" means the government department known as the Charity Commission and existing immediately before commencement.

Section 8	SCHEDULE 3

THE CHARITY TRIBUNAL

1. After Schedule 1A to the 1993 Act (inserted by Schedule 1 to this Act) insert—

Section 2A(3)	SCHEDULE 1B

THE CHARITY TRIBUNAL

Membership

1. (1) The Tribunal shall consist of the President and its other members.

  (2) The Lord Chancellor shall appoint—

    (a) a President of the Tribunal,

    (b) legal members of the Tribunal, and

    (c) ordinary members of the Tribunal.

  (3) A person may be appointed as the President or a legal member of the Tribunal only if he has a seven year general qualification within the meaning of section 71 of the Courts and Legal Services Act 1990.

  (4) A person may be appointed as an ordinary member of the Tribunal only if he appears to the Lord Chancellor to have appropriate knowledge or experience relating to charities.

Deputy President

2. (1) The Lord Chancellor may appoint a legal member as deputy President of the Tribunal.
   (2) The deputy President—
       (a) may act for the President when he is unable to act or unavailable, and
       (b) shall perform such other functions as the President may delegate or assign to him.

Terms of appointment

3. (1) The members of the Tribunal shall hold and vacate office as such in accordance with the terms of their respective appointments.
   (2) A person holding office as a member of the Tribunal—
       (a) may resign that office by giving notice in writing to the Lord Chancellor, and
       (b) may be removed from office by the Lord Chancellor on the ground of incapacity or misbehaviour.
   (3) A previous appointment of a person as a member of the Tribunal does not affect his eligibility for re-appointment as a member of the Tribunal.

Retirement etc.

4. (1) A person shall not hold office as a member of the Tribunal after reaching the age of 70.
   (2) Section 26(5) and (6) of the Judicial Pensions and Retirement Act 1993 (extension to age 75) apply in relation to a member of the Tribunal as they apply in relation to a holder of a relevant office.

Remuneration etc.

5. (1) The Lord Chancellor may pay to the members of the Tribunal such remuneration, and such other allowances, as he may determine.
   (2) The Lord Chancellor may—
       (a) pay such pension, allowances or gratuities as he may determine to or in respect of a person who is or has been a member of the Tribunal, or
       (b) make such payments as he may determine towards provision for the payment of a pension, allowances or gratuities to or in respect of such a person.
   (3) If the Lord Chancellor determines that there are special circumstances which make it right for a person ceasing to hold office as a member of the Tribunal to receive compensation, the Lord Chancellor may pay to him a sum by way of compensation of such amount as may be determined by the Lord Chancellor.

Staff and facilities

6. The Lord Chancellor may make staff and facilities available to the Tribunal.

Panels

7. (1) The functions of the Tribunal shall be exercised by panels of the Tribunal.
   (2) Panels of the Tribunal shall sit at such times and in such places as the President may direct.
   (3) Before giving a direction under sub-paragraph (2) above the President shall consult the Lord Chancellor.
   (4) More than one panel may sit at a time.

Panels

8. (1) The President shall make arrangements for determining which of the members of the Tribunal are to constitute a panel of the Tribunal in relation to the exercise of any function.

   (2) Those arrangements shall, in particular, ensure that each panel is constituted in one of the following ways—

   (a) as the President sitting alone,

   (b) as a legal member sitting alone,

   (c) as the President sitting with two other members,

   (d) as a legal member sitting with two other members,

   (e) as the President sitting with one other member,

   (f) as a legal member sitting with one other member,

   (and references in paragraphs (d) and (f) to other members do not include the President).

   (3) The President shall publish arrangements made under this paragraph.

Practice and procedure

9. (1) Decisions of the Tribunal may be taken by majority vote.

   (2) In the case of a panel constituted in accordance with paragraph 8(2)(e), the President shall have a casting vote.

   (3) In the case of a panel constituted in accordance with paragraph 8(2)(f) which consists of a legal member and an ordinary member, the legal member shall have a casting vote.

   (4) The President shall make and publish arrangements as to who is to have a casting vote in the case of a panel constituted in accordance with paragraph 8(2)(f) which consists of two legal members.

10. The President may, subject to rules under section 2B of this Act, give directions about the practice and procedure of the Tribunal."

House of Commons Disqualification Act 1975 (c. 24)

2. In Part 2 of Schedule 1 to the House of Commons Disqualification Act 1975 (bodies of which all members are disqualified) insert at the appropriate place—
"The Charity Tribunal."

Northern Ireland Assembly Disqualification Act 1975 (c. 25)

3. In Part 2 of Schedule 1 to the Northern Ireland Assembly Disqualification Act 1975 (bodies of which all members are disqualified) insert at the appropriate place—
"The Charity Tribunal."

Courts and Legal Services Act 1990 (c.41)

4. In Schedule 11 to the Courts and Legal Services Act 1990 (judges etc. barred from legal practice) insert at the end—
"President or other member of the Charity Tribunal".

Tribunals and Inquiries Act 1992 (c. 53)

5. In Part 1 of Schedule 1 to the Tribunals and Inquiries Act 1992 (tribunals under general supervision of Council) before paragraph 7 insert—

Charities   6A. The Charity Tribunal constituted under section 2A of, and Schedule 1B to, the Charities Act 1993."

Section 8   SCHEDULE 4

APPEALS AND APPLICATIONS TO CHARITY TRIBUNAL

After Schedule 1B to the 1993 Act (inserted by Schedule 3 to this Act) insert—

Section 2A(4)   "SCHEDULE 1C

APPEALS AND APPLICATIONS TO CHARITY TRIBUNAL

Appeals: general

1. (1) Except in the case of a reviewable matter (see paragraph 3) an appeal may be brought to the Tribunal against any decision, direction or order mentioned in column 1 of the Table.
   (2) Such an appeal may be brought by—
       (a) the Attorney General, or
       (b) any person specified in the corresponding entry in column 2 of the Table.
   (3) The Commission shall be the respondent to such an appeal.
   (4) In determining such an appeal the Tribunal—
       (a) shall consider afresh the decision, direction or order appealed against, and
       (b) may take into account evidence which was not available to the Commission.
   (5) The Tribunal may—
       (a) dismiss the appeal, or
       (b) if it allows the appeal, exercise any power specified in the corresponding entry in column 3 of the Table.

Appeals: orders under section 9

2. (1) Paragraph 1(4)(a) above does not apply in relation to an appeal against an order made under section 9 of this Act.
   (2) On such an appeal the Tribunal shall consider whether the information or document in question—
       (a) relates to a charity;
       (b) is relevant to the discharge of the functions of the Commission or the official custodian.
   (3) The Tribunal may allow such an appeal only if it is satisfied that the information or document in question does not fall within either paragraph (a) or paragraph (b) of sub-paragraph (2) above.

Reviewable matters

3. (1) In this Schedule references to 'reviewable matters' are to—
    (a) decisions to which sub-paragraph (2) applies, and
    (b) orders to which sub-paragraph (3) applies.
  (2) This sub-paragraph applies to decisions of the Commission—
    (a) to institute an inquiry under section 8 of this Act with regard to a particular institution,
    (b) to institute an inquiry under section 8 of this Act with regard to a class of institutions,
    (c) not to make a common investment scheme under section 24 of this Act,
    (d) not to make a common deposit scheme under section 25 of this Act,
    (e) not to make an order under section 26 of this Act in relation to a charity,
    (f) not to make an order under section 36 of this Act in relation to land held by or in trust for a charity,
    (g) not to make an order under section 38 of this Act in relation to a mortgage of land held by or in trust for a charity.
  (3) This sub-paragraph applies to an order made by the Commission under section 69(1) of this Act in relation to a company which is a charity.

Reviews

4. (1) An application may be made to the Tribunal for the review of a reviewable matter.
  (2) Such an application may be made by—
    (a) the Attorney General, or
    (b) any person mentioned in the entry in column 2 of the Table which corresponds to the entry in column 1 which relates to the reviewable matter.
  (3) The Commission shall be the respondent to such an application.
  (4) In determining such an application the Tribunal shall apply the principles which would be applied by the High Court on an application for judicial review.
  (5) The Tribunal may—
    (a) dismiss the application, or
    (b) if it allows the application, exercise any power mentioned in the entry in column 3 of the Table which corresponds to the entry in column 1 which relates to the reviewable matter.

Interpretation: remission of matters to Commission

5. References in column 3 of the Table to the power to remit a matter to the Commission are to the power to remit the matter either—
  (a) generally, or
  (b) for determination in accordance with a finding made or direction given by the Tribunal.

TABLE

1	2	3
Decision of the Commission under section 3 or 3A of this Act—(a) to enter or not to enter an institution in the register of charities, or (b) to remove or not to remove an institution from the register.	The persons are—(a) the persons who are or claim to be the charity trustees of the institution, (b) (if a body corporate) the institution itself, and (c) any other person who is or may be affected by the decision.	Power to quash the decision and (if appropriate)—(a) remit the matter to the Commission, (b) direct the Commission to rectify the register.
Decision of the Commission not to make a determination under section 3(9) of this Act in relation to particular information contained in the register.	The persons are—(a) the charity trustees of the charity to which the information relates, (b) (if a body corporate) the charity itself, and (c) any other person who is or may be affected by the decision.	Power to quash the decision and (if appropriate) remit the matter to the Commission.
Direction given by the Commission under section 6 of this Act requiring the name of a charity to be changed.	The persons are—(a) the charity trustees of the charity to which the direction relates, (b) (if a body corporate) the charity itself, and (c) any other person who is or may be affected by the direction.	Power to—(a) quash the direction and (if appropriate) remit the matter to the Commission, (b) substitute for the direction any other direction which could have been given by the Commission.
Decision of the Commission to institute an inquiry under section 8 of this Act with regard to a particular institution.	The persons are—(a) the persons who have control or management of the institution, and (b) (if a body corporate) the institution itself.	Power to direct the Commission to end the inquiry.
Decision of the Commission to institute an inquiry under section 8 of this Act with regard to a class of institutions.	The persons are—(a) the persons who have control or management of any institution which is a member of the class of institutions, and (b) (if a body corporate) any such institution.	Power to—(a) direct the Commission that the inquiry should not consider a particular institution, (b) direct the Commission to end the inquiry.
Order made by the Commission under section 9 of this Act requiring a person to supply information or a document.	The persons are any person who is required to supply the information or document.	Power to—(a) quash the order, (b) substitute for all or part of the order any other order which could have been made by the Commission.
Order made by the Commission under section 16(1) of this Act (including such an order made by virtue of section 23(1)).	The persons are—(a) in a section 16(1)(a) case, the charity trustees of the charity to which the order relates or (if a body corporate) the charity itself, (b) in a section 16(1)(b) case, any person discharged or removed by the order, and (c) any other person who is or may be affected by the order.	Power to—(a) quash the order in whole or in part and (if appropriate) remit the matter to the Commission, (b) substitute for all or part of the order any other order which could have been made by the Commission, (c) add to the order anything which could have been contained in an order made by the Commission.

171

Order made by the Commission under section 18(1) of this Act in relation to a charity.	The persons are—(a) the charity trustees of the charity, (b) (if a body corporate) the charity itself, (c) in a section 18(1)(i) case, any person suspended by the order, and (d) any other person who is or may be affected by the order.	Power to—(a) quash the order in whole or in part and (if appropriate) remit the matter to the Commission, (b) substitute for all or part of the order any other order which could have been made by the Commission, (c) add to the order anything which could have been contained in an order made by the Commission.
Order made by the Commission under section 18(2) of this Act in relation to a charity.	The persons are—(a) the charity trustees of the charity, (b) (if a body corporate) the charity itself, (c) in a section 18(2)(i) case, any person removed by the order, and (d) any other person who is or may be affected by the order.	Power to—(a) quash the order in whole or in part and (if appropriate) remit the matter to the Commission, (b) substitute for all or part of the order any other order which could have been made by the Commission, (c) add to the order anything which could have been contained in an order made by the Commission.
Order made by the Commission under section 18(4) of this Act removing a charity trustee.	The persons are—(a) the charity trustee, (b) the remaining charity trustees of the charity of which he was a charity trustee, (c) (if a body corporate) the charity itself, and (d) any other person who is or may be affected by the order.	Power to—(a) quash the order in whole or in part and (if appropriate) remit the matter to the Commission, (b) substitute for all or part of the order any other order which could have been made by the Commission, (c) add to the order anything which could have been contained in an order made by the Commission.
Order made by the Commission under section 18(5) of this Act appointing a charity trustee.	The persons are—(a) the other charity trustees of the charity, (b) (if a body corporate) the charity itself, and (c) any other person who is or may be affected by the order.	Power to—(a) quash the order in whole or in part and (if appropriate) remit the matter to the Commission, (b) substitute for all or part of the order any other order which could have been made by the Commission, (c) add to the order anything which could have been contained in an order made by the Commission.
Decision of the Commission—(a) to discharge an order following a review under section 18(13) of this Act, or (b) not to discharge an order following such a review.	The persons are—(a) the charity trustees of the charity to which the order relates, (b) (if a body corporate) the charity itself, (c) if the order in question was made under section 18(1)(i), any person suspended by it, and (d) any other person who is or may be affected by the order.	Power to—(a) quash the decision and (if appropriate) remit the matter to the Commission, (b) make the discharge of the order subject to savings or other transitional provisions, (c) remove any savings or other transitional provisions to which the discharge of the order was

subject, (d) discharge the order in whole or in part (whether subject to any savings or other transitional provisions or not).

Order made by the Commission under section 18A(2) of this Act which suspends a person's membership of a charity.	The persons are—(a) the person whose membership is suspended by the order, and (b) any other person who is or may be affected by the order.	Power to quash the order and (if appropriate) remit the matter to the Commission.
Order made by the Commission under section 19A(2) of this Act which directs a person to take action specified in the order.	The persons are any person who is directed by the order to take the specified action.	Power to quash the order and (if appropriate) remit the matter to the Commission.
Order made by the Commission under section 19B(2) of this Act which directs a person to apply property in a specified manner.	The persons are any person who is directed by the order to apply the property in the specified manner.	Power to quash the order and (if appropriate) remit the matter to the Commission.
Order made by the Commission under section 23(2) of this Act in relation to any land vested in the official custodian in trust for a charity.	The persons are—(a) the charity trustees of the charity, (b) (if a body corporate) the charity itself, and (c) any other person who is or may be affected by the order.	Power to—(a) quash the order and (if appropriate) remit the matter to the Commission, (b) substitute for the order any other order which could have been made by the Commission, (c) add to the order anything which could have been contained in an order made by the Commission.
Decision of the Commission not to make a common investment scheme under section 24 of this Act.	The persons are—(a) the charity trustees of a charity which applied to the Commission for the scheme, (b) (if a body corporate) the charity itself, and (c) any other person who is or may be affected by the decision.	Power to quash the decision and (if appropriate) remit the matter to the Commission.
Decision of the Commission not to make a common deposit scheme under section 25 of this Act.	The persons are—(a) the charity trustees of a charity which applied to the Commission for the scheme, (b) (if a body corporate) the charity itself, and (c) any other person who is or may be affected by the decision.	Power to quash the decision and (if appropriate) remit the matter to the Commission.
Decision by the Commission not to make an order under section 26 of this Act in relation to a charity.	The persons are—(a) the charity trustees of the charity, and (b) (if a body corporate) the charity itself.	Power to quash the decision and (if appropriate) remit the matter to the Commission.

Direction given by the Commission under section 28 of this Act in relation to an account held in the name of or on behalf of a charity.	The persons are—(a) the charity trustees of the charity, (b) (if a body corporate) the charity itself, and (c) any other person who is or may be affected by the order.	Power to—(a) quash the direction and (if appropriate) remit the matter to the Commission, (b) substitute for the direction any other direction which could have been given by the Commission, (c) add to the direction anything which could have been contained in a direction given by the Commission.
Order made by the Commission under section 31 of this Act for the taxation of a solicitor's bill.	The persons are—(a) the solicitor, (b) any person for whom the work was done by the solicitor, and (c) any other person who is or may be affected by the order.	Power to—(a) quash the order, (b) substitute for the order any other order which could have been made by the Commission, (c) add to the order anything which could have been contained in an order made by the Commission.
Decision of the Commission not to make an order under section 36 of this Act in relation to land held by or in trust for a charity.	The persons are—(a) the charity trustees of the charity, (b) (if a body corporate) the charity itself, and (c) any other person who is or may be affected by the decision.	Power to quash the decision and (if appropriate) remit the matter to the Commission.
Decision of the Commission not to make an order under section 38 of this Act in relation to a mortgage of land held by or in trust for a charity.	The persons are—(a) the charity trustees of the charity, (b) (if a body corporate) the charity itself, and (c) any other person who is or may be affected by the decision.	Power to quash the decision and (if appropriate) remit the matter to the Commission.
Order made by the Commission under section 43(4) of this Act requiring the accounts of a charity to be audited.	The persons are—(a) the charity trustees of the charity, (b) (if a body corporate) the charity itself, and (c) any other person who is or may be affected by the order.	Power to— (a) quash the order, (b) substitute for the order any other order which could have been made by the Commission, (c) add to the order anything which could have been contained in an order made by the Commission.
Order made by the Commission under section 44(2) of this Act in relation to a charity, or a decision of the Commission not to make such an order in relation to a charity.	The persons are—(a) the charity trustees of the charity, (b) (if a body corporate) the charity itself, (c) in the case of a decision not to make an order, the auditor, independent examiner or examiner, and (d) any other person who is or may be affected by the order or the decision.	Power to—(a) quash the order or decision and (if appropriate) remit the matter to the Commission, (b) substitute for the order any other order of a kind the Commission could have made, (c) make any order which the Commission could have made.

Decision of the Commission under section 46(5) of this Act to request charity trustees to prepare an annual report for a charity.	The persons are—(a) the charity trustees, and (b) (if a body corporate) the charity itself.	Power to quash the decision and (if appropriate) remit the matter to the Commission.
Decision of the Commission not to dispense with the requirements of section 48(1) in relation to a charity or class of charities.	The persons are the charity trustees of any charity affected by the decision.	Power to quash the decision and (if appropriate) remit the matter to the Commission.
Decision of the Commission—(a) to grant a certificate of incorporation under section 50(1) of this Act to the trustees of a charity, or (b) not to grant such a certificate.	The persons are—(a) the trustees of the charity, and (b) any other person who is or may be affected by the decision.	Power to quash—(a) the decision, (b) any conditions or directions inserted in the certificate, and (if appropriate) remit the matter to the Commission.
Decision of the Commission to amend a certificate of incorporation of a charity under section 56(4) of this Act.	The persons are—(a) the trustees of the charity, and (b) any other person who is or may be affected by the amended certificate of incorporation.	Power to quash the decision and (if appropriate) remit the matter to the Commission.
Decision of the Commission not to amend a certificate of incorporation under section 56(4) of this Act.	The persons are—(a) the trustees of the charity, and (b) any other person who is or may be affected by the decision not to amend the certificate of incorporation.	Power to—(a) quash the decision and (if appropriate) remit the matter to the Commission, (b) make any order the Commission could have made under section 56(4).
Order of the Commission under section 61(1) or (2) of this Act which dissolves a charity which is an incorporated body.	The persons are—(a) the trustees of the charity, (b) the charity itself, and (c) any other person who is or may be affected by the order.	Power to—(a) quash the order and (if appropriate) remit the matter to the Commission, (b) substitute for the order any other order which could have been made by the Commission, (c) add to the order anything which could have been contained in an order made by the Commission.
Decision of the Commission to give, or withhold, consent under section 64(2), 65(4) or 66(1) of this Act in relation to a body corporate which is a charity.	The persons are—(a) the charity trustees of the charity, (b) the body corporate itself, and (c) any other person who is or may be affected by the decision.	Power to quash the decision and (if appropriate) remit the matter to the Commission.
Order made by the Commission under section 69(1) of this Act in relation to a company which is a charity.	The persons are—(a) the directors of the company, (b) the company itself, and (c) any other person who is or may be affected by the order.	Power to—(a) quash the order and (if appropriate) remit the matter to the Commission, (b) substitute for the order any other order which could have been made by the Commission, (c) add to the order anything which could have been contained in an order made by the Commission.

175

Order made by the Commission under section 69(4) of this Act which gives directions to a person or to charity trustees.	The persons are—(a) in the case of directions given to a person, that person, (b) in the case of directions given to charity trustees, those charity trustees and (if a body corporate) the charity of which they are charity trustees, and (c) any other person who is or may be affected by the directions.	Power to—(a) quash the order, (b) substitute for the order any other order which could have been made by the Commission, (c) add to the order anything which could have been contained in an order made by the Commission.
Decision of the Commission under section 69E of this Act to grant an application for the constitution of a CIO and its registration as a charity.	The persons are any person (other than the persons who made the application) who is or may be affected by the decision.	Power to quash the decision and (if appropriate)—(a) remit the matter to the Commission, (b) direct the Commission to rectify the register of charities.
Decision of the Commission under section 69E of this Act not to grant an application for the constitution of a CIO and its registration as a charity.	The persons are—(a) the persons who made the application, and (b) any other person who is or may be affected by the decision.	Power to—(a) quash the decision and (if appropriate) remit the matter to the Commission, (b) direct the Commission to grant the application.
Decision of the Commission under section 69H of this Act not to grant an application for the conversion of a charitable company or a registered society into a CIO and the CIO's registration as a charity.	The persons are—(a) the charity which made the application, (b) the charity trustees of the charity, and (c) any other person who is or may be affected by the decision.	Power to—(a) quash the decision and (if appropriate) remit the matter to the Commission, (b) direct the Commission to grant the application.
Decision of the Commission under section 69K of this Act to grant an application for the amalgamation of two or more CIOs and the incorporation and registration as a charity of a new CIO as their successor.	The persons are any creditor of any of the CIOs being amalgamated.	Power to quash the decision and (if appropriate) remit the matter to the Commission.
Decision of the Commission under section 69K of this Act not to grant an application for the amalgamation of two or more CIOs and the incorporation and registration as a charity of a new CIO as their successor.	The persons are—(a) the CIOs which applied for the amalgamation, (b) the charity trustees of the CIOs, and (c) any other person who is or may be affected by the decision.	Power to—(a) quash the decision and (if appropriate) remit the matter to the Commission, (b) direct the Commission to grant the application.
Decision of the Commission to confirm a resolution passed by a CIO under section 69M(1) of this Act.	The persons are any creditor of the CIO.	Power to quash the decision and (if appropriate) remit the matter to the Commission.
Decision of the Commission not to confirm a resolution passed by a CIO under section 69M(1) of this Act.	The persons are—(a) the CIO, (b) the charity trustees of the CIO, and (c) any other person who is or may be affected by the decision.	Power to—(a) quash the decision and (if appropriate) remit the matter to the Commission, (b) direct the Commission to confirm the resolution.

Decision of the Commission under section 72(4) of this Act to waive, or not to waive, a person's disqualification.	The persons are—(a) the person who applied for the waiver, and (b) any other person who is or may be affected by the decision.	Power to—(a) quash the decision and (if appropriate) remit the matter to the Commission, (b) substitute for the decision any other decision of a kind which could have been made by the Commission.
Order made by the Commission under section 73(4) of this Act in relation to a person who has acted as charity trustee or trustee for a charity.	The persons are—(a) the person subject to the order, and (b) any other person who is or may be affected by the order.	Power to—(a) quash the order and (if appropriate) remit the matter to the Commission, (b substitute for the order any other order which could have been made by the Commission.
Order made by the Commission under section 73C(5) or (6) of this Act requiring a trustee or connected person to repay, or not to receive, remuneration.	The persons are—(a) the trustee or connected person, (b the other charity trustees of the charity concerned, and (c) any other person who is or may be affected by the order.	Power to—(a) quash the order and (if appropriate) remit the matter to the Commission, (b substitute for the order any other order which could have been made by the Commission.
Decision of the Commission to notify charity trustees under section 74A(2) of this Act that it objects to a resolution of the charity trustees under section 74(2) or 74C(2).	The persons are—(a) the charity trustees, and (b any other person who is or may be affected by the decision.	Power to quash the decision.
Decision of the Commission not to concur under section 75A of this Act with a resolution of charity trustees under section 75A(3) or 75B(2).	The persons are—(a) the charity trustees, (b (if a body corporate) the charity itself, and (c) any other person who is or may be affected by the decision.	Power to quash the decision and (if appropriate) remit the matter to the Commission.
Decision of the Commission to withhold approval for the transfer of property from trustees to a parish council under section 79(1) of this Act.	The persons are—(a) the trustees, (b the parish council, and (c) any other person who is or may be affected by the decision.	Power to quash the decision and (if appropriate) remit the matter to the Commission.
Order made by the Commission under section 80(2) of this Act in relation to a person holding property on behalf of a recognised body or of any person concerned in its management or control.	The persons are—(a) the person holding the property in question, and (b any other person who is or may be affected by the order.	Power to quash the order and (if appropriate) remit the matter to the Commission.
Decision of the Commission not to give a direction under section 96(5) or (6) of this Act in relation to an institution or a charity.	The persons are the trustees of the institution or charity concerned.	Power to quash the decision and (if appropriate) remit the matter to the Commission.

Decision of the Commission under paragraph 15 of Schedule 5B to this Act to refuse to register an amendment to the constitution of a CIO.	The persons are—(a) the CIO, (b the charity trustees of the CIO, and (c) any other person who is or may be affected by the decision.	Power to quash the decision and (if appropriate)—(a) remit the matter to the Commission, (b direct the Commission to register the amendment.

Power to amend Table etc.

6. (1)   The Minister may by order—

   (a) amend or otherwise modify an entry in the Table,

   (b) add an entry to the Table, or

   (c) remove an entry from the Table.

   (2)   An order under sub-paragraph (1) may make such amendments, repeals or other modifications of paragraphs 1 to 5 of this Schedule, or of an enactment which applies this Schedule, as the Minister considers appropriate in consequence of any change in the Table made by the order.

   (3)   No order shall be made under this paragraph unless a draft of the order has been laid before and approved by a resolution of each House of Parliament.

7.   Paragraph 6 above applies (with the necessary modifications) in relation to section 57 of the Charities Act 2006 as if—

   (a) the provisions of that section were contained in this Schedule, and

   (b) the reference in that paragraph to paragraphs 1 to 5 of this Schedule included a reference to any other provision relating to appeals to the Tribunal which is contained in Chapter 1 of Part 3 of the Charities Act 2006.

Section 2A(4)   SCHEDULE 1D

REFERENCES TO CHARITY TRIBUNAL

References by Commission

1. (1)   A question which—

   (a) has arisen in connection with the exercise by the Commission of any of its functions, and

   (b) involves either the operation of charity law in any respect or its application to a particular state of affairs,

   may be referred to the Tribunal by the Commission if the Commission considers it desirable to refer the question to the Tribunal.

   (2)   The Commission may make such a reference only with the consent of the Attorney General.

   (3)   The Commission shall be a party to proceedings before the Tribunal on the reference.

   (4)   The following shall be entitled to be parties to proceedings before the Tribunal on the reference—

   (a) the Attorney General, and

   (b) with the Tribunal's permission-

      (i)   the charity trustees of any charity which is likely to be affected by the Tribunal's decision on the reference,

      (ii) any such charity which is a body corporate, and

      (iii) any other person who is likely to be so affected.

References by Attorney General

2. (1)   A question which involves either—

      (a) the operation of charity law in any respect, or

      (b) the application of charity law to a particular state of affairs,

      may be referred to the Tribunal by the Attorney General if the Attorney General considers it desirable to refer the question to the Tribunal.

   (2)   The Attorney General shall be a party to proceedings before the Tribunal on the reference.

   (3)   The following shall be entitled to be parties to proceedings before the Tribunal on the reference—

      (a) the Commission, and

      (b) with the Tribunal's permission—

         (i)   the charity trustees of any charity which is likely to be affected by the Tribunal's decision on the reference,

         (ii) any such charity which is a body corporate, and

         (iii) any other person who is likely to be so affected.

Powers of Commission in relation to matters referred to Tribunal

3. (1)   This paragraph applies where a question which involves the application of charity law to a particular state of affairs has been referred to the Tribunal under paragraph 1 or 2 above.

   (2)   The Commission shall not take any steps in reliance on any view as to the application of charity law to that state of affairs until—

      (a) proceedings on the reference (including any proceedings on appeal) have been concluded, and

      (b) any period during which an appeal (or further appeal) may ordinarily be made has ended.

   (3)   Where—

      (a) paragraphs (a) and (b) of sub-paragraph (2) above are satisfied, and

      (b) the question has been decided in proceedings on the reference, the Commission shall give effect to that decision when dealing with the particular state of affairs to which the reference related.

Suspension of time limits while reference in progress

4. (1)   Sub-paragraph (2) below applies if—

      (a) paragraph 3(2) above prevents the Commission from taking any steps which it would otherwise be permitted or required to take, and

      (b) the steps in question may be taken only during a period specified in an enactment ("the specified period").

   (2)   The running of the specified period is suspended for the period which—

      (a) begins with the date on which the question is referred to the Tribunal, and

(b) ends with the date on which paragraphs (a) and (b) of paragraph 3(2) above are satisfied.

(3) Nothing in this paragraph or section 74A of this Act prevents the specified period being suspended concurrently by virtue of sub-paragraph (2) above and that section.

Agreement for Commission to act while reference in progress

5. (1) Paragraph 3(2) above does not apply in relation to any steps taken by the Commission with the agreement of—
   (a) the persons who are parties to the proceedings on the reference at the time when those steps are taken, and
   (b) (if not within paragraph (a) above) the charity trustees of any charity which—
      (i) is likely to be directly affected by the taking of those steps, and
      (ii) is not a party to the proceedings at that time.

(2) The Commission may take those steps despite the suspension in accordance with paragraph 4(2) above of any period during which it would otherwise be permitted or required to take them.

(3) Paragraph 3(3) above does not require the Commission to give effect to a decision as to the application of charity law to a particular state of affairs to the extent that the decision is inconsistent with any steps already taken by the Commission in relation to that state of affairs in accordance with this paragraph.

Appeals and applications in respect of matters determined on references

6. (1) No appeal or application may be made to the Tribunal by a person to whom sub-paragraph (2) below applies in respect of an order or decision made, or direction given, by the Commission in accordance with paragraph 3(3) above.

(2) This sub-paragraph applies to a person who was at any stage a party to the proceedings in which the question referred to the Tribunal was decided.

(3) Rules under section 2B(1) of this Act may include provision as to who is to be treated for the purposes of sub-paragraph (2) above as being (or not being) a party to the proceedings.

(4) Any enactment (including one contained in this Act) which provides for an appeal or application to be made to the Tribunal has effect subject to sub-paragraph (1) above.

Interpretation

7. (1) In this Schedule—
   'charity law' means—
      (a) any enactment contained in, or made under, this Act or the Charities Act 2006,
      (b) any other enactment specified in regulations made by the Minister, and
      (c) any rule of law which relates to charities, and
   'enactment' includes an enactment comprised in subordinate legislation (within the meaning of the Interpretation Act 1978), and includes an enactment whenever passed or made.

(2) The exclusions contained in section 96(2) of this Act (ecclesiastical corporations etc.) do not have effect for the purposes of this Schedule."

Section 12   SCHEDULE 5

EXEMPT CHARITIES: INCREASED REGULATION UNDER 1993 ACT

Power to require charity's name to be changed

1. In section 6 of the 1993 Act (power of Commission to require charity's name to be changed) omit subsection (9) (exclusion of exempt charities).

Power to institute inquiries

2. In section 8(1) of the 1993 Act (power of Commission to institute inquiries with regard to charities but not in relation to any exempt charity) after "any exempt charity" insert "except where this has been requested by its principal regulator."

Power to call for documents etc.

3. In section 9 of the 1993 Act (power of Commission to call for documents and search records) omit subsection (4) (exclusion of documents relating only to exempt charities).

Concurrent jurisdiction of Commission with High Court

4. (1) Section 16 of the 1993 Act (concurrent jurisdiction of Commission with High Court for certain purposes) is amended as follows.
   (2) In subsection (4)(c) (application for Commission to exercise powers may be made by Attorney General except in case of exempt charity) omit "in the case of a charity other than an exempt charity,".
   (3) In subsection (5) (jurisdiction exercisable in case of charity which is not an exempt charity and whose annual income does not exceed £500) omit "which is not an exempt charity and".

Further powers of Commission

5. In section 17(7) of the 1993 Act (expenditure by charity on promoting Parliamentary Bill needs consent of court or Commission except in case of exempt charity) omit the words from "but this subsection" onwards.

Power to act for protection of charities

6. In section 18 of the 1993 Act (power of Commission to act for protection of charities) for subsection (16) substitute—

   "(16) In this section—
         (a) subsections (1) to (3) apply in relation to an exempt charity, and
         (b) subsections (4) to (6) apply in relation to such a charity at any time after the Commission have instituted an inquiry under section 8 with respect to it,
         and the other provisions of this section apply accordingly."

Power to give directions about dormant bank accounts

7. In section 28 of the 1993 Act (power of Commission to give directions about dormant bank accounts of charities), omit subsection (10) (exclusion of accounts held by or on behalf of exempt charity).

Proceedings by persons other than Commission

8. (1) Section 33 of the 1993 Act (charity proceedings by persons other than Commission) is amended as follows.

(2) In subsection (2) (proceedings relating to a charity other than an exempt charity must be authorised by the Commission) omit "(other than an exempt charity)".

(3) In subsection (7) (participation by Attorney General in proceedings relating to charity other than exempt charity) omit "(other than an exempt charity)".

Power to order disqualified person to repay sums received from charity

9. In section 73 of the 1993 Act (consequences of person acting as charity trustee while disqualified), in subsection (4) (power of Commission to order disqualified person to repay sums received from a charity other than an exempt charity) omit "(other than an exempt charity)".

Section 30   SCHEDULE 6

                         GROUP ACCOUNTS

After Schedule 5 to the 1993 Act insert—

Section 49A   SCHEDULE 5A

                         GROUP ACCOUNTS

Interpretation

1. (1) This paragraph applies for the purposes of this Schedule.

(2) A charity is a "parent charity" if—

(a) it is (or is to be treated as) a parent undertaking in relation to one or more other undertakings in accordance with the provisions of section 258 of, and Schedule 10A to, the Companies Act 1985, and

(b) it is not a company.

(3) Each undertaking in relation to which a parent charity is (or is to be treated as) a parent undertaking in accordance with those provisions is a "subsidiary undertaking" in relation to the parent charity.

(4) But sub-paragraph (3) does not have the result that any of the following is a 'subsidiary undertaking'—

(a) any special trusts of a charity,

(b) any institution which, by virtue of a direction under section 96(5) of this Act, is to be treated as forming part of a charity for the purposes of this Part of this Act, or

(c) any charity to which a direction under section 96(6) of this Act applies for those purposes.

(5) 'The group', in relation to a parent charity, means that charity and its subsidiary undertaking or undertakings, and any reference to the members of the group is to be construed accordingly.

(6) For the purposes of—

(a) this paragraph, and

(b) the operation of the provisions mentioned in sub-paragraph (2) above for the purposes of this paragraph,

'undertaking' has the meaning given by sub-paragraph (7) below.

(7) For those purposes 'undertaking' means—

(a) an undertaking as defined by section 259(1) of the Companies Act 1985, or

(b) a charity which is not an undertaking as so defined.

Accounting records

2. (1) The charity trustees—

(a) of a parent charity, or

(b) of any charity which is a subsidiary undertaking,

must ensure that the accounting records kept in respect of the charity under section 41(1) of this Act not only comply with the requirements of that provision but also are such as to enable the charity trustees of the parent charity to ensure that, where any group accounts are prepared by them under paragraph 3(2), those accounts comply with the relevant requirements.

(2) If a parent charity has a subsidiary undertaking in relation to which the requirements of section 41(1) of this Act do not apply, the charity trustees of the parent charity must take reasonable steps to secure that the undertaking keeps such accounting records as to enable the trustees to ensure that, where any group accounts are prepared by them under paragraph 3(2), those accounts comply with the relevant requirements.

(3) In this paragraph 'the relevant requirements' means the requirements of regulations under paragraph 3.

Preparation of group accounts

3. (1) This paragraph applies in relation to a financial year of a charity if it is a parent charity at the end of that year.

(2) The charity trustees of the parent charity must prepare group accounts in respect of that year.

(3) 'Group accounts' means consolidated accounts—

(a) relating to the group, and

(b) complying with such requirements as to their form and contents as may be prescribed by regulations made by the Minister.

(4) Without prejudice to the generality of sub-paragraph (3), regulations under that sub-paragraph may make provision—

(a) for any such accounts to be prepared in accordance with such methods and principles as are specified or referred to in the regulations;

     (b) for dealing with cases where the financial years of the members of the group do not all coincide;

     (c) as to any information to be provided by way of notes to the accounts.

  (5) Regulations under that sub-paragraph may also make provision—

     (a) for determining the financial years of subsidiary undertakings for the purposes of this Schedule;

     (b) for imposing on the charity trustees of a parent charity requirements with respect to securing that such financial years coincide with that of the charity.

  (6) If the requirement in sub-paragraph (2) applies to the charity trustees of a parent charity in relation to a financial year—

     (a) that requirement so applies in addition to the requirement in section 42(1) of this Act, and

     (b) the option of preparing the documents mentioned in section 42(3) of this Act is not available in relation to that year (whatever the amount of the charity's gross income for that year).

  (7) Sub-paragraph (2) has effect subject to paragraph 4.

Exceptions relating to requirement to prepare group accounts

4. (1) The requirement in paragraph 3(2) does not apply to the charity trustees of a parent charity in relation to a financial year if at the end of that year it is itself a subsidiary undertaking in relation to another charity.

  (2) The requirement in paragraph 3(2) does not apply to the charity trustees of a parent charity in relation to a financial year if the aggregate gross income of the group for that year does not exceed such sum as is specified in regulations made by the Minister.

  (3) Regulations made by the Minister may prescribe circumstances in which a subsidiary undertaking may or (as the case may be) must be excluded from group accounts required to be prepared under paragraph 3(2) for a financial year.

  (4) Where, by virtue of such regulations, each of the subsidiary undertakings which are members of a group is either permitted or required to be excluded from any such group accounts for a financial year, the requirement in paragraph 3(2) does not apply to the charity trustees of the parent charity in relation to that year.

Preservation of group accounts

5. (1) The charity trustees of a charity shall preserve any group accounts prepared by them under paragraph 3(2) for at least six years from the end of the financial year to which the accounts relate.

  (2) Subsection (4) of section 41 of this Act shall apply in relation to the preservation of any such accounts as it applies in relation to the preservation of any accounting records (the references to subsection (3) of that section being construed as references to sub-paragraph (1) above).

Audit of accounts of larger groups

6. (1) This paragraph applies where group accounts are prepared for a financial year of a parent charity under paragraph 3(2) and—

     (a) the aggregate gross income of the group in that year exceeds the relevant income threshold, or

     (b) the aggregate gross income of the group in that year exceeds the relevant income threshold and at the end of the year the aggregate value of the assets of the group (before deduction of liabilities) exceeds the relevant assets threshold.

(2) In sub-paragraph (1)—

    (a) the reference in paragraph (a) or (b) to the relevant income threshold is a reference to the sum prescribed as the relevant income threshold for the purposes of that paragraph, and

    (b) the reference in paragraph (b) to the relevant assets threshold is a reference to the sum prescribed as the relevant assets threshold for the purposes of that paragraph.

'Prescribed' means prescribed by regulations made by the Minister.

(3) This paragraph also applies where group accounts are prepared for a financial year of a parent charity under paragraph 3(2) and the appropriate audit provision applies in relation to the parent charity's own accounts for that year.

(4) If this paragraph applies in relation to a financial year of a parent charity by virtue of sub-paragraph (1) or (3), the group accounts for that year shall be audited—

    (a) (subject to paragraph (b) or (c) below) by a person within section 43(2)(a) or (b) of this Act;

    (b) if section 43A of this Act applies in relation to that year, by a person appointed by the Audit Commission (see section 43A(7));

    (c) if section 43B of this Act applies in relation to that year, by the Auditor General for Wales.

(5) Where it appears to the Commission that sub-paragraph (4)(a) above has not been complied with in relation to that year within ten months from the end of that year—

    (a) the Commission may by order require the group accounts for that year to be audited by a person within section 43(2)(a) or (b) of this Act, and

    (b) if it so orders, the auditor shall be a person appointed by the Commission.

(6) Section 43(6) of this Act shall apply in relation to any such audit as it applies in relation to an audit carried out by an auditor appointed under section 43(5) (reading the reference to the funds of the charity as a reference to the funds of the parent charity).

(7) Section 43A(4) and (6) of this Act apply in relation to any appointment under sub-paragraph (4)(b) above as they apply in relation to an appointment under section 43A(2).

(8) If this paragraph applies in relation to a financial year of a parent charity by virtue of sub-paragraph (1), the appropriate audit provision shall apply in relation to the parent charity's own accounts for that year (whether or not it would otherwise so apply).

(9) In this paragraph 'the appropriate audit provision', in relation to a financial year of a parent charity, means—

    (a) (subject to paragraph (b) or (c) below) section 43(2) of this Act;

    (b) if section 43A of this Act applies in relation to that year, section 43A(2);

    (c) if section 43B of this Act applies in relation to that year, section 43B(2).

Examination of accounts of smaller groups

7. (1) This paragraph applies where—

    (a) group accounts are prepared for a financial year of a parent charity under paragraph 3(2), and

(b) paragraph 6 does not apply in relation to that year.

(2) If—

    (a) this paragraph applies in relation to a financial year of a parent charity, and

    (b) sub-paragraph (4) or (5) below does not apply in relation to it,

subsections (3) to (7) of section 43 of this Act shall apply in relation to the group accounts for that year as they apply in relation to the accounts of a charity for a financial year in relation to which subsection (2) of that section does not apply, but subject to the modifications in sub-paragraph (3) below.

(3) The modifications are—

    (a) any reference to the charity trustees of the charity is to be construed as a reference to the charity trustees of the parent charity;

    (b) any reference to the charity's gross income in the financial year in question is to be construed as a reference to the aggregate gross income of the group in that year; and

    (c) any reference to the funds of the charity is to be construed as a reference to the funds of the parent charity.

(4) If—

    (a) this paragraph applies in relation to a financial year of a parent charity, and

    (b) section 43A of this Act also applies in relation to that year,

subsections (3) to (6) of that section shall apply in relation to the group accounts for that year as they apply in relation to the accounts of a charity for a financial year in relation to which subsection (2) of that section does not apply.

(5) If—

    (a) this paragraph applies in relation to a financial year of a parent charity, and

    (b) section 43B of this Act also applies in relation to that year,

subsection (3) of that section shall apply in relation to the group accounts for that year as they apply in relation to the accounts of a charity for a financial year in relation to which subsection (2) of that section does not apply.

(6) If the group accounts for a financial year of a parent charity are to be examined or audited in accordance with section 43(3) of this Act (as applied by sub-paragraph (2) above), section 43(3) shall apply in relation to the parent charity's own accounts for that year (whether or not it would otherwise so apply).

(7) Nothing in sub-paragraph (4) or (5) above affects the operation of section 43A(3) to (6) or (as the case may be) section 43B(3) in relation to the parent charity's own accounts for the financial year in question.

Supplementary provisions relating to audits etc.

8. (1) Section 44(1) of this Act shall apply in relation to audits and examinations carried out under or by virtue of paragraph 6 or 7, but subject to the modifications in sub-paragraph (2) below.

(2) The modifications are—

    (a) in paragraph (b), the reference to section 43, 43A or 43B of this Act is to be construed as a reference to paragraph 6 above or to any of those sections as applied by paragraph 7 above;

    (b) also in paragraph (b), the reference to any such statement of accounts as is mentioned in sub-paragraph (i) of that paragraph is to be construed as a reference to group accounts prepared for a financial year under paragraph 3(2) above;

(c) in paragraph (c), any reference to section 43, 43A or 43B of this Act is to be construed as a reference to that section as applied by paragraph 7 above;

(d) in paragraphs (d) and (e), any reference to the charity concerned or a charity is to be construed as a reference to any member of the group; and

(e) in paragraph (f), the reference to the requirements of section 43(2) or (3) of this Act is to be construed as a reference to the requirements of paragraph 6(4)(a) or those applied by paragraph 7(2) above.

(3) Without prejudice to the generality of section 44(1)(e), as modified by sub-paragraph (2)(d) above, regulations made under that provision may make provision corresponding or similar to any provision made by section 389A of the Companies Act 1985 (c. 6) in connection with the rights exercisable by an auditor of a company in relation to a subsidiary undertaking of the company.

(4) In section 44(2) of this Act the reference to section 44(1)(d) or (e) includes a reference to that provision as it applies in accordance with this paragraph.

Duty of auditors etc. to report matters to Commission

9. (1) Section 44A(2) to (5) and (7) of this Act shall apply in relation to a person appointed to audit, or report on, any group accounts under or by virtue of paragraph 6 or 7 above as they apply in relation to a person such as is mentioned in section 44A(1).

(2) In section 44A(2)(a), as it applies in accordance with sub-paragraph (1) above, the reference to the charity or any connected institution or body is to be construed as a reference to the parent charity or any of its subsidiary undertakings.

Annual reports

10. (1) This paragraph applies where group accounts are prepared for a financial year of a parent charity under paragraph 3(2).

(2) The annual report prepared by the charity trustees of the parent charity in respect of that year under section 45 of this Act shall include—

(a) such a report by the trustees on the activities of the charity's subsidiary undertakings during that year, and

(b) such other information relating to any of those undertakings,

as may be prescribed by regulations made by the Minister.

(3) Without prejudice to the generality of sub-paragraph (2), regulations under that sub-paragraph may make provision—

(a) for any such report as is mentioned in paragraph (a) of that sub-paragraph to be prepared in accordance with such principles as are specified or referred to in the regulations;

(b) enabling the Commission to dispense with any requirement prescribed by virtue of sub-paragraph (2)(b) in the case of a particular subsidiary undertaking or a particular class of subsidiary undertaking.

(4) Section 45(3) to (3B) shall apply in relation to the annual report referred to in sub-paragraph (2) above as if any reference to the charity's gross income in the financial year in question were a reference to the aggregate gross income of the group in that year.

(5) When transmitted to the Commission in accordance with sub-paragraph (4) above, the copy of the annual report shall have attached to it both a copy of the group accounts prepared for that year under paragraph 3(2) and—

(a) a copy of the report made by the auditor on those accounts; or

(b) where those accounts have been examined under section 43, 43A or 43B of this Act (as applied by paragraph 7 above), a copy of the report made by the person carrying out the examination.

(6) The requirements in this paragraph are in addition to those in section 45 of this Act.

Excepted charities

11. (1) This paragraph applies where—

    (a) a charity is required to prepare an annual report in respect of a financial year by virtue of section 46(5) of this Act,

    (b) the charity is a parent charity at the end of the year, and

    (c) group accounts are prepared for that year under paragraph 3(2) by the charity trustees of the charity.

(2) When transmitted to the Commission in accordance with section 46(7) of this Act, the copy of the annual report shall have attached to it both a copy of the group accounts and—

    (a) a copy of the report made by the auditor on those accounts; or

    (b) where those accounts have been examined under section 43, 43A or 43B of this Act (as applied by paragraph 7 above), a copy of the report made by the person carrying out the examination.

(3) The requirement in sub-paragraph (2) is in addition to that in section 46(6) of this Act.

Exempt charities

12. Nothing in the preceding provisions of this Schedule applies to an exempt charity.

Public inspection of annual reports etc.

13. In section 47(2) of this Act, the reference to a charity's most recent accounts includes, in relation to a charity whose charity trustees have prepared any group accounts under paragraph 3(2), the group accounts most recently prepared by them.

Offences

14. (1) Section 49(1) of this Act applies in relation to a requirement within sub-paragraph (2) as it applies in relation to a requirement within section 49(1)(a).

(2) A requirement is within this sub-paragraph where it is imposed by section 45(3) or (3A) of this Act, taken with—

    (a) section 45(3B), (4) and (5), and

    (b) paragraph 10(5) or 11(2) above,

as applicable.

(3) In sub-paragraph (2) any reference to section 45(3), (3A) or (3B) of this Act is a reference to that provision as applied by paragraph 10(4) above.

(4) In section 49(1)(b) the reference to section 47(2) of this Act includes a reference to that provision as extended by paragraph 13 above.

Aggregate gross income

15. The Minister may by regulations make provision for determining for the purposes of this Schedule the amount of the aggregate gross income for a financial year of a group consisting of a parent charity and its subsidiary undertaking or undertakings."

Section 34   SCHEDULE 7

CHARITABLE INCORPORATED ORGANISATIONS

PART 1
NEW PART 8A OF AND SCHEDULE 5B TO 1993 ACT

1. After Part 8 of the 1993 Act insert the following new Part—

"PART 8A
CHARITABLE INCORPORATED ORGANISATIONS

69A Charitable incorporated organisations

(1) In this Act, a charitable incorporated organisation is referred to as a 'CIO'.

(2) A CIO shall be a body corporate.

(3) A CIO shall have a constitution.

(4) A CIO shall have a principal office, which shall be in England or in Wales.

(5) A CIO shall have one or more members.

(6) The members may be either—

(a) not liable to contribute to the assets of the CIO if it is wound up, or

(b) liable to do so up to a maximum amount each.

69B Constitution

(1) A CIO's constitution shall state—

(a) its name,

(b) its purposes,

(c) whether its principal office is in England or in Wales, and

(d) whether or not its members are liable to contribute to its assets if it is wound up, and (if they are) up to what amount.

(2) A CIO's constitution shall make provision-

(a) about who is eligible for membership, and how a person becomes a member,

(b) about the appointment of one or more persons who are to be charity trustees of the CIO, and about any conditions of eligibility for appointment, and

(c) containing directions about the application of property of the CIO on its dissolution.

(3) A CIO's constitution shall also provide for such other matters, and comply with such requirements, as are specified in regulations made by the Minister.

(4) A CIO's constitution—

(a) shall be in English if its principal office is in England,

(b) may be in English or in Welsh if its principal office is in Wales.

(5) A CIO's constitution shall be in the form specified in regulations made by the Commission, or as near to that form as the circumstances admit.

(6) Subject to anything in a CIO's constitution: a charity trustee of the CIO may, but need not, be a member of it; a member of the CIO may, but need not, be one of its charity trustees; and those who are members of the CIO and those who are its charity trustees may, but need not, be identical.

69C Name and status

(1) The name of a CIO shall appear in legible characters—

(a) in all business letters of the CIO,

(b) in all its notices and other official publications,

(c) in all bills of exchange, promissory notes, endorsements, cheques and orders for money or goods purporting to be signed on behalf of the CIO,

(d) in all conveyances purporting to be executed by the CIO, and

(e) in all bills rendered by it and in all its invoices, receipts, and letters of credit.

(2) In subsection (1)(d), 'conveyance' means any instrument creating, transferring, varying or extinguishing an interest in land.

(3) Subsection (5) applies if the name of a CIO does not include—

(a) 'charitable incorporated organisation', or

(b) 'CIO', with or without full stops after each letter, or

(c) a Welsh equivalent mentioned in subsection (4) (but this option applies only if the CIO's constitution is in Welsh),

and it is irrelevant, in any such case, whether or not capital letters are used.

(4) The Welsh equivalents referred to in subsection (3)(c) are-

(a) 'sefydliad elusennol corfforedig', or

(b) 'SEC', with or without full stops after each letter.

(5) If this subsection applies, the fact that a CIO is a CIO shall be stated in legible characters in all the documents mentioned in subsection (1).

(6) The statement required by subsection (5) shall be in English, except that in the case of a document which is otherwise wholly in Welsh, the statement may be in Welsh.

69D Offences connected with name and status

(1) A charity trustee of a CIO or a person on the CIO's behalf who issues or authorises the issue of any document referred to in paragraph (a), (b), (d) or (e) of section 69C(1) above which fails to comply with the requirements of section 69C(1), (5) or (6) is liable on summary conviction to a fine not exceeding level 3 on the standard scale.

(2) A charity trustee of a CIO or a person on the CIO's behalf who signs or authorises to be signed on behalf of the CIO any document referred to in paragraph (c) of section 69C(1) above which fails to comply with the requirements of section 69C(1), (5) or (6)—

(a) is liable on summary conviction to a fine not exceeding level 3 on the standard scale, and

(b) is personally liable to the holder of the bill of exchange (etc.) for the amount of it, unless it is duly paid by the CIO.

(3) A person who holds any body out as being a CIO when it is not (however he does this) is guilty of an offence and is liable on summary conviction to a fine not exceeding level 3 on the standard scale.

(4) It is a defence for a person charged with an offence under subsection (3) to prove that he believed on reasonable grounds that the body was a CIO.

Registration

69E Application for registration

(1) Any one or more persons ('the applicants') may apply to the Commission for a CIO to be constituted and for its registration as a charity.

(2) The applicants shall supply the Commission with—

(a) a copy of the proposed constitution of the CIO,

(b) such other documents or information as may be prescribed by regulations made by the Minister, and

(c) such other documents or information as the Commission may require for the purposes of the application.

(3) The Commission shall refuse such an application if—
  (a) it is not satisfied that the CIO would be a charity at the time it would be registered, or
  (b) the CIO's proposed constitution does not comply with one or more of the requirements of section 69B above and any regulations made under that section.
(4) The Commission may refuse such an application if—
  (a) the proposed name of the CIO is the same as, or is in the opinion of the Commission too like, the name of any other charity (whether registered or not), or
  (b) the Commission is of the opinion referred to in any of paragraphs (b) to (e) of section 6(2) above (power of Commission to require change in charity's name) in relation to the proposed name of the CIO (reading paragraph (b) as referring to the proposed purposes of the CIO and to the activities which it is proposed it should carry on).

69F Effect of registration
(1) If the Commission grants an application under section 69E above it shall register the CIO to which the application relates as a charity in the register of charities.
(2) Upon the registration of the CIO in the register of charities, it becomes by virtue of the registration a body corporate—
  (a) whose constitution is that proposed in the application,
  (b) whose name is that specified in the constitution, and
  (c) whose first member is, or first members are, the applicants referred to in section 69E above.
(3) All property for the time being vested in the applicants (or, if more than one, any of them) on trust for the charitable purposes of the CIO (when incorporated) shall by virtue of this subsection become vested in the CIO upon its registration.
(4) The entry relating to the charity's registration in the register of charities shall include-
  (a) the date of the charity's registration, and
  (b) a note saying that it is constituted as a CIO.
(5) A copy of the entry in the register shall be sent to the charity at the principal office of the CIO.

Conversion, amalgamation and transfer

69G Conversion of charitable company or registered industrial and provident society
(1) The following may apply to the Commission to be converted into a CIO, and for the CIO's registration as a charity, in accordance with this section—
  (a) a charitable company,
  (b) a charity which is a registered society within the meaning of the Industrial and Provident Societies Act 1965.
(2) But such an application may not be made by—
  (a) a company or registered society having a share capital if any of the shares are not fully paid up, or
  (b) an exempt charity.
(3) Such an application is referred to in this section and sections 69H and 69I below as an 'application for conversion'.
(4) The Commission shall notify the following of any application for conversion—
  (a) the appropriate registrar, and
  (b) such other persons (if any) as the Commission thinks appropriate in the particular case.

(5)   The company or registered society shall supply the Commission with—

    (a) a copy of a resolution of the company or registered society that it be converted into a CIO,

    (b) a copy of the proposed constitution of the CIO,

    (c) a copy of a resolution of the company or registered society adopting the proposed constitution of the CIO,

    (d) such other documents or information as may be prescribed by regulations made by the Minister, and

    (e) such other documents or information as the Commission may require for the purposes of the application.

(6)   The resolution referred to in subsection (5)(a) shall be—

    (a) a special resolution of the company or registered society, or

    (b) a unanimous written resolution signed by or on behalf of all the members of the company or registered society who would be entitled to vote on a special resolution.

(7)   In the case of a registered society, 'special resolution' has the meaning given in section 52(3) of the Industrial and Provident Societies Act 1965.

(8)   In the case of a company limited by guarantee which makes an application for conversion (whether or not it also has a share capital), the proposed constitution of the CIO shall (unless subsection (10) applies) provide for the CIO's members to be liable to contribute to its assets if it is wound up, and for the amount up to which they are so liable.

(9)   That amount shall not be less than the amount up to which they were liable to contribute to the assets of the company if it was wound up.

(10) If the amount each member of the company is liable to contribute to its assets on its winding up is £10 or less, the guarantee shall be extinguished on the conversion of the company into a CIO, and the requirements of subsections (8) and (9) do not apply.

(11) In subsection (4), and in sections 69H and 69I below, 'the appropriate registrar' means—

    (a) in the case of an application for conversion by a charitable company, the registrar of companies,

    (b) in the case of an application for conversion by a registered society, the Financial Services Authority.

(12) In this section, 'charitable company' means a company which is a charity.

69H Conversion: consideration of application

(1)   The Commission shall consult those to whom it has given notice of an application for conversion under section 69G(4) above about whether the application should be granted.

(2)   The Commission shall refuse an application for conversion if—

    (a) it is not satisfied that the CIO would be a charity at the time it would be registered,

    (b) the CIO's proposed constitution does not comply with one or more of the requirements of section 69B above and any regulations made under that section, or

    (c) in the case of an application for conversion made by a company limited by guarantee, the CIO's proposed constitution does not comply with the requirements of subsections (8) and (9) of section 69G above.

(3) The Commission may refuse an application for conversion if—

    (a) the proposed name of the CIO is the same as, or is in the opinion of the Commission too like, the name of any other charity (whether registered or not),

    (b) the Commission is of the opinion referred to in any of paragraphs (b) to (e) of section 6(2) above (power of Commission to require change in charity's name) in relation to the proposed name of the CIO (reading paragraph (b) as referring to the proposed purposes of the CIO and to the activities which it is proposed it should carry on), or

    (c) having considered any representations received from those whom it has consulted under subsection (1), the Commission considers (having regard to any regulations made under subsection (4)) that it would not be appropriate to grant the application.

(4) The Minister may make provision in regulations about circumstances in which it would not be appropriate to grant an application for conversion.

(5) If the Commission refuses an application for conversion, it shall so notify the appropriate registrar (see section 69G(11) above).

69I Conversion: supplementary

(1) If the Commission grants an application for conversion, it shall—

    (a) register the CIO to which the application related in the register of charities, and

    (b) send to the appropriate registrar (see section 69G(11) above) a copy of each of the resolutions of the converting company or registered society referred to in section 69G(5)(a) and (c) above, and a copy of the entry in the register relating to the CIO.

(2) The registration of the CIO in the register shall be provisional only until the appropriate registrar cancels the registration of the company or registered society as required by subsection (3)(b).

(3) The appropriate registrar shall—

    (a) register the documents sent to him under subsection (1)(b), and

    (b) cancel the registration of the company in the register of companies, or of the society in the register of friendly societies,

and shall notify the Commission that he has done so.

(4) When the appropriate registrar cancels the registration of the company or of the registered society, the company or registered society is thereupon converted into a CIO, being a body corporate—

    (a) whose constitution is that proposed in the application for conversion,

    (b) whose name is that specified in the constitution, and

    (c) whose first members are the members of the converting company or society immediately before the moment of conversion.

(5) If the converting company or registered society had a share capital, upon the conversion of the company or registered society all the shares shall by virtue of this subsection be cancelled, and no former holder of any cancelled share shall have any right in respect of it after its cancellation.

(6) Subsection (5) does not affect any right which accrued in respect of a share before its cancellation.

(7) The entry relating to the charity's registration in the register shall include—

    (a) a note that it is constituted as a CIO,

(b) the date on which it became so constituted, and

(c) a note of the name of the company or society which was converted into the CIO, but the matters mentioned in paragraphs (a) and (b) are to be included only when the appropriate registrar has notified the Commission as required by subsection (3).

(8) A copy of the entry in the register shall be sent to the charity at the principal office of the CIO.

(9) The conversion of a charitable company or of a registered society into a CIO does not affect, in particular, any liability to which the company or registered society was subject by virtue of its being a charitable company or registered society.

69J Conversion of community interest company

(1) The Minister may by regulations make provision for the conversion of a community interest company into a CIO, and for the CIO's registration as a charity.

(2) The regulations may, in particular, apply, or apply with modifications specified in the regulations, or disapply, anything in sections 53 to 55 of the Companies (Audit, Investigations and Community Enterprise) Act 2004 or in sections 69G to 69I above.

69K Amalgamation of CIOs

(1) Any two or more CIOs ('the old CIOs') may, in accordance with this section, apply to the Commission to be amalgamated, and for the incorporation and registration as a charity of a new CIO ('the new CIO') as their successor.

(2) Such an application is referred to in this section and section 69L below as an 'application for amalgamation'.

(3) Subsections (2) to (4) of section 69E above apply in relation to an application for amalgamation as they apply to an application for a CIO to be constituted, but in those subsections—

(a) 'the applicants' shall be construed as meaning the old CIOs, and

(b) references to the CIO are to the new CIO.

(4) In addition to the documents and information referred to in section 69E(2) above, the old CIOs shall supply the Commission with—

(a) a copy of a resolution of each of the old CIOs approving the proposed amalgamation, and

(b) a copy of a resolution of each of the old CIOs adopting the proposed constitution of the new CIO.

(5) The resolutions referred to in subsection (4) must have been passed—

(a) by a 75% majority of those voting at a general meeting of the CIO (including those voting by proxy or by post, if voting that way is permitted), or

(b) unanimously by the CIO's members, otherwise than at a general meeting.

(6) The date of passing of such a resolution is—

(a) the date of the general meeting at which it was passed, or

(b) if it was passed otherwise than at a general meeting, the date on which provision in the CIO's constitution or in regulations made under paragraph 13 of Schedule 5B to this Act deems it to have been passed (but that date may not be earlier than that on which the last member agreed to it).

(7) Each old CIO shall—

(a) give notice of the proposed amalgamation in the way (or ways) that in the opinion of its charity trustees will make it most likely to come to the attention of those who would be affected by the amalgamation, and

(b) send a copy of the notice to the Commission.

(8)   The notice shall invite any person who considers that he would be affected by the proposed amalgamation to make written representations to the Commission not later than a date determined by the Commission and specified in the notice.

(9)   In addition to being required to refuse it on one of the grounds mentioned in section 69E(3) above as applied by subsection (3) of this section, the Commission shall refuse an application for amalgamation if it considers that there is a serious risk that the new CIO would be unable properly to pursue its purposes.

(10) The Commission may refuse an application for amalgamation if it is not satisfied that the provision in the constitution of the new CIO about the matters mentioned in subsection (11) is the same, or substantially the same, as the provision about those matters in the constitutions of each of the old CIOs.

(11) The matters are—
     (a) the purposes of the CIO,
     (b) the application of property of the CIO on its dissolution, and
     (c) authorisation for any benefit to be obtained by charity trustees or members of the CIO or persons connected with them.

(12) For the purposes of subsection (11)(c)—
     (a) 'benefit' means a direct or indirect benefit of any nature, except that it does not include any remuneration (within the meaning of section 73A below) whose receipt may be authorised under that section, and
     (b) the same rules apply for determining whether a person is connected with a charity trustee or member of the CIO as apply, in accordance with section 73B(5) and (6) below, for determining whether a person is connected with a charity trustee for the purposes of section 73A.

69L Amalgamation: supplementary

(1)   If the Commission grants an application for amalgamation, it shall register the new CIO in the register of charities.

(2)   Upon the registration of the new CIO it thereupon becomes by virtue of the registration a body corporate—
     (a) whose constitution is that proposed in the application for amalgamation,
     (b) whose name is that specified in the constitution, and
     (c) whose first members are the members of the old CIOs immediately before the new CIO was registered.

(3)   Upon the registration of the new CIO—
     (a) all the property, rights and liabilities of each of the old CIOs shall become by virtue of this subsection the property, rights and liabilities of the new CIO, and
     (b) each of the old CIOs shall be dissolved.

(4)   Any gift which—
     (a) is expressed as a gift to one of the old CIOs, and
     (b) takes effect on or after the date of registration of the new CIO,
     takes effect as a gift to the new CIO.

(5)   The entry relating to the registration in the register of the charity constituted as the new CIO shall include—
     (a) a note that it is constituted as a CIO,
     (b) the date of the charity's registration, and
     (c) a note that the CIO was formed following amalgamation, and of the name of each of the old CIOs.

(6)   A copy of the entry in the register shall be sent to the charity at the principal office of the new CIO.

69M Transfer of CIO's undertaking

(1)   A CIO may resolve that all its property, rights and liabilities should be transferred to another CIO specified in the resolution.

(2)   Where a CIO has passed such a resolution, it shall send to the Commission—
(a) a copy of the resolution, and
(b) a copy of a resolution of the transferee CIO agreeing to the transfer to it.

(3)   Subsections (5) and (6) of section 69K above apply to the resolutions referred to in subsections (1) and (2)(b) as they apply to the resolutions referred to in section 69K(4).

(4)   Having received the copy resolutions referred to in subsection (2), the Commission—
(a) may direct the transferor CIO to give public notice of its resolution in such manner as is specified in the direction, and
(b) if it gives such a direction, must take into account any representations made to it by persons appearing to it to be interested in the transferor CIO, where those representations are made to it within the period of 28 days beginning with the date when public notice of the resolution is given by the transferor CIO.

(5)   The resolution shall not take effect until confirmed by the Commission.

(6)   The Commission shall refuse to confirm the resolution if it considers that there is a serious risk that the transferee CIO would be unable properly to pursue the purposes of the transferor CIO.

(7)   The Commission may refuse to confirm the resolution if it is not satisfied that the provision in the constitution of the transferee CIO about the matters mentioned in section 69K(11) above is the same, or substantially the same, as the provision about those matters in the constitution of the transferor CIO.

(8)   If the Commission does not notify the transferor CIO within the relevant period that it is either confirming or refusing to confirm the resolution, the resolution is to be treated as confirmed by the Commission on the day after the end of that period.

(9)   Subject to subsection (10), 'the relevant period' means—
(a) in a case where the Commission directs the transferor CIO under subsection (4) to give public notice of its resolution, the period of six months beginning with the date when that notice is given, or
(b) in any other case, the period of six months beginning with the date when both of the copy resolutions referred to in subsection (2) have been received by the Commission.

(10)   The Commission may at any time within the period of six months mentioned in subsection (9)(a) or (b) give the transferor CIO a notice extending the relevant period by such period (not exceeding six months) as is specified in the notice.

(11)   A notice under subsection (10) must set out the Commission's reasons for the extension.

(12)   If the resolution is confirmed (or treated as confirmed) by the Commission—

(a) all the property, rights and liabilities of the transferor CIO shall become by virtue of this subsection the property, rights and liabilities of the transferee CIO in accordance with the resolution, and

(b) the transferor CIO shall be dissolved.

(13) Any gift which—

(a) is expressed as a gift to the transferor CIO, and

(b) takes effect on or after the date on which the resolution is confirmed (or treated as confirmed),

takes effect as a gift to the transferee CIO.

Winding up, insolvency and dissolution

69N Regulations about winding up, insolvency and dissolution

(1) The Minister may by regulations make provision about—

(a) the winding up of CIOs,

(b) their insolvency,

(c) their dissolution, and

(d) their revival and restoration to the register following dissolution.

(2) The regulations may, in particular, make provision—

(a) about the transfer on the dissolution of a CIO of its property and rights (including property and rights held on trust for the CIO) to the official custodian or another person or body,

(b) requiring any person in whose name any stocks, funds or securities are standing in trust for a CIO to transfer them into the name of the official custodian or another person or body,

(c) about the disclaiming, by the official custodian or other transferee of a CIO's property, of title to any of that property,

(d) about the application of a CIO's property cy-près,

(e) about circumstances in which charity trustees may be personally liable for contributions to the assets of a CIO or for its debts,

(f) about the reversal on a CIO's revival of anything done on its dissolution.

(3) The regulations may—

(a) apply any enactment which would not otherwise apply, either without modification or with modifications specified in the regulations,

(b) disapply, or modify (in ways specified in the regulations) the application of, any enactment which would otherwise apply.

(4) In subsection (3), 'enactment' includes a provision of subordinate legislation within the meaning of the Interpretation Act 1978.

Miscellaneous

69O Power to transfer all property of unincorporated charity to one or more CIOs

Section 74 below (power to transfer all property of unincorporated charity) applies with the omission of paragraph (a) of subsection (1) in relation to a resolution by the charity trustees of a charity to transfer all its property to a CIO or to divide its property between two or more CIOs.

69P Further provision about CIOs

The provisions of Schedule 5B to this Act shall have effect with respect to CIOs.

69N Regulations

(1)   The Minister may by regulations make further provision about applications for registration of CIOs, the administration of CIOs, the conversion of charitable companies, registered societies and community interest companies into CIOs, the amalgamation of CIOs, and in relation to CIOs generally.

(2)   The regulations may, in particular, make provision about—

(a) the execution of deeds and documents,

(b) the electronic communication of messages or documents relevant to a CIO or to any dealing with the Commission in relation to one,

(c) the maintenance of registers of members and of charity trustees,

(d) the maintenance of other registers (for example, a register of charges over the CIO's assets).

(3)   The regulations may, in relation to charities constituted as CIOs—

(a) disapply any of sections 3 to 4 above,

(b) modify the application of any of those sections in ways specified in the regulations.

(4)   Subsections (3) and (4) of section 69N above apply for the purposes of this section as they apply for the purposes of that."

2. After the Schedule 5A inserted in the 1993 Act by Schedule 6 to this Act, insert the following Schedule—

Section 69P   "SCHEDULE 5B

FURTHER PROVISION ABOUT CHARITABLE INCORPORATED ORGANISATIONS

Powers

1. (1) Subject to anything in its constitution, a CIO has power to do anything which is calculated to further its purposes or is conducive or incidental to doing so.

(2) The CIO's charity trustees shall manage the affairs of the CIO and may for that purpose exercise all the powers of the CIO.

Constitutional requirements

2. A CIO shall use and apply its property in furtherance of its purposes and in accordance with its constitution.

3. If the CIO is one whose members are liable to contribute to its assets if it is wound up, its constitution binds the CIO and its members for the time being to the same extent as if its provisions were contained in a contract—

(a) to which the CIO and each of its members was a party, and

(b) which contained obligations on the part of the CIO and each member to observe all the provisions of the constitution.

4. Money payable by a member to the CIO under the constitution is a debt due from him to the CIO, and is of the nature of a specialty debt.

Third parties

5. (1) Sub-paragraphs (2) and 3) are subject to sub-paragraph (4).

(2) The validity of an act done (or purportedly done) by a CIO shall not be called into question on the ground that it lacked constitutional capacity.

(3) The power of the charity trustees of a CIO to act so as to bind the CIO (or authorise others to do so) shall not be called into question on the ground of any constitutional limitations on their powers.

(4) But sub-paragraphs (2) and (3) apply only in favour of a person who gives full consideration in money or money's worth in relation to the act in question, and does not know—

(a) in a sub-paragraph (2) case, that the act is beyond the CIO's constitutional capacity, or

(b) in a sub-paragraph (3) case, that the act is beyond the constitutional powers of its charity trustees,

and (in addition) sub-paragraph (3) applies only if the person dealt with the CIO in good faith (which he shall be presumed to have done unless the contrary is proved).

(5) A party to an arrangement or transaction with a CIO is not bound to inquire—

(a) whether it is within the CIO's constitutional capacity, or

(b) as to any constitutional limitations on the powers of its charity trustees to bind the CIO or authorise others to do so.

(6) If a CIO purports to transfer or grant an interest in property, the fact that the act was beyond its constitutional capacity, or that its charity trustees in connection with the act exceeded their constitutional powers, does not affect the title of a person who subsequently acquires the property or any interest in it for full consideration without actual notice of any such circumstances affecting the validity of the CIO's act.

(7) In any proceedings arising out of sub-paragraphs (2) to (4), the burden of proving that a person knew that an act—

(a) was beyond the CIO's constitutional capacity, or

(b) was beyond the constitutional powers of its charity trustees,

lies on the person making that allegation.

(8) In this paragraph and paragraphs 6 to 8—

(a) references to a CIO's lack of 'constitutional capacity' are to lack of capacity because of anything in its constitution, and

(b) references to 'constitutional limitations' on the powers of a CIO's charity trustees are to limitations on their powers under its constitution, including limitations deriving from a resolution of the CIO in general meeting, or from an agreement between the CIO's members, and 'constitutional powers' is to be construed accordingly.

6. (1) Nothing in paragraph 5 prevents a person from bringing proceedings to restrain the doing of an act which would be—

(a) beyond the CIO's constitutional capacity, or

(b) beyond the constitutional powers of the CIO's charity trustees.

(2) But no such proceedings may be brought in respect of an act to be done in fulfilment of a legal obligation arising from a previous act of the CIO.

(3) Sub-paragraph (2) does not prevent the Commission from exercising any of its powers.

7. Nothing in paragraph 5(3) affects any liability incurred by the CIO's charity trustees (or any one of them) for acting beyond his or their constitutional powers.

8. Nothing in paragraph 5 absolves the CIO's charity trustees from their duty to act within the CIO's constitution and in accordance with any constitutional limitations on their powers.

Duties

9. It is the duty of—

    (a) each member of a CIO, and

    (b) each charity trustee of a CIO,

    to exercise his powers, and (in the case of a charity trustee) to perform his functions, in his capacity as such, in the way he decides, in good faith, would be most likely to further the purposes of the CIO.

10. (1) Subject to any provision of a CIO's constitution permitted by virtue of regulations made under sub-paragraph (2), each charity trustee of a CIO shall in the performance of his functions in that capacity exercise such care and skill as is reasonable in the circumstances, having regard in particular—

    (a) to any special knowledge or experience that he has or holds himself out as having, and

    (b) if he acts as a charity trustee in the course of a business or profession, to any special knowledge or experience that it is reasonable to expect of a person acting in the course of that kind of business or profession.

    (2) The Minister may make regulations permitting a CIO's constitution to provide that the duty in sub-paragraph (1) does not apply, or does not apply in so far as is specified in the constitution.

    (3) Regulations under sub-paragraph (2) may provide for limits on the extent to which, or the cases in which, a CIO's constitution may disapply the duty in sub-paragraph (1).

Personal benefit and payments

11. (1) A charity trustee of a CIO may not benefit personally from any arrangement or transaction entered into by the CIO if, before the arrangement or transaction was entered into, he did not disclose to all the charity trustees of the CIO any material interest of his in it or in any other person or body party to it (whether that interest is direct or indirect).

    (2) Nothing in sub-paragraph (1) confers authority for a charity trustee of a CIO to benefit personally from any arrangement or transaction entered into by the CIO.

12.   A charity trustee of a CIO—

    (a) is entitled to be reimbursed by the CIO, or

    (b) may pay out of the CIO's funds,

    expenses properly incurred by him in the performance of his functions as such.

Procedure

13. (1) The Minister may by regulations make provision about the procedure of CIOs.

    (2) Subject to—

    (a) any such regulations,

    (b) any other requirement imposed by or by virtue of this Act or any other enactment, and

    (c) anything in the CIO's constitution,

    a CIO may regulate its own procedure.

    (3) But a CIO's procedure shall include provision for the holding of a general meeting

of its members, and the regulations referred to in sub-paragraph (1) may in particular make provision about such meetings.

Amendment of constitution

14. (1) A CIO may by resolution of its members amend its constitution (and a single resolution may provide for more than one amendment).

(2) Such a resolution must be passed—

(a) by a 75% majority of those voting at a general meeting of the CIO (including those voting by proxy or by post, if voting that way is permitted), or

(b) unanimously by the CIO's members, otherwise than at a general meeting.

(3) The date of passing of such a resolution is—

(a) the date of the general meeting at which it was passed, or

(b) if it was passed otherwise than at a general meeting, the date on which provision in the CIO's constitution or in regulations made under paragraph 13 deems it to have been passed (but that date may not be earlier than that on which the last member agreed to it).

(4) The power of a CIO to amend its constitution is not exercisable in any way which would result in the CIO's ceasing to be a charity.

(5) Subject to paragraph 15(5) below, a resolution containing an amendment which would make any regulated alteration is to that extent ineffective unless the prior written consent of the Commission has been obtained to the making of the amendment.

(6) The following are regulated alterations—

(a) any alteration of the CIO's purposes,

(b) any alteration of any provision of the CIO's constitution directing the application of property of the CIO on its dissolution,

(c) any alteration of any provision of the CIO's constitution where the alteration would provide authorisation for any benefit to be obtained by charity trustees or members of the CIO or persons connected with them.

(7) For the purposes of sub-paragraph (6)(c)—

(a) 'benefit' means a direct or indirect benefit of any nature, except that it does not include any remuneration (within the meaning of section 73A of this Act) whose receipt may be authorised under that section, and

(b) the same rules apply for determining whether a person is connected with a charity trustee or member of the CIO as apply, in accordance with section 73B(5) and (6) of this Act, for determining whether a person is connected with a charity trustee for the purposes of section 73A.

Registration and coming into effect of amendments

15. (1) A CIO shall send to the Commission a copy of a resolution containing an amendment to its constitution, together with—

(a) a copy of the constitution as amended, and

(b) such other documents and information as the Commission may require,

by the end of the period of 15 days beginning with the date of passing of the resolution (see paragraph 14(3)).

(2) An amendment to a CIO's constitution does not take effect until it has been registered.

(3) The Commission shall refuse to register an amendment if—

      (a) in the opinion of the Commission the CIO had no power to make it (for example, because the effect of making it would be that the CIO ceased to be a charity, or that the CIO or its constitution did not comply with any requirement imposed by or by virtue of this Act or any other enactment), or

      (b) the amendment would change the name of the CIO, and the Commission could have refused an application under section 69E of this Act for the constitution and registration of a CIO with the name specified in the amendment on a ground set out in subsection (4) of that section.

   (4) The Commission may refuse to register an amendment if the amendment would make a regulated alteration and the consent referred to in paragraph 14(5) had not been obtained.

   (5) But if the Commission does register such an amendment, paragraph 14(5) does not apply."

PART 2
OTHER AMENDMENTS OF 1993 ACT

3. The 1993 Act is further amended as follows.

4. In section 45 (annual reports), after subsection (3A) insert—

   "(3B) But in the case of a charity which is constituted as a CIO—

      (a) the requirement imposed by subsection (3) applies whatever the charity's gross income is, and

      (b) subsection (3A) does not apply."

5. In section 48 (annual returns), in subsection (1A), at the end add "(but this subsection does not apply if the charity is constituted as a CIO)".

6. In section 86 (regulations and orders)—

      (a) in subsection (2), after paragraph (a) insert—

      "(aa) to regulations under section 69N above; and no regulations shall be made under that section unless a draft of the regulations has been laid before and approved by a resolution of each House of Parliament; or",

      (b) in subsection (4), for "or 45" substitute ", 45, 69N or 69Q".

7. In section 97 (general interpretation), in subsection (1), at the appropriate place insert— " 'CIO' means charitable incorporated organisation;".

Section 75   SCHEDULE 8

MINOR AND CONSEQUENTIAL AMENDMENTS

Literary and Scientific Institutions Act 1854 (c. 112)

1. In section 6 of the Literary and Scientific Institutions Act 1854 (power of corporations etc. to convey land for the purposes of that Act) for "without the consent of the Charity Commissioners" substitute "except with the consent of the Charity Commission or in accordance with such provisions of section 36(2) to (8) of the Charities Act 1993 as are applicable".

Places of Worship Registration Act 1855 (c. 81)

2. In section 9(1) of the Places of Worship Registration Act 1855 (certified places exempt from requirement to register)—
   (a) for "shall be excepted under subsection (5) of section 3 of the Charities Act 1993, from registration under that section" substitute "shall, so far as it is a charity, be treated for the purposes of section 3A(4)(b) of the Charities Act 1993 (institutions to be excepted from registration under that Act) as if that provision applied to it", and
   (b) for "Charity Commissioners" substitute "Charity Commission".

Bishops Trusts Substitution Act 1858 (c. 71)

3. The Bishops Trusts Substitution Act 1858 has effect subject to the following amendments.
4. In section 1 (substitution of one bishop for another as trustee)—
   (a) for "Charity Commissioners" substitute "Charity Commission", and
   (b) for "them" substitute "it".
5. In section 3 (how costs are to be defrayed) for "said Charity Commissioners" (in both places) substitute "Charity Commission".

Places of Worship Sites Amendment Act 1882 (c. 21)

6. In section 1(d) of the Places of Worship Sites Amendment Act 1882 (conveyance of lands by corporations and other public bodies) for "without the consent of the Charity Commissioners" substitute "except with the consent of the Charity Commission or in accordance with such provisions of section 36(2) to (8) of the Charities Act 1993 as are applicable".

Municipal Corporations Act 1882 (c. 50)

7. In section 133(2) of the Municipal Corporations Act 1882 (administration of charitable trusts and vesting of legal estate) for "Charity Commissioners" substitute "Charity Commission".

Technical and Industrial Institutions Act 1892 (c. 29)

8. In section 9(1) of the Technical and Industrial Institutions Act 1892 (site may be sold or exchanged) for "with the consent of the Charity Commissioners" substitute "with the consent of the Charity Commission or in accordance with such provisions of section 36(2) to (8) of the Charities Act 1993 as are applicable".

Local Government Act 1894 (c. 73)

9. (1) In section 75(2) of the Local Government Act 1894 (construction of that Act) the definition of "ecclesiastical charity" is amended as follows.
   (2) In the second paragraph (proviso)—
   (a) for "Charity Commissioners" substitute "Charity Commission", and
   (b) for "them" substitute "it".
   (3) In the third paragraph (inclusion of other buildings) for "Charity Commissioners" substitute "Charity Commission".

Commons Act 1899 (c. 30)

10. In section 18 of the Commons Act 1899 (power to modify provisions as to recreation grounds)—
   (a) for "Charity Commissioners" substitute "Charity Commission", and

(b) for "their" substitute "its".

Open Spaces Act 1906 (c. 25)

11. The Open Spaces Act 1906 has effect subject to the following amendments.

12. In section 3(1) (transfer to local authority of spaces held by trustees for purposes of public recreation) for "Charity Commissioners" substitute "Charity Commission".

13. (1) Section 4 (transfer by charity trustees of open space to local authority) is amended as follows.

   (2) In subsection (1), for the words from "and with the sanction" to "as hereinafter provided" substitute "and in accordance with subsection (1A)".

   (3) After subsection (1) insert—

   "(1A) The trustees act in accordance with this subsection if they convey or demise the open space as mentioned in subsection (1)—

   (a) with the sanction of an order of the Charity Commission or with that of an order of the court to be obtained as provided in the following provisions of this section, or

   (b) in accordance with such provisions of section 36(2) to (8) of the Charities Act 1993 as are applicable."

   (4) In subsection (4)—

   (a) for "Charity Commissioners" substitute "Charity Commission", and

   (b) for "them" substitute "it".

14. In section 21(1) (application to Ireland)—

   (a) for "Charity Commissioners" substitute "Charity Commission", and

   (b) for "Commissioners of Charity Donations and Bequests for Ireland" substitute "the Department for Social Development".

Police, Factories, &c. (Miscellaneous Provisions) Act 1916 (c. 31)

15. (1) Section 5 of the Police, Factories, &c. (Miscellaneous Provisions) Act 1916 (regulation of street collections) is amended as follows.

   (2) In subsection (1) for "the benefit of charitable or other purposes," substitute "any purposes in circumstances not involving the making of a charitable appeal,".

   (3) In paragraph (b) of the proviso to subsection (1) omit the words from ", and no representation" onwards.

   (4) In subsection (4) before the definition of "street" insert—

   "'charitable appeal' has the same meaning as in Chapter 1 of Part 3 of the Charities Act 2006;".

National Trust Charity Scheme Confirmation Act 1919 (c. lxxxiv)

16. The National Trust Charity Scheme Confirmation Act 1919 has effect subject to the following amendments.

17. In section 1 (confirmation of the scheme) for "Charity Commissioners" substitute "Charity Commission".

18. In paragraph 3 of the scheme set out in the Schedule, for "Charity Commissioners upon such application made to them for the purpose as they think" substitute "Charity Commission upon such application made to it for the purpose as it thinks".

Settled Land Act 1925 (c. 18)

19. In section 29(3) of the Settled Land Act 1925 (charitable and public trusts: saving) for "Charity Commissioners" substitute "Charity Commission".

Landlord and Tenant Act 1927 (c. 36)

20. In Part 2 of the Second Schedule to the Landlord and Tenant Act 1927 (application to ecclesiastical and charity land), in paragraph 2, for "Charity Commissioners" substitute "Charity Commission".

Voluntary Hospitals (Paying Patients) Act 1936 (c. 17)

21. The Voluntary Hospitals (Paying Patients) Act 1936 has effect subject to the following amendments.
22. In section 1 (definitions), in the definition of "Order", for "Charity Commissioners" substitute "Charity Commission".
23. (1) Section 2 (accommodation for and charges to paying patients) is amended as follows.
    (2) In subsections (1), (3) and (4) for "Charity Commissioners" substitute "Charity Commission".
    (3) In subsection (4)—
        (a) for "the Commissioners" (in both places) substitute "the Commission",
        (b) for "they" substitute "it", and
        (c) for "their" substitute "its".
24. In section 3(1) (provision for patients able to make some, but not full, payment)—
    (a) for "Charity Commissioners are" substitute "Charity Commission is", and
    (b) for "they" substitute "it".
25. In section 4 (provisions for protection of existing trusts)—
    (a) for "Charity Commissioners" substitute "Charity Commission", and
    (b) in paragraphs (a), (b) and (c) for "they are" substitute "it is".
26. (1) Section 5 (power to make rules) is amended as follows.
    (2) In subsection (1)—
        (a) for "Charity Commissioners" substitute "Charity Commission", and
        (b) for "they" substitute "it".
    (3) In subsection (3)—
        (a) for "Charity Commissioners" (in both places) substitute "Charity Commission",
        (b) for "they" and "them" (in each place) substitute "it", and
        (c) for "an officer" substitute "a member of staff".
    (4) In the sidenote, for "Charity Commissioners" substitute "Charity Commission".
27. In section 6(2) (savings)—
    (a) for "Charity Commissioners" substitute "Charity Commission", and
    (b) for "them" substitute "it".

Green Belt (London and Home Counties) Act 1938 (c. xciii)

28. In section 20 of the Green Belt (London and Home Counties) Act 1938 (lands held on charitable trusts) for "Charity Commissioners" substitute "Charity Commission".

New Parishes Measure 1943 (No. 1)

29. The New Parishes Measure 1943 has effect subject to the following amendments.
30. In section 14(1)(b) (power of corporations etc. to give or grant land for sites of churches, etc.) for "with the sanction of an order of the Charity Commissioners" substitute—

"(i) with the sanction of an order of the Charity Commission, or

(ii) in accordance with such provisions of section 36(2) to (8) of the Charities Act 1993 as are applicable;".

31. In section 31 (charitable trusts)—

(a) for "the Board of Charity Commissioners" substitute "the Charity Commission", and

(b) for "the Charity Commissioners" substitute "the Charity Commission".

Crown Proceedings Act 1947 (c. 44)

32. In section 23(3) of the Crown Proceedings Act 1947 (proceedings with respect to which Part 2 of the Act does not apply) for "Charity Commissioners" substitute "Charity Commission".

London County Council (General Powers) Act 1947 (c. xlvi)

33. (1) Section 6 of the London County Council (General Powers) Act 1947 (saving for certain trusts) is amended as follows.

(2) In subsection (2)—

(a) for "Charity Commissioners" substitute "Charity Commission", and

(b) at the end add "; but this is subject to subsection (3)".

(3) After subsection (2) add—

"(3) In relation to any disposition of land falling within section 36(1) of the Charities Act 1993, the Council or the borough council may, instead of acting with the sanction of an order of the court or of the Charity Commission, make the disposition in accordance with such provisions of section 36(2) to (8) of that Act as are applicable."

London County Council (General Powers) Act 1951 (c. xli)

34. In section 33(6) of the London County Council (General Powers) Act 1951 (improvement of roadside amenities: saving for certain land) for "Charity Commissioners" substitute "Charity Commission".

City of London (Various Powers) Act 1952 (c. vi)

35. In section 4(6) of the City of London (Various Powers) Act 1952 (improvement of amenities) for "Charity Commissioners" substitute "Charity Commission".

City of London (Guild Churches) Act 1952 (c. xxxviii)

36. In section 35 of the City of London (Guild Churches) Act 1952 (saving of rights of certain persons) for "Charity Commissioners" substitute "Charity Commission".

London County Council (General Powers) Act 1955 (c. xxix)

37. (1) Section 34 of the London County Council (General Powers) Act 1955 (powers as to erection of buildings: saving for certain land and buildings) is amended as follows.

(2) In subsection (2)—

(a) for "Charity Commissioners" substitute "Charity Commission", and

(b) at the end add "; but this is subject to subsection (3)".

(3) After subsection (2) add—

"(3) In relation to any disposition of land falling within section 36(1) of the Charities Act 1993, the Council may, instead of acting with the sanction of an order of the court or of the Charity Commission, make the disposition in accordance with such provisions of section 36(2) to (8) of that Act as are applicable."

Parochial Church Councils (Powers) Measure 1956 (No. 3)

38. In section 6(5) of the Parochial Church Councils (Powers) Measure 1956 (consents required for transactions relating to certain property) for "Charity Commissioners" substitute "Charity Commission".

Recreational Charities Act 1958 (c. 17)

39. In section 6 of the Recreational Charities Act 1958 (short title and extent) for subsection (2) substitute—
"(2) Section 1 of this Act, as amended by section 5 of the Charities Act 2006, has the same effect in relation to the law of Scotland or Northern Ireland as section 5 of that Act has by virtue of section 80(3) to (6) of that Act.
(3) Sections 1 and 2 of this Act, as in force before the commencement of section 5 of that Act, continue to have effect in relation to the law of Scotland or Northern Ireland so far as they affect the construction of any references to charities or charitable purposes which—
(a) are to be construed in accordance with the law of England and Wales, but
(b) are not contained in enactments relating to matters of the kind mentioned in section 80(4) or (6) of that Act."

Church Funds Investment Measure 1958 (No. 1)

40. Section 5 of the Church Funds Investment Measure 1958 (jurisdiction of Charity Commissioners) is omitted.

Incumbents and Churchwardens (Trusts) Measure 1964 (No. 2)

41. The Incumbents and Churchwardens (Trusts) Measure 1964 has effect subject to the following amendments.

42. In section 2(3) (property to which Measure applies) for "Charity Commissioners" substitute "Charity Commission".

43. In section 3(6) (vesting of property in diocesan authority: saving) for "Charity Commissioners" substitute "Charity Commission".

44. In section 5 (provisions as to property vested in the diocesan authority) for "Charity Commissioners" substitute "Charity Commission".

45. (1) The Schedule (procedure where diocesan authority is of the opinion that Measure applies to an interest) is amended as follows.
(2) In paragraph 2 for "Charity Commissioners" substitute "Charity Commission".
(3) In paragraph 3—
(a) for "Charity Commissioners" substitute "Charity Commission",
(b) for "they think" (in both places) substitute "it thinks", and
(c) for "the Commissioners" substitute "the Commission".
(4) In paragraph 5—
(a) for "Charity Commissioners have" substitute "Charity Commission has", and
(b) for "they" substitute "it".

Faculty Jurisdiction Measure 1964 (No. 5)

46. In section 4(2) of the Faculty Jurisdiction Measure 1964 (sale of books in parochial

libraries under a faculty) for "Charity Commissioners" substitute "Charity Commission".

Industrial and Provident Societies Act 1965 (c. 12)

47. In section 7D(4) of the Industrial and Provident Societies Act 1965 (application of sections 7A and 7B to charitable societies) for "Charity Commissioners" substitute "Charity Commission".

Clergy Pensions (Amendment) Measure 1967 (No. 1)

48. In section 4(5) of the Clergy Pensions (Amendment) Measure 1967 (amendments of powers of Board relating to provision of residences) for "Charity Commissioners" and "said Commissioners" substitute "Charity Commission".

Ministry of Housing and Local Government Provisional Order Confirmation (Greater London Parks and Open Spaces) Act 1967 (c. xxix)

49. In article 11(3) of the order set out in the Schedule to the Ministry of Housing and Local Government Provisional Order Confirmation (Greater London Parks and Open Spaces) Act 1967 (exercise of powers under articles 7 to 10 of the order) for "Charity Commissioners" substitute "Charity Commission".

Redundant Churches and other Religious Buildings Act 1969 (c. 22)

50. The Redundant Churches and other Religious Buildings Act 1969 has effect subject to the following amendments.

51. (1) Section 4 (transfer of certain redundant places of worship) is amended as follows.
    (2) In subsections (6), (7) and (8) for "Charity Commissioners" substitute "Charity Commission".
    (3) In subsection (6) for "Commissioners'" substitute "Commission's".
    (4) In subsection (8) for "they have" substitute "it has".
    (5) After subsection (8) insert—

    "(8A) Schedule 1C to the Charities Act 1993 shall apply in relation to an order made by virtue of subsection (8) above as it applies in relation to an order made under section 16(1) of that Act."

52. In section 7(2) (saving) for "Charity Commissioners" (in both places) substitute "Charity Commission".

Children and Young Persons Act 1969 (c. 54)

53. In Schedule 3 to the Children and Young Persons Act 1969 (approved schools and other institutions), in paragraph 6(3), for "Charity Commissioners" substitute "Charity Commission".

Synodical Government Measure 1969 (No. 2)

54. (1) Schedule 3 to the Synodical Government Measure 1969 (which sets out the Church Representation Rules) is amended as follows.
    (2) In Rule 46A(a)—
        (a) for "Charity Commissioners" substitute "Charity Commission", and
        (b) for "them" substitute "it".
    (3) In Section 4 of Appendix I to those Rules (which sets out certain forms), in Note 3—

    (a) for "Charity Commissioners" substitute "Charity Commission", and
    (b) for "them" substitute "it".
  (4) In Section 6 of that Appendix, in the Note—
    (a) for "Charity Commissioners" substitute "Charity Commission", and
    (b) for "them" substitute "it".
  (5) In Appendix II to those Rules (general provisions relating to parochial church councils), in paragraph 16, for "Charity Commissioners" substitute "Charity Commission".

Local Government Act 1972 (c. 70)

55. In section 131(3) of the Local Government Act 1972 (savings in relation to charity land) for "Charity Commissioners" substitute "Charity Commission".

Consumer Credit Act 1974 (c. 39)

56. In section 16 of the Consumer Credit Act 1974 (exempt agreements), in the table in subsection (3A) and in subsections (8) and (9), for "Charity Commissioners" substitute "Charity Commission".

Sex Discrimination Act 1975 (c. 65)

57. In section 21A of the Sex Discrimination Act 1975 (public authorities) in paragraph 14 in the Table of Exceptions in subsection (9), for "Charity Commissioners for England and Wales" substitute "Charity Commission".

Endowments and Glebe Measure 1976 (No. 4)

58. The Endowments and Glebe Measure 1976 has effect subject to the following amendments.
59. In section 11(2) (extinguishment of certain trusts) for "the Charity Commissioners" substitute "the Charity Commission or in accordance with such provisions of section 36(2) to (8) of the Charities Act 1993 as are applicable".
60. In section 18(2) (means by which land may become diocesan) for "Charity Commissioners" substitute "Charity Commission".

Interpretation Act 1978 (c. 30)

61. In Schedule 1 to the Interpretation Act 1978 (words and expressions defined) for the definition of "Charity Commissioners" substitute—
" 'Charity Commission' means the Charity Commission for England and Wales established by section 1A of the Charities Act 1993."

Dioceses Measure 1978 (No. 1)

62. The Dioceses Measure 1978 has effect subject to the following amendments.
63. In section 5(1) (preparation of draft scheme: meaning of "interested parties"), in paragraph (e), for "the Charity Commissioners" substitute "the Charity Commission".
64. In section 19(4) (schemes with respect to discharge of functions of diocesan bodies corporate, etc.) for "Charity Commissioners" substitute "Charity Commission".

Disused Burial Grounds (Amendment) Act 1981 (c. 18)

65. In section 6 of the Disused Burial Grounds (Amendment) Act 1981 (saving for Charity Commission) for "Charity Commissioners" substitute "Charity Commission".

Local Government (Miscellaneous Provisions) Act 1982 (c. 30)

66. In Schedule 4 to the Local Government (Miscellaneous Provisions) Act 1982 (street trading) for paragraph 1(2)(j) substitute—

> "(j)   conducting a public charitable collection that—
>
>> (i)   is conducted in accordance with section 48 or 49 of the Charities Act 2006, or
>>
>> (ii)   is an exempt collection by virtue of section 50 of that Act."

Administration of Justice Act 1982 (c. 53)

67. In section 41(1) of the Administration of Justice Act 1982 (transfer of funds in court to official custodian for charities and Church Commissioners) for "Charity Commissioners" substitute "Charity Commission".

Pastoral Measure 1983 (No. 1)

68. The Pastoral Measure 1983 has effect subject to the following amendments.

69. In section 55(1) (schemes under the Charities Act 1993 for redundant chapels belonging to charities) for "Charity Commissioners" substitute "Charity Commission".

70. In section 63(4) (trusts for the repair etc. of redundant buildings and contents) for "the Charity Commissioners given under the hand of an Assistant Commissioner" substitute "the Charity Commission".

71. In section 76(1) (grant of land for new churches etc. and vesting of certain churches) for "Charity Commissioners" substitute "Charity Commission".

72. In Schedule 3, in paragraph 11(1), (2), (6) and (7), for "Charity Commissioners" substitute "Charity Commission".

Rates Act 1984 (c. 33)

73. In section 3(9) of the Rates Act 1984 (expenditure levels) for ", or excepted from registration, under section 3 of the Charities Act 1993" substitute "in accordance with section 3A of the Charities Act 1993 or not required to be registered (by virtue of subsection (2) of that section)".

Companies Act 1985 (c. 6)

74. The Companies Act 1985 has effect subject to the following amendments.

75. (1) Section 380 (registration of resolutions) is amended as follows.

(2) In subsection (4), at the beginning insert "Except as mentioned in subsection (4ZB),".

(3) After subsection (4ZA) insert—

> "(4ZB) Paragraphs (a) and (c) of subsection (4) do not apply to the resolutions of a charitable company mentioned in paragraphs (a) and (b) respectively of section 69G(6) of the Charities Act 1993."

76. In Schedule 15D (permitted disclosures of information), in paragraph 21, for "Charity Commissioners to exercise their" substitute "Charity Commission to exercise its".

Housing Act 1985 (c. 68)

77. (1) Section 6A of the Housing Act 1985 (definition of "Relevant Authority") is amended as follows.

(2) In subsection (2) for "Charity Commissioners" substitute "Charity Commission".

(3) In subsection (5)—

(a) for "under section 3" substitute "in accordance with section 3A", and

(b) omit the words from "and is not" onwards.

Housing Associations Act 1985 (c. 69)

78. In section 10(1) of the Housing Associations Act 1985 (dispositions excepted from section 9 of that Act) for "Charity Commissioners" (in both places) substitute "Charity Commission".

Agricultural Holdings Act 1986 (c. 5)

79. In section 86(4) of the Agricultural Holdings Act 1986 (power of landlord to obtain charge on holding) for "Charity Commissioners" substitute "Charity Commission".

Coal Industry Act 1987 (c. 3)

80. (1) Section 5 of the Coal Industry Act 1987 (coal industry trusts) is amended as follows.

(2) In subsection (1)—

(a) for "Charity Commissioners" (in the first place) substitute "Charity Commission ("the Commission")",

(b) for "to them" substitute "to the Commission",

(c) for "Charity Commissioners" (in the second place) substitute "Commission", and

(d) for "they consider" substitute "the Commission considers".

(3) In subsection (2) for "Charity Commissioners consider" (in both places) substitute "Commission considers".

(4) In subsections (4) and (6) for "Charity Commissioners" substitute "Commission".

(5) In subsection (7)—

(a) for "Charity Commissioners" substitute "Commission",

(b) for "their powers" substitute "its powers",

(c) for "they consider" substitute "it considers", and

(d) for "the Charities Act 1960" substitute "the Charities Act 1993".

(6) In subsection (8)—

(a) for "16(3), (9), (11) to (14)" substitute "16(3) and (9)",

(b) for "and 20" substitute ", 20 and 20A",

(c) for "Charity Commissioners" substitute "Commission",

(d) for "their powers" substitute "its powers", and

(e) for "91 and 92" substitute "and 91".

(7) In subsection (8A)—

(a) for "Commissioners" (in both places) substitute "Commission",

(b) for "they were proceeding" substitute "the Commission was proceeding", and

(c) for "to them" substitute "to it".

(8) After subsection (8A) insert—

"(8B) Schedule 1C to the Charities Act 1993 shall apply in relation to an order made under this section as it applies in relation to an order made under section 16(1) of that Act."

(9) In subsection (9) for "Charity Commissioners" substitute "Commission".

(10) In subsection (10)(b) for "Charity Commissioners" substitute "Commission".

Reverter of Sites Act 1987 (c. 15)

81. The Reverter of Sites Act 1987 has effect subject to the following amendments.

82. (1) Section 2 (Charity Commissioners' schemes) is amended as follows.

(2) In subsection (1) for "Charity Commissioners" substitute "Charity Commission".

(3) For subsection (3) substitute—

> "(3) The charitable purposes specified in an order made under this section on an application with respect to any trust shall be such as the Charity Commission consider appropriate, having regard to the matters set out in subsection (3A).
>
> (3A) The matters are—
>> (a) the desirability of securing that the property is held for charitable purposes ('the new purposes') which are close to the purposes, whether charitable or not, for which the trustees held the relevant land before the cesser of use in consequence of which the trust arose ('the former purposes'); and
>> (b) the need for the new purposes to be capable of having a significant social or economic effect.
>
> (3B) In determining the character of the former purposes, the Commission may, if they think it appropriate to do so, give greater weight to the persons or locality benefited by those purposes than to the nature of the benefit."

(4) In subsection (5)—

    (a) for "Charity Commissioners" substitute "Charity Commission",

    (b) in paragraph (c), for "Commissioners'" and "them" substitute "Commission's" and "it", and

    (c) in paragraph (d), for "Commissioners have" substitute "Commission has".

(5) In subsection (7) for "Charity Commissioners" substitute "Charity Commission".

(6) In subsection (8)—

    (a) for "Commissioners'" substitute "Commission's",

    (b) for "they think" substitute "it thinks", and

    (c) for "Commissioners decide" substitute "Commission decides".

(7) In the sidenote, for "Charity Commissioners'" substitute "Charity Commission's".

83. (1) Section 4 (provisions supplemental to sections 2 and 3) is amended as follows.

(2) In subsection (1)—

    (a) for "Charity Commissioners think" substitute "Charity Commission thinks";

    (b) for "Commissioners'" substitute "Commission's"; and

    (c) for "the Commissioners think" substitute "the Commission thinks".

(3) For subsections (2) and (3) substitute—

> "(2) Schedule 1C to the Charities Act 1993 shall apply in relation to an order made under section 2 above as it applies in relation to an order made under section 16(1) of that Act, except that the persons who may bring an appeal against an order made under section 2 above are—
>
> (a) the Attorney General;
>
> (b) the trustees of the trust established under the order;
>
> (c) a beneficiary of, or the trustees of, the trust in respect of which the application for the order had been made;
>
> (d) any person interested in the purposes for which the last-mentioned trustees or any of their predecessors held the relevant land before the cesser of use in consequence of which the trust arose under section 1 above;
>
> (e) any two or more inhabitants of the locality where that land is situated;
>
> (f) any other person who is or may be affected by the order."

(4) In subsection (4)—

(a) for "Sections 89, 91 and 92" substitute "Sections 89 and 91", and

(b) omit "and appeals" and (in both places) ", and to appeals against,".

84.   In section 5(3) (orders under section 554 of the Education Act 1996)—

(a) for "Charity Commissioners" (in both places) substitute "Charity Commission";

(b) for "the Commissioners" substitute "the Commission"; and

(c) for "them" substitute "it".

Education Reform Act 1988 (c. 40)

85.   For section 125A of the Education Reform Act 1988 substitute—

"125A Charitable status of a higher education corporation
A higher education corporation shall be a charity within the meaning of the Charities Act 1993 (and in accordance with Schedule 2 to that Act is an exempt charity for the purposes of that Act)."

Courts and Legal Services Act 1990 (c. 41)

86. In Schedule 11 to the Courts and Legal Services Act 1990 (judges etc. barred from legal practice) for the entry beginning "Charity Commissioner" substitute "Member of the Charity Commission appointed as provided in Schedule 1A to the Charities Act 1993".

London Local Authorities Act 1991 (c. xiii)

87. In section 4 of the London Local Authorities Act 1991 (interpretation of Part 2), in paragraph (d) of the definition of "establishment for special treatment", for the words from "under section 3" to "that section" substitute "in accordance with section 3A of the Charities Act 1993 or is not required to be registered (by virtue of subsection (2) of that section)".

Further and Higher Education Act 1992 (c. 13)

88. For section 22A of the Further and Higher Education Act 1992 substitute—

"22A Charitable status of a further education corporation
A further education corporation shall be a charity within the meaning of the Charities Act 1993 (and in accordance with Schedule 2 to that Act is an exempt charity for the purposes of that Act)."

Charities Act 1992 (c. 41)

89. The 1992 Act has effect subject to the following amendments.

90. (1) Section 58 (interpretation of Part 2) is amended as follows.

(2) In subsection (1) after the definition of "institution" insert—
"'the Minister' means the Minister for the Cabinet Office;".

(3) In subsection (2)—

(a) in paragraph (c) for "to be treated as a promoter of such a collection by virtue of section 65(3)" substitute "a promoter of such a collection as defined in section 47(1) of the Charities Act 2006", and

      (b) for "Part III of this Act" substitute "Chapter 1 of Part 3 of the Charities Act 2006".

    (4) In subsection (4) for "whether or not the purposes are charitable within the meaning of any rule of law" substitute "as defined by section 2(1) of the Charities Act 2006".

91. Omit Part 3 (public charitable collections).

92. In section 76(1) (service of documents) omit paragraph (c) and the "and" preceding it.

93. (1) Section 77 (regulations and orders) is amended as follows.

    (2) In subsection (1)(b) for "subsection (2)" substitute "subsections (2) and (2A)".

    (3) After subsection (2) insert—

        "(2A) Subsection (1)(b) does not apply to regulations under section 64A, and no such regulations may be made unless a draft of the statutory instrument containing the regulations has been laid before, and approved by a resolution of, each House of Parliament."

    (4) In subsection (4)—

        (a) after "64" insert "or 64A"; and

        (b) omit "or 73".

94. In section 79 (short title, commencement and extent) omit-

        (a) in subsection (6), the words "(subject to subsection (7))", and

        (b) subsection (7).

95. In Schedule 7 (repeals) omit the entry relating to the Police, Factories, &c. (Miscellaneous Provisions) Act 1916 (c. 31).

Charities Act 1993 (c. 10)

96. The 1993 Act has effect subject to the following amendments.

97. In the heading for Part 1, for "CHARITY COMMISSIONERS" substitute "CHARITY COMMISSION".

98. (1) Section 2 (official custodian for charities) is amended as follows.

    (2) For subsection (2) substitute—

        "(2) Such individual as the Commission may from time to time designate shall be the official custodian."

    (3) In subsection (3), for "Commissioners" (in both places) substitute "Commission".

    (4) In subsection (4)—

        (a) for "officer of the Commissioners" substitute "member of the staff of the Commission", and

        (b) for "by them" substitute "by it".

    (5) In subsection (7) omit the words from ", and the report" onwards.

    (6) After subsection (7) add—

        "(8) The Comptroller and Auditor General shall send to the Commission a copy of the accounts as certified by him together with his report on them.

        (9) The Commission shall publish and lay before Parliament a copy of the documents sent to it under subsection (8) above."

99. (1) Section 4 (claims and objections to registration) is amended as follows.

    (2) In subsection (2)—

        (a) for "the Commissioners" substitute "the Commission", and

        (b) for "to them" substitute "to the Commission".

    (3) Omit subsection (3).

(4) In subsection (4)—
  (a) for "High Court" substitute "Tribunal",
  (b) for "the Commissioners" (in the first and third places) substitute "the Commission", and
  (c) for "the Commissioners are" substitute "the Commission is".
(5) In subsection (5)—
  (a) for "subsection (3) above" substitute "Schedule 1C to this Act",
  (b) for "the Commissioners" (in both places) substitute "the Commission", and
  (c) omit ", whether given on such an appeal or not".

100. (1) Section 6 (power to require charity's name to be changed) is amended as follows.
  (2) For "Commissioners" (in each place including the sidenote) substitute "Commission".
  (3) In subsection (5) for "section 3(7)(b) above" substitute "section 3B(3)".

101. For the heading for Part 3 substitute "INFORMATION POWERS".

102. (1) Section 8 (power to institute inquiries) is amended as follows.
  (2) In subsection (1) for "The Commissioners" substitute "The Commission".
  (3) In subsection (2)—
    (a) for "The Commissioners" substitute "The Commission",
    (b) for "themselves" substitute "itself", and
    (c) for "to them" substitute "to the Commission".
  (4) In subsection (3) for "the Commissioners, or a person appointed by them" substitute "the Commission, or a person appointed by the Commission".
  (5) In subsection (5) for "The Commissioners" substitute "The Commission".
  (6) In subsection (6)—
    (a) for "the Commissioners" substitute "the Commission",
    (b) for "they think" substitute "the Commission thinks",
    (c) for "their opinion" substitute "the Commission's opinion", and
    (d) for "to them" substitute "to the Commission".
  (7) In subsection (7) for "the Commissioners" substitute "the Commission".

103. (1) Section 9 (power to call for documents and search records) is amended as follows.
  (2) In subsection (1)—
    (a) for "The Commissioners" substitute "The Commission",
    (b) for "furnish them" (in both places) substitute "furnish the Commission",
    (c) for "their functions" (in both places) substitute "the Commission's functions", and
    (d) for "them for their" substitute "the Commission for its".
  (3) In subsection (2)—
    (a) for "officer of the Commissioners, if so authorised by them" substitute "member of the staff of the Commission, if so authorised by it", and
    (b) for "the Commissioners" (in the second place) substitute "the Commission".
  (4) In subsection (3)—
    (a) for "The Commissioners" substitute "The Commission",
    (b) for "to them" (in the first place) substitute "to it",
    (c) for "to them" (in the second place) substitute "to the Commission",
    (d) for "their inspection" substitute "it to inspect", and
    (e) for "the Commissioners" substitute "the Commission".
  (5) After subsection (5) add—

"(6) In subsection (2) the reference to a member of the staff of the Commission includes the official custodian even if he is not a member of the staff of the Commission."

104. For section 10 substitute—

"10 Disclosure of information to Commission

(1) Any relevant public authority may disclose information to the Commission if the disclosure is made for the purpose of enabling or assisting the Commission to discharge any of its functions.

(2) But Revenue and Customs information may be disclosed under subsection (1) only if it relates to an institution, undertaking or body falling within one (or more) of the following paragraphs—

(a) a charity;

(b) an institution which is established for charitable, benevolent or philanthropic purposes;

(c) an institution by or in respect of which a claim for exemption has at any time been made under section 505(1) of the Income and Corporation Taxes Act 1988;

(d) a subsidiary undertaking of a charity;

(e) a body entered in the Scottish Charity Register which is managed or controlled wholly or mainly in or from England or Wales.

(3) In subsection (2)(d) above 'subsidiary undertaking of a charity' means an undertaking (as defined by section 259(1) of the Companies Act 1985) in relation to which—

(a) a charity is (or is to be treated as) a parent undertaking in accordance with the provisions of section 258 of, and Schedule 10A to, the Companies Act 1985, or

(b) two or more charities would, if they were a single charity, be (or be treated as) a parent undertaking in accordance with those provisions.

(4) For the purposes of the references to a parent undertaking—

(a) in subsection (3) above, and

(b) in section 258 of, and Schedule 10A to, the Companies Act 1985 as they apply for the purposes of that subsection,

'undertaking' includes a charity which is not an undertaking as defined by section 259(1) of that Act.

10A Disclosure of information by Commission

(1) Subject to subsections (2) and (3) below, the Commission may disclose to any relevant public authority any information received by the Commission in connection with any of the Commission's functions—

(a) if the disclosure is made for the purpose of enabling or assisting the relevant public authority to discharge any of its functions, or

(b) if the information so disclosed is otherwise relevant to the discharge of any of the functions of the relevant public authority.

(2) In the case of information disclosed to the Commission under section 10(1) above, the Commission's power to disclose the information under subsection (1) above is exercisable subject to any express restriction subject to which the information was disclosed to the Commission.

(3) Subsection (2) above does not apply in relation to Revenue and Customs information disclosed to the Commission under section 10(1) above; but any such information may not be further disclosed (whether under subsection (1) above or otherwise) except with the consent of the Commissioners for Her Majesty's Revenue and Customs.

(4) Any responsible person who discloses information in contravention of subsection (3) above is guilty of an offence and liable—

(a) on summary conviction, to imprisonment for a term not exceeding 12 months or to a fine not exceeding the statutory maximum, or both;

(b) on conviction on indictment, to imprisonment for a term not exceeding two years or to a fine, or both.

(5) It is a defence for a responsible person charged with an offence under subsection (4) above of disclosing information to prove that he reasonably believed—

(a) that the disclosure was lawful, or

(b) that the information had already and lawfully been made available to the public.

(6) In the application of this section to Scotland or Northern Ireland, the reference to 12 months in subsection (4) is to be read as a reference to 6 months.

(7) In this section 'responsible person' means a person who is or was—

(a) a member of the Commission,

(b) a member of the staff of the Commission,

(c) a person acting on behalf of the Commission or a member of the staff of the Commission, or

(d) a member of a committee established by the Commission.

10B Disclosure to and by principal regulators of exempt charities

(1) Sections 10 and 10A above apply with the modifications in subsections (2) to (4) below in relation to the disclosure of information to or by the principal regulator of an exempt charity.

(2) References in those sections to the Commission or to any of its functions are to be read as references to the principal regulator of an exempt charity or to any of the functions of that body or person as principal regulator in relation to the charity.

(3) Section 10 above has effect as if for subsections (2) and (3) there were substituted—

'(2) But Revenue and Customs information may be disclosed under subsection (1) only if it relates to—

(a) the exempt charity in relation to which the principal regulator has functions as such, or

(b) a subsidiary undertaking of the exempt charity.

(3) In subsection (2)(b) above "subsidiary undertaking of the exempt charity" means an undertaking (as defined by section 259(1) of the Companies Act 1985) in relation to which—

(a) the exempt charity is (or is to be treated as) a parent undertaking in accordance with the provisions of section 258 of, and Schedule 10A to, the Companies Act 1985, or

(b) the exempt charity and one or more other charities would, if they were a single charity, be (or be treated as) a parent undertaking in accordance with those provisions.'

(4) Section 10A above has effect as if for the definition of 'responsible person' in subsection (7) there were substituted a definition specified by regulations under section 13(4)(b) of the Charities Act 2006 (regulations prescribing principal regulators).

(5) Regulations under section 13(4)(b) of that Act may also make such amendments or other modifications of any enactment as the Secretary of State considers appropriate for securing that any disclosure provisions that would otherwise apply in relation to the principal regulator of an exempt charity do not apply in relation to that body or person in its or his capacity as principal regulator.

(6) In subsection (5) above 'disclosure provisions' means provisions having effect for authorising, or otherwise in connection with, the disclosure of information by or to the principal regulator concerned.

10C Disclosure of information: supplementary

(1) In sections 10 and 10A above 'relevant public authority' means—

(a) any government department (including a Northern Ireland department),

(b) any local authority,

(c) any constable, and

(d) any other body or person discharging functions of a public nature (including a body or person discharging regulatory functions in relation to any description of activities).

(2) In section 10A above 'relevant public authority' also includes any body or person within subsection (1)(d) above in a country or territory outside the United Kingdom.

(3) In sections 10 to 10B above and this section—

'enactment' has the same meaning as in the Charities Act 2006;

'Revenue and Customs information' means information held as mentioned in section 18(1) of the Commissioners for Revenue and Customs Act 2005.

(4) Nothing in sections 10 and 10A above (or in those sections as applied by section 10B(1) to (4) above) authorises the making of a disclosure which—

(a) contravenes the Data Protection Act 1998, or

(b) is prohibited by Part 1 of the Regulation of Investigatory Powers Act 2000."

105. (1) Section 11 (supply of false or misleading information) is amended as follows.

(2) For "Commissioners" (in each place including the sidenote) substitute "Commission".

(3) In subsection (1)(b) for "their functions" substitute "its functions".

106. In the heading for Part 4 for "AND COMMISSIONERS" substitute "AND COMMISSION".

107. (1) Section 14 (application cy-près of gifts of donors unknown or disclaiming) is amended as follows.

(2) In subsection (6) for "the Commissioners so direct" substitute "the Commission so directs".

(3) In subsection (8) for "the Commissioners" substitute "the Commission".

(4) In subsection (9)—

(a) for "the Commissioners" (in both places) substitute "the Commission", and

(b) for "they think fit" substitute "it thinks fit".

108. In the heading preceding section 16 for "*Powers of Commissioners*" substitute "*Powers of Commission*".

109. (1) Section 16 (concurrent jurisdiction of Commissioners with High Court) is amended as follows.

(2) In subsection (1) for "the Commissioners" substitute "the Commission".

(3) In subsection (2)—
(a) for "the Commissioners for them" substitute "the Commission for it", and
(b) for "the Commissioners" (in the second place) substitute "the Commission".

(4) In subsection (3) for "The Commissioners" substitute "The Commission".

(5) In subsection (4) for "the Commissioners shall not exercise their" substitute "the Commission shall not exercise its".

(6) In subsection (5)—
(a) for "income from all sources does not in aggregate" substitute "gross income does not", and
(b) for "the Commissioners may exercise their" substitute "the Commission may exercise its".

(7) In subsection (6)—
(a) for "the Commissioners are" substitute "the Commission is",
(b) for "the Commissioners have" substitute "the Commission has",
(c) for "the Commissioners" (in the third and fourth places) substitute "the Commission", and
(d) for "they act" substitute "it acts".

(8) In subsection (7)—
(a) for "the Commissioners" (in the first and third places) substitute "the Commission", and
(b) for "the Commissioners consider" substitute "the Commission considers".

(9) In subsection (8)—
(a) for "The Commissioners" substitute "The Commission", and
(b) for "their jurisdiction" substitute "its jurisdiction".

(10) In subsection (9) for "the Commissioners shall give notice of their" substitute "the Commission shall give notice of its".

(11) In subsection (10)—
(a) for "The Commissioners shall not exercise their" substitute "The Commission shall not exercise its", and
(b) for "the Commissioners" (in the second place) substitute "the Commission".

(12) Omit subsections (11) to (14).

(13) In subsection (15)(b) for "the Commissioners may exercise their" substitute "the Commission may exercise its".

110. (1) Section 17 (further power to make schemes or alter application of charitable property) is amended as follows.

(2) In subsection (1)—
(a) for "the Commissioners" (in both places) substitute "the Commission", and
(b) for "by them" substitute "by the Commission".

(3) In subsection (2) for "the Commissioners" substitute "the Commission".

(4) In subsection (4) for "the Commissioners" (in both places) substitute "the Commission".

(5) In subsection (6)—
(a) for "Commissioners" (in both places) substitute "Commission",
(b) for "if they were" substitute "if the Commission was",

(c) for "they act" substitute "it acts", and

(d) for "to them" substitute "to it".

(6) In subsection (7) for "the Commissioners" substitute "the Commission".

(7) In subsection (8)—

(a) for "the Commissioners are" substitute "the Commission is", and

(b) for "the Commissioners" (in the second place) substitute "the Commission".

111. (1) Section 18 (power to act for protection of charities) is amended as follows.

(2) In subsection (1)—

(a) for "after they have" substitute "after it has",

(b) for "the Commissioners are" substitute "the Commission is",

(c) for "the Commissioners may of their" substitute "the Commission may of its",

(d) for "as they consider" substitute "as it considers",

(e) for "the Commissioners" (in the third, fourth and fifth places) substitute "the Commission", and

(f) for "a receiver" substitute "an interim manager, who shall act as receiver".

(3) In subsection (2)—

(a) for "they have" substitute "it has",

(b) for "the Commissioners are" substitute "the Commission is", and

(c) for "the Commissioners may of their" substitute "the Commission may of its".

(4) In subsection (4)—

(a) for "The Commissioners" substitute "The Commission", and

(b) for "their own motion" substitute "its own motion".

(5) In subsection (5)—

(a) for "The Commissioners may by order made of their" substitute "The Commission may by order made of its",

(b) for "removed by them" substitute "removed by the Commission", and

(c) for "the Commissioners are of" (in both places) substitute "the Commission is of".

(6) In subsection (6)—

(a) for "the Commissioners" (in both places) substitute "the Commission",

(b) for "their own motion" substitute "its own motion", and

(c) for "by them" substitute "by it".

(7) Omit subsections (8) to (10).

(8) In subsection (11) for "the Commissioners" substitute "the Commission".

(9) In subsection (12)—

(a) for "the Commissioners" substitute "the Commission", and

(b) for "their intention" substitute "its intention".

(10) In subsection (13)—

(a) for "The Commissioners" substitute "The Commission",

(b) for "they think fit" substitute "it thinks fit",

(c) for "by them" substitute "by it",

(d) for "to them" substitute "to the Commission", and

(e) for "they shall" substitute "the Commission shall".

112. (1) Section 19 (supplementary provisions relating to receiver and manager appointed for a charity) is amended as follows.

(2) For subsection (1) substitute—

"(1) The Commission may under section 18(1)(vii) above appoint to be interim manager in respect of a charity such person (other than a member of its staff) as it thinks fit."

(3) In subsection (2)—
     (a) for "the Commissioners" (in both places) substitute "the Commission", and
     (b) for "receiver and manager" substitute "interim manager".

(4) In subsection (3) for "receiver and manager" (in both places) substitute "interim manager".

(5) In subsection (4)—
     (a) for "receiver and manager" substitute "interim manager", and
     (b) for "the Commissioners" substitute "the Commission".

(6) In subsections (6)(c) and (7) for "the Commissioners" substitute "the Commission".

(7) In the sidenote for "receiver and manager" substitute "interim manager".

113. After section 19B (inserted by section 21 of this Act) insert—

"**19C Copy of order under section 18, 18A, 19A or 19B, and Commission's reasons, to be sent to charity**

(1) Where the Commission makes an order under section 18, 18A, 19A or 19B, it must send the documents mentioned in subsection (2) below—
     (a) to the charity concerned (if a body corporate), or
     (b) (if not) to each of the charity trustees.

(2) The documents are—
     (a) a copy of the order, and
     (b) a statement of the Commission's reasons for making it.

(3) The documents must be sent to the charity or charity trustees as soon as practicable after the making of the order.

(4) The Commission need not, however, comply with subsection (3) above in relation to the documents, or (as the case may be) the statement of its reasons, if it considers that to do so—
     (a) would prejudice any inquiry or investigation, or
     (b) would not be in the interests of the charity;
     but, once the Commission considers that this is no longer the case, it must send the documents, or (as the case may be) the statement, to the charity or charity trustees as soon as practicable.

(5) Nothing in this section requires any document to be sent to a person who cannot be found or who has no known address in the United Kingdom.

(6) Any documents required to be sent to a person under this section may be sent to, or otherwise served on, that person in the same way as an order made by the Commission under this Act could be served on him in accordance with section 91 below."

114. In section 22(3) (property vested in official custodian) for "the Commissioners" substitute "the Commission".

115. (1) Section 23 (divestment in case of land subject to Reverter of Sites Act 1987 (c. 15)) is amended as follows.

    (2) In subsection (1)—
        (a) for "the Commissioners" (in both places) substitute "the Commission",
        (b) for "by them of their own" substitute "by the Commission of its own", and
        (c) for "appear to them" substitute "appear to the Commission".

    (3) In subsection (2)—

        (a) for "the Commissioners (of their own motion)" substitute "the Commission (of its own motion)", and

        (b) omit "or them".

    (4) In subsection (3)—

        (a) for "the Commissioners" (in the first and second places) substitute "the Commission", and

        (b) for "the Commissioners is or are" substitute "the Commission is".

116. In section 24 (schemes to establish common investment funds), in subsections (1) and (2), for "the Commissioners" substitute "the Commission".

117. In section 25(1) (schemes to establish common deposit funds) for "the Commissioners" substitute "the Commission".

118. For the heading preceding section 26 substitute "*Additional powers of Commission*".

119. In section 26(1) (power to authorise dealings with charity property)—

    (a) for "the Commissioners" substitute "the Commission", and

    (b) for "they may" substitute "the Commission may".

120. (1) Section 27 (power to authorise ex gratia payments) is amended as follows.

    (2) In subsection (1) for "the Commissioners" substitute "the Commission".

    (3) In subsection (2)—

        (a) for "the Commissioners" (in both places) substitute "the Commission", and

        (b) for "by them" substitute "by the Commission".

    (4) In subsection (3)—

        (a) for "the Commissioners for them" substitute "the Commission for it",

        (b) for "they are not" substitute "it is not",

        (c) for "they consider" substitute "the Commission considers",

        (d) for "by them" substitute "by the Commission", and

        (e) for "they shall" substitute "the Commission shall".

    (5) In subsection (4)—

        (a) for "to them" substitute "to the Commission", and

        (b) for "the Commissioners determine" substitute "the Commission determines".

121. (1) Section 28 (power to give directions about dormant bank accounts) is amended as follows.

    (2) In subsection (1)—

        (a) for "the Commissioners" substitute "the Commission",

        (b) for "are informed" substitute "is informed",

        (c) for "are unable" substitute "is unable", and

        (d) for "they may give" substitute "it may give".

    (3) In subsection (3)—

        (a) for "Commissioners" (in both places) substitute "Commission",

        (b) for "they consider" substitute "it considers",

        (c) for "to them" substitute "to the Commission", and

        (d) for "they have received" substitute "it has received".

    (4) In subsection (5)—

        (a) for "the Commissioners have been" substitute "the Commission has been",

        (b) for "the Commissioners" (in the second and third places) substitute "the Commission",

        (c) for "they shall revoke" substitute "it shall revoke", and

(d) for "by them" substitute "by it".
(5) In subsection (7)—
(a) for "the Commissioners" substitute "the Commission", and
(b) for "them to discharge their functions" substitute "the Commission to discharge its functions".
(6) In subsection (8)(a) for "the Commissioners are informed" substitute "the Commission is informed".
(7) In subsection (9)—
(a) for "the Commissioners have" substitute "the Commission has", and
(b) for "the Commissioners" (in the second place) substitute "the Commission".
122. (1) Section 30 (powers for preservation of charity documents) is amended as follows.
(2) In subsection (1) for "The Commissioners" substitute "The Commission".
(3) In subsection (2) for "Commissioners" (in each place) substitute "Commission".
(4) In subsection (3)—
(a) for "the Commissioners" (in the first place) substitute "the Commission",
(b) for "with them" substitute "with the Commission",
(c) for "officer of the Commissioners generally or specially authorised by them" substitute "member of the staff of the Commission generally or specially authorised by the Commission".
(5) In subsection (4) for "the Commissioners" substitute "the Commission".
(6) In subsection (5)—
(a) for "the Commissioners" substitute "the Commission",
(b) for "by them" substitute "by the Commission", and
(c) for "with them" substitute "with the Commission".
123. (1) Section 31 (power to order taxation of solicitor's bill) is amended as follows.
(2) In subsection (1) for "The Commissioners" substitute "The Commission".
(3) In subsection (3) for "the Commissioners are" substitute "the Commission is".
124. (1) Section 32 (proceedings by Commissioners) is amended as follows.
(2) In subsections (1) and (3) for "the Commissioners" substitute "the Commission".
(3) In subsection (5)—
(a) for "the Commissioners" substitute "the Commission", and
(b) for "by them of their own" substitute "by the Commission of its own".
(4) In the sidenote, for "Commissioners" substitute "Commission".
125. (1) Section 33 (proceedings by other persons) is amended as follows.
(2) In subsection (2) for "the Commissioners" substitute "the Commission".
(3) In subsection (3)—
(a) for "The Commissioners" substitute "The Commission",
(b) for "their opinion" substitute "its opinion", and
(c) for "by them" substitute "by the Commission".
(4) In subsections (5) and (6) for "the Commissioners" substitute "the Commission".
(5) In subsection (7)—
(a) for "the Commissioners" (in both places) substitute "the Commission", and
(b) for "they think" substitute "the Commission thinks".
126. In section 34 (report of inquiry to be evidence in certain proceedings), in subsections (1) and (2), for "the Commissioners" substitute "the Commission".
127. In section 35(1) (application of certain provisions to trust corporations) for "the Commissioners" substitute "the Commission".

128. (1) Section 36 (restrictions on dispositions) is amended as follows.
    (2) In subsection (1)—
        (a) for "sold" substitute "conveyed, transferred", and
        (b) for "the Commissioners" substitute "the Commission".
    (3) In subsection (3) after "subsection (5) below," insert "the requirements mentioned in subsection (2)(b) above are that".
    (4) In subsection (5) after "consideration of a fine)," insert "the requirements mentioned in subsection (2)(b) above are that".
    (5) In subsection (6)—
        (a) for "sold" substitute "conveyed, transferred", and
        (b) for "previously" substitute "before the relevant time".
    (6) After subsection (6) insert—
        "(6A) In subsection (6) above "the relevant time" means—

            (a) where the charity trustees enter into an agreement for the sale, or (as the case may be) for the lease or other disposition, the time when they enter into that agreement, and

            (b) in any other case, the time of the disposition."

    (7) In subsection (8)—
        (a) for "The Commissioners" substitute "The Commission",
        (b) for "the Commissioners are satisfied" substitute "the Commission is satisfied", and
        (c) for "for them" substitute "for the Commission".

129. In section 37 (supplementary provisions relating to dispositions), in subsections (2) and (4)—
    (a) for "sold" substitute "conveyed, transferred", and
    (b) for "the Commissioners" substitute "the Commission".

130. In section 38(1) (restrictions on mortgaging) for "the Commissioners" substitute "the Commission".

131. (1) Section 39 (supplementary provisions relating to mortgaging) is amended as follows.
    (2) In subsections (2)(a) and (4) for "the Commissioners" substitute "the Commission".
    (3) After subsection (4) insert—

        "(4A) Where subsection (3D) of section 38 above applies to any mortgage of land held by or in trust for a charity, the charity trustees shall certify in relation to any transaction falling within that subsection that they have obtained and considered such advice as is mentioned in that subsection.

        (4B) Where subsection (4A) above has been complied with in relation to any transaction, then, in favour of a person who (whether under the mortgage or afterwards) has acquired or acquires an interest in the land for money or money's worth, it shall be conclusively presumed that the facts were as stated in the certificate."

132. In section 41(4) (obligation to preserve accounting records) for "the Commissioners consent" substitute "the Commission consents".

133. (1) Section 42 (annual statements of accounts) is amended as follows.

(2) After subsection (2) insert—

"(2A) Such regulations may, however, not impose on the charity trustees of a charity that is a charitable trust created by any person ('the settlor') any requirement to disclose, in any statement of accounts prepared by them under subsection (1)—

(a) the identities of recipients of grants made out of the funds of the charity, or

(b) the amounts of any individual grants so made,

if the disclosure would fall to be made at a time when the settlor or any spouse or civil partner of his was still alive."

(3) After subsection (7) add—

"(8) Provisions about the preparation of accounts in respect of groups consisting of certain charities and their subsidiary undertakings, and about other matters relating to such groups, are contained in Schedule 5A to this Act (see section 49A below)."

134. (1) Section 43 (annual audit or examination of charity accounts) is amended as follows.

(2) In subsection (4) for "the Commissioners" (in both places) substitute "the Commission".

(3) In subsection (5)—

(a) for "the Commissioners make" substitute "the Commission makes", and

(b) for "the Commissioners" (in the second place) substitute "the Commission".

(4) In subsection (6) for "the Commissioners" (in each place) substitute "the Commission".

(5) In subsection (7)—

(a) for "The Commissioners" substitute "The Commission", and

(b) for "they think" substitute "it thinks".

135. (1) Section 43A (annual audit or examination of English NHS charity accounts) is amended as follows.

(2) In subsection (2) for "the criterion set out in subsection (1) of section 43 is met in respect of" substitute "paragraph (a) or (b) of section 43(1) is satisfied in relation to".

(3) In subsection (5)—

(a) for "The Commissioners" substitute "The Commission", and

(b) for "they think" substitute "it thinks".

136. (1) Section 43B (annual audit or examination of Welsh NHS charity accounts) is amended as follows.

(2) In subsection (2) for "the criterion set out in subsection (1) of section 43 is met in respect of" substitute "paragraph (a) or (b) of section 43(1) is satisfied in relation to".

(3) After subsection (4) add—

"(5) References in this Act to an auditor or an examiner have effect in relation to this section as references to the Auditor General for Wales acting under this section as an auditor or examiner."

137. (1) Section 44 (supplementary provisions relating to audits) is amended as follows.

(2) In subsection (1)—

(a) in paragraph (b) after "section 43" insert ", 43A or 43B",

(b) for paragraph (c) substitute—

"(c) with respect to the making of a report—

    (i) by an independent examiner in respect of an examination carried out by him under section 43 above; or

    (ii) by an examiner in respect of an examination carried out by him under section 43A or 43B above;"

(c) in each of paragraphs (d) and (e) after "independent examiner" insert "or examiner", and

(d) in paragraph (f) for "the Commissioners" substitute "the Commission".

(3) In subsection (2)—

    (a) after "independent examiner" insert "or examiner",

    (b) for "the Commissioners" (in the first place) substitute "the Commission", and

    (c) for "the Commissioners think" substitute "the Commission thinks".

(4) Omit subsection (3).

138. (1) Section 45 (annual reports) is amended as follows.

(2) In subsection (2)(b) for "the Commissioners" substitute "the Commission".

(3) In subsection (3)—

    (a) for the words from "in any" to "expenditure" substitute "a charity's gross income in any financial year",

    (b) before "the annual report" insert "a copy of", and

    (c) for "the Commissioners" (in both places) substitute "the Commission".

(4) In subsection (3A)—

    (a) for the words from "in any" to "exceeds" substitute "a charity's gross income in any financial year does not exceed",

    (b) before "the annual report" insert "a copy of",

    (c) for "the Commissioners so request, be transmitted to them" substitute "the Commission so requests, be transmitted to it", and

    (d) for "the Commissioners" (in the second place) substitute "the Commission".

(5) In subsection (4)—

    (a) for "annual report transmitted to the Commissioners" substitute "copy of an annual report transmitted to the Commission", and

    (b) before "the statement", and before "the account and statement", insert "a copy of".

(6) In subsection (5) before "annual report" insert "copy of an".

(7) In subsection (6)—

    (a) after "Any" insert "copy of an",

    (b) for "the Commissioners" (in both places) substitute "the Commission", and

    (c) for "they think fit" substitute "it thinks fit".

(8) In subsection (7) for the words from "which they have not" onwards substitute "of which they have not been required to transmit a copy to the Commission."

(9) In subsection (8) for "in subsection (3)" substitute "to subsection (3)".

139. (1) Section 46 (special provisions as respects accounts etc. of excepted charities) is amended as follows.

(2) In subsection (2) for "the Commissioners consent" substitute "the Commission consents".

(3) For subsection (3) substitute—

"(3) Except in accordance with subsections (3A) and (3B) below, nothing in section 43, 44, 44A or 45 applies to any charity which—

    (a) falls within section 3A(2)(d) above (whether or not it also falls within section 3A(2)(b) or (c)), and

    (b) is not registered.

(3A) Section 44A above applies in accordance with subsections (2A) and (2B) above to a charity mentioned in subsection (3) above which is also an exempt charity.

(3B) Sections 44 and 44A above apply to a charity mentioned in subsection (3) above which is also an English National Health Service charity or a Welsh National Health Service charity (as defined in sections 43A and 43B above)."

   (4) In subsection (4) for the words from "(other than" onwards substitute "which—

    (a) falls within section 3A(2)(b) or (c) above but does not fall within section 3A(2)(d), and

    (b) is not registered."

   (5) In subsection (5)—

    (a) for "the Commissioners" (in the first place) substitute "the Commission", and

    (b) for "the Commissioners' request" substitute "the Commission's request".

   (6) For subsection (7) substitute—

"(7) The following provisions of section 45 above shall apply in relation to any report required to be prepared under subsection (5) above as if it were an annual report required to be prepared under subsection (1) of that section—

    (a) subsection (3), with the omission of the words preceding "a copy of the annual report", and

    (b) subsections (4) to (6)."

   (7) Omit subsection (8).

140. (1) Section 47 (public inspection of annual reports etc.) is amended as follows.

   (2) In subsection (1)—

    (a) for "Any annual report or other document kept by the Commissioners" substitute "Any document kept by the Commission",

    (b) for "the Commissioners so determine" substitute "the Commission so determines", and

    (c) for "they may" substitute "it may".

   (3) In subsection (2)(a) after "accounts" insert "or (if subsection (4) below applies) of its most recent annual report".

   (4) After subsection (3) add—

"(4) This subsection applies if an annual report has been prepared in respect of any financial year of a charity in pursuance of section 45(1) or 46(5) above.

   (5) In subsection (2) above the reference to a charity's most recent annual report is a reference to the annual report prepared in pursuance of section 45(1) or 46(5) in respect of the last financial year of the charity in respect of which an annual report has been so prepared."

141. (1) Section 48 (annual returns by registered charities) is amended as follows.

   (2) In subsection (1) for "the Commissioners" substitute "the Commission".

   (3) In subsection (1A) for the words from "neither" to "exceeds" substitute "the charity's gross income does not exceed".

   (4) In subsection (2)—

    (a) for "the Commissioners" substitute "the Commission", and

(b) for "to them" substitute "to the Commission".

(5) In subsection (3) for "The Commissioners" substitute "The Commission".

142. For section 49 (offences) substitute—

"49 **Offences**

(1) If any requirement imposed—

    (a) by section 45(3) or (3A) above (taken with section 45(3B), (4) and (5), as applicable), or

    (b) by section 47(2) or 48(2) above,

is not complied with, each person who immediately before the date for compliance specified in the section in question was a charity trustee of the charity shall be guilty of an offence and liable on summary conviction to the penalty mentioned in subsection (2).

(2) The penalty is—

    (a) a fine not exceeding level 4 on the standard scale, and

    (b) for continued contravention, a daily default fine not exceeding 10% of level 4 on the standard scale for so long as the person in question remains a charity trustee of the charity.

(3) It is a defence for a person charged with an offence under subsection (1) to prove that he took all reasonable steps for securing that the requirement in question would be complied with in time."

143. (1) Section 50 (incorporation of trustees of charity) is amended as follows.

(2) In subsection (1)—

    (a) for "the Commissioners" (in the first and third places) substitute "the Commission",

    (b) for "the Commissioners consider" substitute "the Commission considers", and

    (c) for "they think fit" substitute "the Commission thinks fit".

(3) In subsection (2)—

    (a) for "The Commissioners" substitute "The Commission",

    (b) for "to them" substitute "to the Commission", and

    (c) for "under section 3" substitute "in accordance with section 3A".

144. (1) Section 52 (applications for incorporation) is amended as follows.

(2) In subsection (1) for "the Commissioners" (in both places) substitute "the Commission".

(3) In subsection (2)—

    (a) for "The Commissioners" substitute "The Commission", and

    (b) for "they may specify" substitute "it may specify".

145. In section 53(1) (nomination of trustees, and filling up vacancies) for "the Commissioners" substitute "the Commission".

146. (1) Section 56 (power of Commissioners to amend certificate of incorporation) is amended as follows.

(2) In subsection (1)—

    (a) for "The Commissioners" substitute "The Commission", and

    (b) for "of their own motion" substitute "of the Commission's own motion".

(3) In subsection (2)—

    (a) for "of their own motion, the Commissioners" substitute "of its own motion, the Commission",

    (b) for "their proposals" substitute "its proposals", and
    (c) for "to them" substitute "to it".
(4) In subsection (3)—
    (a) for "The Commissioners" substitute "The Commission",
    (b) for "their proposals" substitute "its proposals", and
    (c) for "to them" substitute "to it".
(5) In subsection (4) for "The Commissioners" substitute "The Commission".
(6) In the sidenote, for "Commissioners" substitute "Commission".

147. (1) Section 57 (records of applications and certificates) is amended as follows.
(2) In subsection (1)—
    (a) for "The Commissioners" substitute "The Commission", and
    (b) for "to them" substitute "to it".
(3) In subsection (2)—
    (a) for "the Commissioners" (in the first place) substitute "the Commission", and
    (b) for "the secretary of the Commissioners" substitute "a member of the staff of the Commission".

148. In section 58 (enforcement of orders and directions) for "the Commissioners" substitute "the Commission".

149. (1) Section 61 (power of Commissioners to dissolve incorporated body) is amended as follows.
(2) In subsection (1)—
    (a) for "the Commissioners are" substitute "the Commission is",
    (b) for "treated by them" substituted "treated by the Commission", and
    (c) for "they may of their own motion" substitute "the Commission may of its own motion".
(3) In subsection (2)—
    (a) for "the Commissioners are" substitute "the Commission is", and
    (b) for "the Commissioners" (in the second place) substitute "the Commission".
(4) In subsection (4)—
    (a) for "the Commissioners so direct" substitute "the Commission so directs", and
    (b) for "the Commissioners" (in the second place) substitute "the Commission".
(5) Omit subsection (7).
(6) In the sidenote, for "Commissioners" substitute "Commission".

150. (1) Section 63 (winding up) is amended as follows.
(2) In subsection (2)—
    (a) for "the Commissioners" substitute "the Commission",
    (b) for "they have instituted" substitute "it has instituted", and
    (c) for "they are satisfied" substitute "it is satisfied".
(3) In subsection (3) for "the Commissioners" (in both places) substitute "the Commission".
(4) In subsection (4) for "the Commissioners" (in both places) substitute "the Commission".
(5) In subsection (5)—
    (a) for "the Commissioners" substitute "the Commission", and
    (b) for "by them of their own motion" substitute "by the Commission of its own motion".

151. In section 64(3) (alteration of objects clause) for "the Commissioner's consent" substitute "the Commission's consent".
152. In section 65(4) (invalidity of certain transactions) for "the Commissioners" substitute "the Commission".
153. In section 66 (requirement of consent of Commissioners to certain acts), in subsection (1) and the sidenote, for "Commissioners" substitute "Commission".
154. (1) Section 69 (investigation of accounts) is amended as follows.
    (2) In subsection (1)—
        (a) for "the Commissioners" substitute "the Commission",
        (b) for "they think fit" substitute "the Commission thinks fit", and
        (c) for "by them" substitute "by the Commission".
    (3) In subsections (2)(c) and (3) for "the Commissioners" substitute "the Commission".
    (4) In subsection (4)—
        (a) for "the Commissioners" (in the first place) substitute "the Commission", and
        (b) for "the Commissioners think" substitute "the Commission thinks".
155. For the heading preceding section 72 substitute "*Charity trustees*".
156. (1) Section 72 (persons disqualified for being trustees of a charity) is amended as follows.
    (2) In subsection (1)(d)(i) after "by the" insert "Commission or".
    (3) In subsection (4) for "The Commissioners" substitute "The Commission".
    (4) In subsection (6)—
        (a) for "the Commissioners" (in the first place) substitute "the Commission",
        (b) for "they think fit" substitute "it thinks fit",
        (c) after "order of" insert "the Commission or", and
        (d) for "the Commissioners" (in the third place) substitute "the Commission".
    (5) After subsection (7) add—
        "(8) In this section "the Commissioners" means the Charity Commissioners for England and Wales."
157. In section 73(4) (person acting as charity trustee while disqualified)—
        (a) for "the Commissioners are" substitute "the Commission is",
        (b) for "they may by order" substitute "the Commission may by order", and
        (c) for "(as determined by them)" substitute "(as determined by the Commission)".
158. For the heading preceding section 74 substitute "*Miscellaneous powers of charities*".
159. In section 76(2) (local authority's index of local charities)—
        (a) for "the Commissioners" (in both places) substitute "the Commission", and
        (b) for "they will" substitute "it will".
160. In section 77(1) (reviews of local charities by local authority) for "the Commissioners" substitute "the Commission".
161. (1) Section 79 (parochial charities) is amended as follows.
    (2) In subsection (1) for "the Commissioners" substitute "the Commission".
    (3) In subsection (2) for "the Commissioners" (in both places) substitute "the Commission".
162. (1) Section 80 (supervision by Commissioners of certain Scottish charities) is amended as follows.
    (2) In subsection (1) for paragraph (c) and the "and" preceding it substitute—
        "(c) sections 19 to 19C, and

(d) section 31A,".

(3) In subsection (2)—
(a) for "the Commissioners are satisfied" substitute "the Commission is satisfied",
(b) for "they may make" substitute "it may make", and
(c) for "their approval" substitute "the Commission's approval".

(4) In subsection (3)—
(a) for "the Commissioners" substitute "the Commission",
(b) for "their being" substitute "the Commission being", and
(c) for "supplied to them" substitute "supplied to it".

(5) In subsection (4)—
(a) for "the Commissioners are satisfied" substitute "the Commission is satisfied",
(b) for "supplied to them" substitute "supplied to it", and
(c) for "the Commissioners" (in the second place) substitute "the Commission".

(6) In subsection (5)—
(a) for "Commissioners" (in each place) substitute "Commission",
(b) for "they consider" substitute "it considers", and
(c) for "they have received" substitute "it has received".

(7) In the sidenote, for "Commissioners" substitute "Commission".

163. (1) Section 84 (supply by Commissioners of copies of documents open to public inspection) is amended as follows.
(2) For "The Commissioners" substitute "The Commission".
(3) For "their possession" substitute "the Commission's possession".
(4) At the end add "or section 75D".
(5) In the sidenote, for "Commissioners" substitute "Commission".

164. (1) Section 85 (fees and other amounts payable to Commissioners) is amended as follows.
(2) In subsection (1)—
(a) for "the Commissioners" (in both places) substitute "the Commission", and
(b) for "kept by them" substitute "kept by the Commission".
(3) In subsection (4)—
(a) for "The Commissioners" substitute "The Commission",
(b) for "they consider" substitute "it considers", and
(c) for "by them" substitute "by it".
(4) In subsection (5) for "the Commissioners" substitute "the Commission".
(5) In the sidenote, for "Commissioners" substitute "Commission".

165. (1) Section 86 (regulations and orders) is amended as follows.
(2) In subsection (2)(a)—
(a) after "17(2)," insert "73F(6)", and
(b) after "99(2)" insert "or paragraph 6 of Schedule 1C".
(3) In subsection (3)—
(a) for "the Commissioners" (in the first place) substitute "the Commission", and
(b) for "the Commissioners consider" substitute "the Commission considers".
(4) In subsection (4) after "above" insert "or Schedule 5A,".

166. (1) Section 87 (enforcement of requirement by order of Commissioners) is amended as follows.
(2) In subsection (1)—
(a) for "the Commissioners" substitute "the Commission", and

     (b) for "they consider" substitute "it considers".

   (3) In subsection (2) for "the Commissioners" (in both places) substitute "the Commission".

   (4) In the sidenote, for "Commissioners" substitute "Commission".

167. (1) Section 88 (enforcement of orders of Commissioners) is amended as follows.

   (2) For paragraph (a) substitute—

     "(a) to an order of the Commission under section 9(1), 19A, 19B, 44(2), 61, 73, 73C or 80 above; or".

   (3) In paragraphs (b) and (c) for "the Commissioners" substitute "the Commission".

   (4) For "the Commissioners to" substitute "the Commission to".

   (5) In the sidenote, for "Commissioners" substitute "Commission".

168. (1) Section 89 (other provisions as to orders of Commissioners) is amended as follows.

   (2) In subsection (1)—

     (a) for "the Commissioners" (in the first place) substitute "the Commission",

     (b) for "the Commissioners think" substitute "the Commission thinks",

     (c) for "the Commissioners exercise" substitute "the Commission exercises", and

     (d) for "to them, they may" substitute "to it, it may".

   (3) In subsection (2)—

     (a) for "the Commissioners make" substitute "the Commission makes",

     (b) for "they may themselves" substitute "the Commission may itself", and

     (c) for "they think fit" substitute "it thinks fit".

   (4) In subsection (3)—

     (a) for "The Commissioners" substitute "The Commission",

     (b) for "they have" substitute "it has",

     (c) for "they are" substitute "it is", and

     (d) for "to them" substitute "to it".

   (5) In subsection (4) for "the Commissioners" substitute "the Commission".

   (6) At the end add—

     "(5) Any order made by the Commission under any provision of this Act may be varied or revoked by a subsequent order so made."

   (7) In the sidenote, for "Commissioners" substitute "Commission".

169. In section 90 (directions of the Commissioners) for "the Commissioners" (in each place including the sidenote) substitute "the Commission".

170. In section 91 (service of orders and directions), in subsections (1), (4) and (5), for "the Commissioners" (in each place) substitute "the Commission".

171. Omit section 92 (appeals from Commissioners).

172. In section 93 (miscellaneous provisions as to evidence), for subsection (3) substitute—

    "(3) Evidence of any order, certificate or other document issued by the Commission may be given by means of a copy which it retained, or which is taken from a copy so retained, and evidence of an entry in any register kept by it may be given by means of a copy of the entry, if (in each case) the copy is certified in accordance with subsection (4).

    (4) The copy shall be certified to be a true copy by any member of the staff of the Commission generally or specially authorised by the Commission to act for that purpose.

    (5) A document purporting to be such a copy shall be received in evidence without proof of the official position, authority or handwriting of the person certifying it.

(6) In subsection (3) above "the Commission" includes the Charity Commissioners for England and Wales."

173. (1) Section 96 (construction of references to a "charity" etc.) is amended as follows.

(2) In subsection (1) for the definition of "charity" substitute—

"charity" has the meaning given by section 1(1) of the Charities Act 2006;".

(3) Omit—

(a) in the definition of "exempt charity" in subsection (1), the words "(subject to section 24(8) above)", and

(b) subsection (4).

(4) In subsections (5) and (6) for "The Commissioners" substitute "The Commission".

174. In section 97(1) (interpretation)—

(a) in the definition of "charitable purposes", for "charitable according to the law of England and Wales;" substitute "charitable purposes as defined by section 2(1) of the Charities Act 2006;";

(b) for the definition of "the Commissioners" substitute—

"'the Commission' means the Charity Commission;";

(c) in the definition of "institution", after "'institution'" insert "means an institution whether incorporated or not, and"; and

(d) at the appropriate place insert—

"'members', in relation to a charity with a body of members distinct from the charity trustees, means any of those members;"

"'the Minister' means the Minister for the Cabinet Office;"

"'principal regulator', in relation to an exempt charity, means the charity's principal regulator within the meaning of section 13 of the Charities Act 2006;"

"'the Tribunal' means the Charity Tribunal;".

175. In section 97(3) (general interpretation) for "Part IV or IX" substitute "Part 4, 7, 8A or 9".

176. In section 100(3) (extent) for "Section 10" substitute "Sections 10 to 10C".

177. In paragraph (a) of Schedule 2 (exempt charities) for "the Commissioners" (in the first place) substitute "the Charity Commissioners for England and Wales".

178. (1) Schedule 5 (meaning of "connected person" for the purposes of section 36(2)) is amended as follows.

(2) In paragraph 1 for the words preceding paragraphs (a) to (g) substitute—

"(1) In section 36(2) of this Act 'connected person', in relation to a charity, means any person who falls within sub-paragraph (2)—

(a) at the time of the disposition in question, or

(b) at the time of any contract for the disposition in question.

(2) The persons falling within this sub-paragraph are—".

(3) Paragraphs (a) to (g) of paragraph 1 become paragraphs (a) to (g) of sub-paragraph (2) (as inserted by sub-paragraph (2) above).

(4) After paragraph (e) of sub-paragraph (2) (as so inserted) insert—

"(ea) a person carrying on business in partnership with any person falling within any of sub-paragraphs (a) to (e) above;";

and in paragraph (f)(i) of that sub-paragraph, for "(e)" substitute "(ea)".

(5) In paragraph 2—

(a) in sub-paragraph (1), for "1(c)" substitute "1(2)(c)",

(b) in sub-paragraph (2), for "1(e)" substitute "1(2)(e)", and

(c) after that sub-paragraph add—

"(3) Where two persons of the same sex are not civil partners but live together as if they were, each of them shall be treated for those purposes as the civil partner of the other."

(6) In paragraph 3 for "1(f)" substitute "1(2)(f)".

(7) In paragraph 4(1) for "1(g)" substitute "1(2)(g)".

Deregulation and Contracting Out Act 1994 (c. 40)

179. (1) Section 79 of the Deregulation and Contracting Out Act 1994 (interpretation of Part 2) is amended as follows.

(2) For subsection (3)(a) substitute—

"(a) any reference to a Minister included a reference to the Forestry Commissioners or to the Charity Commission;

(b) any reference to an officer in relation to the Charity Commission were a reference to a member or member of staff of the Commission; and."

(3) In subsection (4) after "those Commissioners" insert "or that Commission".

Pensions Act 1995 (c. 26)

180. In section 107(1) of the Pensions Act 1995 (disclosure for facilitating discharge of functions by other supervisory authorities), for the entry in the Table relating to the Charity Commissioners substitute—

"The Charity Commission.	Functions under the Charities Act 1993 or the Charities Act 2006."

Reserve Forces Act 1996 (c. 14)

181. (1) Schedule 5 to the Reserve Forces Act 1996 (charitable property on disbanding of units) is amended as follows.

(2) In paragraph 1(2) for "the Charity Commissioners" substitute "the Charity Commission".

(3) In paragraph 4(1)—

(a) for "Charity Commissioners consider" substitute "Charity Commission considers", and

(b) for "they" substitute "it".

(4) In paragraph 5(2)—

(a) for "Charity Commissioners" substitute "Charity Commission", and

(b) for "the Commissioners" (in both places) substitute "the Commission".

(5) In paragraph 6—

(a) for "Charity Commissioners" substitute "Charity Commission",

(b) for "the Commissioners" substitute "the Commission", and

(c) for "their" substitute "its".

Trusts of Land and Appointment of Trustees Act 1996 (c. 47)

182. In section 6(7) of the Trusts of Land and Appointment of Trustees Act 1996 (limitation on general powers of trustees) for "Charity Commissioners" substitute "Charity Commission".

Housing Act 1996 (c. 52)

183. The Housing Act 1996 has effect subject to the following amendments.
184. In section 3(3) (registration as social landlord) for "Charity Commissioners" substitute "Charity Commission".
185. In section 4(6) (removal from the register of social landlords) for "Charity Commissioners" substitute "Charity Commission".
186. In section 6(3) (notice of appeal against decision on removal) for "Charity Commissioners" substitute "Charity Commission".
187. In section 44(3) (consultation on proposals as to ownership and management of landlord's land) for "Charity Commissioners" substitute "Charity Commission".
188. In section 45(4) (service of copy of agreed proposals) for "Charity Commissioners" substitute "Charity Commission".
189. In section 46(2) (notice of appointment of manager to implement agreed proposals) for "Charity Commissioners" substitute "Charity Commission".
190. In section 56(2) (meaning of "the Relevant Authority") for "Charity Commissioners" substitute "Charity Commission".
191. In section 58(1)(b) (definitions relating to charities)—
    (a) for "under section 3" substitute "in accordance with section 3A", and
    (b) omit the words from "and is not" onwards.
192. (1) Schedule 1 (regulation of registered social landlords) is amended as follows.
    (2) In paragraph 6(2) (exercise of power to appoint new director or trustee) for "Charity Commissioners" substitute "Charity Commission".
    (3) In paragraph 10 (change of objects by certain charities)—
        (a) in sub-paragraphs (1) and (2) for "Charity Commissioners" (in each place) substitute "Charity Commission", and
        (b) in sub-paragraph (2) for "their" substitute "its".
    (4) In paragraph 18(4), for paragraphs (a) and (b) and the words following them substitute—
    "(a) the charity's gross income arising in connection with its housing activities exceeds the sum for the time being specified in section 43(1)(a) of the Charities Act 1993, or
    (b) the charity's gross income arising in that connection exceeds the accounts threshold and at the end of that period the aggregate value of its assets (before deduction of liabilities) in respect of its housing activities exceeds the sum for the time being specified in section 43(1)(b) of that Act;
    and in this sub-paragraph 'gross income' and 'accounts threshold' have the same meanings as in section 43 of the Charities Act 1993."
    (5) In paragraph 28(4) (notification upon exercise of certain powers in relation to registered charities) for "Charity Commissioners" substitute "Charity Commission".

School Standards and Framework Act 1998 (c. 31)

193. The School Standards and Framework Act 1998 has effect subject to the following amendments.
194. (1) Section 23 is amended as follows.
    (2) In subsection (1) (certain school bodies to be charities that are exempt charities) omit "which are exempt charities for the purposes of the Charities Act 1993".
    (3) After that subsection insert—
    "(1A) Any body to which subsection (1)(a) or (b) applies is an institution to which

section 3A(4)(b) of the Charities Act 1993 applies (institutions to be excepted from registration under that Act).''

(4) In subsection (2) (connected bodies that are to be exempt charities) for the words from "also" onwards substitute "be treated for the purposes of section 3A(4)(b) of the Charities Act 1993 as if it were an institution to which that provision applies.''

(5) In subsection (3) (status of certain foundations) for the words from "which (subject" onwards substitute ", and is an institution to which section 3A(4)(b) of the Charities Act 1993 applies.''

195. In Schedule 1 (education action forums), in paragraph 10, for the words from "which is" onwards substitute "within the meaning of the Charities Act 1993, and is an institution to which section 3A(4)(b) of that Act applies (institutions to be excepted from registration under that Act).''

Cathedrals Measure 1999 (No. 1)

196. In section 34 of the Cathedrals Measure 1999 (charities) for "Charity Commissioners" substitute "Charity Commission".

Trustee Act 2000 (c. 29)

197. In section 19(4) of the Trustee Act 2000 (guidance concerning persons who may be appointed as nominees or custodians) for "Charity Commissioners" substitute "Charity Commission".

Churchwardens Measure 2001 (No. 1)

198. In section 2(1) of the Churchwardens Measure 2001 (person disqualified from being churchwarden if disqualified from being a charity trustee)—

(a) for "Charity Commissioners" substitute "Charity Commission", and

(b) for "them" substitute "it".

Licensing Act 2003 (c. 17)

199. In Schedule 2 to the Licensing Act 2003 (provision of late night refreshment) in paragraph 5(4)—

(a) for "under section 3" substitute "in accordance with section 3A", and

(b) for "subsection (5)" substitute "subsection (2)".

Companies (Audit, Investigations and Community Enterprise) Act 2004 (c. 27)

200. The Companies (Audit, Investigations and Community Enterprise) Act 2004 has effect subject to the following amendments.

201. In section 39 (existing companies: charities), in subsections (1) and (2), for "Charity Commissioners" substitute "Charity Commission".

202. In section 40 (existing companies: Scottish charities), in subsections (4)(b) and (6), for "Charity Commissioners" substitute "Charity Commission".

203. In section 54(7) (requirements for becoming a charity or a Scottish charity)—

(a) for "Charity Commissioners" substitute "Charity Commission", and

(b) for "their" substitute "its".

204. In paragraph 4 of Schedule 3 (regulator of community interest companies)—

(a) for "Chief Charity Commissioner" substitute "chairman of the Charity Commission", and

(b) for "any officer or employee appointed under paragraph 2(1) of Schedule 1 to the

Charities Act 1993 (c. 10)" substitute "any other member of the Commission appointed under paragraph 1(2) of Schedule 1A to the Charities Act 1993 or any member of staff of the Commission appointed under paragraph 5(1) of that Schedule".

Pensions Act 2004 (c. 35)

205. The Pensions Act 2004 has effect subject to the following amendments.
206. In Schedule 3 (certain permitted disclosures of restricted information held by the Regulator), for the entry relating to the Charity Commissioners substitute—

"The Charity Commission.	Functions under the Charities Act 1993 (c. 10) or the Charities Act 2006."

207. In Schedule 8 (certain permitted disclosures of restricted information held by the Board), for the entry relating to the Charity Commissioners substitute—

"The Charity Commission.	Functions under the Charities Act 1993 (c. 10) or the Charities Act 2006."

Constitutional Reform Act 2005 (c. 4)

208. In Part 3 of Schedule 14 to the Constitutional Reform Act 2005 (the Judicial Appointments Commission: relevant offices etc.) after the entries relating to section 6(5) of the Tribunals and Inquiries Act 1992 insert—

"President of the Charity Tribunal	Paragraph 1(2) of Schedule 1B to the Charities Act 1993 (c. 10)."
Legal member of the Charity Tribunal	
Ordinary member of the Charity Tribunal	

Charities and Trustee Investment (Scotland) Act 2005 (asp 10)

209. The Charities and Trustee Investment (Scotland) Act 2005 has effect subject to the following amendments.
210. In section 36(1) (powers of OSCR in relation to English and Welsh charities)—
    (a) for "Charity Commissioners for England and Wales inform" substitute "Charity Commission for England and Wales informs",
    (b) for "under section 3" substitute "in accordance with section 3A", and
    (c) for "section 3(5) of that Act," substitute "subsection (2) of that section,".
211. In section 69(2)(d)(i) (persons disqualified from being charity trustees)—
    (a) at the beginning insert "by the Charity Commission for England and Wales under section 18(2)(i) of the Charities Act 1993 or", and

(b) for "under section 18(2)(i) of the Charities Act 1993 (c. 10)," substitute ", whether under section 18(2)(i) of that Act or under".

Equality Act 2006 (c. 3)

212. (1) The Equality Act 2006 has effect subject to the following amendments.

(2) In section 58(2) (charities relating to religion or belief)—

(a) for "Charity Commissioners for England and Wales" substitute "Charity Commission", and

(b) for "the Commissioners" substitute "the Commission".

(3) In section 79(1)(a) (interpretation) after "given by" insert "section 1(1) of".

Section 75

SCHEDULE 9

REPEALS AND REVOCATIONS

Short title and chapter or title and number	Extent of repeal or revocation
Police, Factories, &c. (Miscellaneous Provisions) Act 1916 (c. 31)	In section 5(1), in paragraph (b) of the proviso, the words from ", and no representation" onwards.
Recreational Charities Act 1958 (c. 17)	Section 2.
Church Funds Investment Measure 1958 (No. 1)	Section 5.
Charities Act 1960 (c. 58)	The whole Act.
Housing Act 1985 (c. 68)	In section 6A(5), the words from "and is not" onwards.
Reverter of Sites Act 1987 (c. 15)	In section 4(4), the words "and appeals" and (in both places) ", and to appeals against,".
Charities Act 1992 (c. 41)	Part 1 (so far as unrepealed). Part 3. Section 76(1)(c) and the word "and" preceding it. In section 77(4), "or 73". In section 79, in subsection (6) the words "(subject to subsection (7))", and subsection (7). Schedule 5. In Schedule 6, paragraph 9. In Schedule 7, the entry relating to the Police, Factories, &c. (Miscellaneous Provisions) Act 1916.
Charities Act 1993 (c. 10)	Section 1. In section 2(7), the words from ", and the report" onwards. In section 4, subsection (3) and, in subsection (5), the words ", whether given on such an appeal or not".

Section 6(9).
Section 9(4).
In section 16, in subsection (4)(c) the words "in the case of a charity other than an exempt charity,", in subsection (5) the words "which is not an exempt charity and", and subsections (11) to (14).
In section 17(7), the words from "but this subsection" onwards.
Section 18(8) to (10).
In section 23(2), the words "or them".
In section 24(8), the words from "; and if the scheme" onwards.
Section 28(10).
In section 33, in each of subsections (2) and (7) the words "(other than an exempt charity)".
Section 44(3).
Section 46(8).
Section 61(7).
In section 73(4), the words "(other than an exempt charity)".
Section 92.
In section 96, in the definition of "exempt charity" in subsection (1) the words "(subject to section 24(8) above)", and subsection (4). Schedule 1. In Schedule 2, in paragraph (b) the words "and the colleges of Winchester and Eton", and paragraph (x).
In Schedule 6, paragraphs 1(2), 26, 28 and 29(2) to (4), (7) and (8).

National Lottery etc. Act 1993 (c. 39)	In Schedule 5, paragraph 12.
Local Government (Wales) Act 1994 (c. 19)	In Schedule 16, paragraph 99.
Deregulation and Contracting Out Act 1994 (c. 40)	Section 28. Section 29(7) and (8).
Housing Act 1996 (c. 52)	In section 58(1)(b), the words from "and is not" onwards.
Teaching and Higher Education Act 1998 (c. 30)	Section 41. In Schedule 3, paragraph 9.
School Standards and Framework Act 1998 (c. 31)	In section 23(1), the words "which are exempt charities for the purposes of the Charities Act 1993". In Schedule 30, paragraph 48.
Intervention Board for Agricultural Produce (Abolition) Regulations 2001 (S.I. 2001/3686)	Regulation 6(11)(a).

Regulatory Reform (National Health Service Charitable and Non-Charitable Trust Accounts and Audit) Order 2005 (S.I. 2005/1074)	Article 3(5).

Section 75   SCHEDULE 10

TRANSITIONAL PROVISIONS AND SAVINGS

Section 4: guidance as to operation of public benefit requirement

1. Any consultation initiated by the Charity Commissioners for England and Wales before the day on which section 4 of this Act comes into force is to be as effective for the purposes of section 4(4)(a) as if it had been initiated by the Commission on or after that day.

Section 5: recreational charities etc.

2. Where section 2 of the Recreational Charities Act 1958 (c. 17) applies to any trusts immediately before the day on which subsection (3) of section 5 of this Act comes into force, that subsection does not prevent the trusts from continuing to be charitable if they constitute a charity in accordance with section 1(1) of this Act.

Section 18: cy-près schemes

3. The amendment made by section 18 applies to property given for charitable purposes whether before or on or after the day on which that section comes into force.

Section 19: suspension or removal of trustee etc. from membership of charity

4. The amendment made by section 19 applies where the misconduct or other relevant conduct on the part of the person suspended or removed from his office or employment took place on or after the day on which section 19 comes into force.

Section 20: specific directions for protection of charity

5. The amendment made by section 20 applies whether the inquiry under section 8 of the 1993 Act was instituted before or on or after the day on which section 20 comes into force.

Section 26: offence of obstructing power of entry

6. In relation to an offence committed before the commencement of section 281(5) of the Criminal Justice Act 2003 (c. 44) (alteration of penalties for summary offences), the reference to 51 weeks in section 31A(11) of the 1993 Act (as inserted by section 26 of this Act) is to be read as a reference to 3 months.

Section 28: audit or examination of accounts of charity which is not a company

7. The amendments made by section 28 apply in relation to any financial year of a charity which begins on or after the day on which that section comes into force.

Section 29: auditor etc. of charity which is not a company to report matters to Commission

8. (1) The amendments made by section 29 apply in relation to matters ("pre-commencement matters") of which a person became aware at any time falling—

   (a) before the day on which that section comes into force, and

240

(b) during a financial year ending on or after that day,
as well as in relation to matters of which he becomes aware on or after that day.

(2) Any duty imposed by or by virtue of the new section 44A(2) or 46(2A) of the 1993 Act inserted by section 29 must be complied with in relation to any such pre-commencement matters as soon as practicable after section 29 comes into force.

Section 32: audit or examination of accounts of charitable companies

9. The amendments made by section 32 apply in relation to any financial year of a charity which begins on or after the day on which that section comes into force.

Section 33: auditor etc. of charitable company to report matters to Commission

10. (1) The amendment made by section 33 applies in relation to matters ("pre-commencement matters") of which a person became aware at any time falling—
   (a) before the day on which that section comes into force, and
   (b) during a financial year ending on or after that day,
   as well as in relation to matters of which he becomes aware on or after that day.

   (2) Any duty imposed by virtue of the new section 68A(1) of the 1993 Act inserted by section 33 must be complied with in relation to any such pre-commencement matters as soon as practicable after section 33 comes into force.

Section 35: waiver of trustee's disqualification

11. The amendment made by section 35 applies whether the disqualification took effect before, on or after the day on which that section comes into force.

Section 36: remuneration of trustees etc. providing services to charity

12. The amendment made by section 36 does not affect the payment of remuneration or provision of services in accordance with an agreement made before the day on which that section comes into force.

Section 38: relief from liability for breach of trust or duty

13. Sections 73D and 73E of the 1993 Act (as inserted by section 38 of this Act) have effect in relation to acts or omissions occurring before the day on which section 38 comes into force as well as in relation to those occurring on or after that day.

Section 44: registration of charity mergers

14. Section 75C of the 1993 Act (as inserted by section 44 of this Act) applies to relevant charity mergers taking place before the day on which section 44 comes into force as well as to ones taking place on or after that day.

Section 67: statements relating to fund-raising

15. The amendments made by section 67 apply in relation to any solicitation or representation to which section 60(1), (2) or (3) of the 1992 Act applies and which is made on or after the day on which section 67 comes into force.

Section 72: Disclosure of information to and by Northern Ireland regulator

16. In relation to an offence committed in England and Wales before the commencement of section 154(1) of the Criminal Justice Act 2003 (c. 44) (general limit on magistrates' court's power to impose imprisonment), the reference to 12 months in section 72(6) is to be read as a reference to 6 months.

Schedule 6: group accounts

17. Paragraph 3(2) of the new Schedule 5A inserted in the 1993 Act by Schedule 6 to this

Act does not apply in relation to any financial year of a parent charity beginning before the day on which paragraph 3(2) comes into force.

Schedule 8: minor and consequential amendments

18. The following provisions, namely—
    (a) paragraphs 80(6) and (8), 83(3) and (4), 99(3), (4)(a) and (5)(a) and (c), 109(12), 111(7) and 171 of Schedule 8, and
    (b) the corresponding entries in Schedule 9,
    do not affect the operation of the Coal Industry Act 1987 (c. 3), the Reverter of Sites Act 1987 (c. 15) or the 1993 Act in relation to any appeal brought in the High Court before the day on which those provisions come into force.

19. Paragraph 98(2) of Schedule 8 does not affect the validity of any designation made by the Charity Commissioners for England and Wales under section 2(2) of the 1993 Act which is in effect immediately before that paragraph comes into force.

20. In relation to an offence committed in England and Wales before the commencement of section 154(1) of the Criminal Justice Act 2003 (c. 44) (general limit on magistrates' court's power to impose imprisonment), the reference to 12 months in section 10A(4) of the 1993 Act (as inserted by paragraph 104 of Schedule 8 to this Act) is to be read as a reference to 6 months.

Schedule 9: savings on repeal of provisions of Charities Act 1960

21. (1) This paragraph applies where, immediately before the coming into force of the repeal by this Act of section 35(6) of the Charities Act 1960 (c. 58) (transfer and evidence of title to property vested in trustees), any relevant provision had effect, in accordance with that provision, as if contained in a conveyance or other document declaring the trusts on which land was held at the commencement of that Act.
    (2) In such a case the relevant provision continues to have effect as if so contained despite the repeal of section 35(6) of that Act.
    (3) A "relevant provision" means a provision of any of the following Acts providing for the appointment of trustees—
        (a) the Trustee Appointment Act 1850 (c.28),
        (b) the Trustee Appointment Act 1869 (c.26),
        (c) the Trustees Appointment Act 1890 (c.19), or
        (d) the School Sites Act 1852 (c. 49) so far as applying any of the above Acts,
    as in force at the commencement of the Charities Act 1960.

22. The repeal by this Act of section 39(2) of the Charities Act 1960 (repeal of obsolete enactments) does not affect the continued operation of any trusts which, at the commencement of that Act, were wholly or partly comprised in an enactment specified in Schedule 5 to that Act (enactments repealed as obsolete).

23. The repeal by this Act of section 48(1) of, and Schedule 6 to, the Charities Act 1960 (consequential amendments etc.) does not affect the amendments made by Schedule 6 in—
    (a) section 9 of the Places of Worship Registration Act 1855 (c. 81),
    (b) section 4(1) of the Open Spaces Act 1906 (c. 25),
    (c) section 24(4) of the Landlord and Tenant Act 1927 (c. 36), or
    (d) section 14(1) or 31 of the New Parishes Measure 1943.

24. Despite the repeal by this Act of section 48(3) of the Charities Act 1960, section 30(3)

to (5) of the 1993 Act continue to apply to documents enrolled by or deposited with the Charity Commissioners under the Charitable Trusts Acts 1853 to 1939.

25. Despite the repeal by this Act of section 48(4) of the Charities Act 1960—

(a) any scheme, order, certificate or other document issued under or for the purposes of the Charitable Trusts Acts 1853 to 1939 and having effect in accordance with section 48(4) immediately before the commencement of that repeal continues to have the same effect (and to be enforceable or liable to be discharged in the same way) as would have been the case if that repeal had not come into force, and

(b) any such document, and any document under the seal of the official trustees of charitable funds, may be proved as if the 1960 Act had not been passed.

26. (1) Despite the repeal by this Act of section 48(6) of the Charities Act 1960 (c. 58), the official custodian for charities is to continue to be treated as the successor for all purposes both of the official trustee of charity lands and of the official trustees of charitable funds as if—

(a) the functions of the official trustee or trustees had been functions of the official custodian, and

(b) as if the official trustee or trustees had been, and had discharged his or their functions as, holder of the office of the official custodian.

(2) Despite the repeal of section 48(6) (and without affecting the generality of sub-paragraph (1))—

(a) any property which immediately before the commencement of that repeal was, by virtue of section 48(6), held by the official custodian as if vested in him under section 21 of the 1993 Act continues to be so held, and

(b) any enactment or document referring to the official trustee or trustees mentioned above continues to have effect, so far as the context permits, as if the official custodian had been mentioned instead.

27. The repeal by this Act of the Charities Act 1960 does not affect any transitional provision or saving contained in that Act which is capable of having continuing effect but whose effect is not preserved by any other provision of this Schedule.

Schedule 9: savings on repeal of provisions of Charities Act 1992

28. The repeal by this Act of section 49 of, and Schedule 5 to, the 1992 Act (amendments relating to redundant churches etc.) does not affect the amendments made by that Schedule in the Redundant Churches and Other Religious Buildings Act 1969.

Schedule 9: repeal of certain repeals made by Charities Acts 1960 and 1992

29. (1) It is hereby declared that (in accordance with sections 15 and 16 of the Interpretation Act 1978 (c. 30)) the repeal by this Act of any of the provisions mentioned in sub-paragraph (2) does not revive so much of any enactment or document as ceased to have effect by virtue of that provision.

(2) The provisions are—

(a) section 28(9) of the Charities Act 1960 (repeal of provisions regulating taking of charity proceedings),

(b) section 36 of the 1992 Act (repeal of provisions requiring Charity Commissioners' consent to dealings with charity land), and

(c) section 50 of that Act (repeal of provisions requiring amount of contributions towards maintenance etc. of almshouses to be sanctioned by Charity Commissioners).

The Charity Commission's Approach to Public Benefit[1]

(October 2006)

The Charities Bill and public benefit

The Bill requires organisations to pass two tests if they are to be charities. Firstly that their objects are charitable, and secondly that they operate for the public benefit. For the first time, the law will require charities which advance education, religion OF relieve poverty to explicitly demonstrate they deliver public benefit, The law has previously presumed this to be the case for these types of charities.

The Bill does not contain any new definition of public benefit or suggest how charities should demonstrate public benefit. Decisions on how the public benefit test will operate will, rightly, rest with the Commission, as the independent regulator for charities in England and Wales.

The new public benefit test is not a green-field site. Our decisions must be based on underlying case law. But we will follow the courts' approach and develop our decisions on public benefit in the context of changing economic and social conditions, including public attitudes.

It is a helpful development that, in future, easier and less expensive appeals against our decisions can be made to the new Charity Tribunal proposed in the Bill and ultimately, of course, to the courts..

Our broad approach

There are considerable advantages which arise from charitable status:

- Reputational—people are more likely to offer time, energy or money to a registered charity;
- Opportunity—many grant-makers only give to charities; and
- Fiscal—charities receive a wide range of tax advantages.

There is a clear relationship between these benefits of charitable status and the need for charities to deliver benefit for the public. Charities are precious, and play a vital and unique role at the heart of our society, but like all bodies in which the public places its trust, they should be accountable to everyone for what they do. That is the essence of the public benefit test. It also fits squarely with the Commission's new objectives in the Bill, particularly the objective to enhance the accountability of charities to donors, beneficiaries and the public.

---

[1] http://www.charity-commission.gov.uk/spr/pubben.asp

Our aim will be to ensure both that charities demonstrate public benefit in what they do and, beyond that, continue to increase the value they bring to the communities they serve.

We need to articulate and explain the concept of public benefit in a way which is consistent with the law and clear to the public.

In taking forward our work on public benefit, we also need to ensure that wherever we can we make use of existing accountability processes. For instance, we think that all charities should report what they do for public benefit and we will be recommending that all charities report once a year on this, using the existing reporting framework, as many already do. There is no point in duplication and, in any case, we are committed as an organisation to achieving at least a 25% reduction in the administrative burden of regulation over the next four years.

Consultation process

We will consult widely with the charity sector and the public about the public benefit test.

We have already met some key parts of the sector, including fee-charging and religious organisations, to begin to identify with them:

- the public benefit they bring;
- what might be good practice in their context; and
- what issues should be covered in guidance the Commission publishes on this.

We have also convened a group of public policy experts independently chaired, to think through the meaning of the concept and application of public benefit.

We have commissioned a citizens' forum to research public perceptions and expectations of public benefit.

All these strands will inform our preparation of the guidance which we will issue for public consultation early in the new year.

The need for continuing improvement

It is in the interests of everyone if charities become more effective over time. That is why we are keen to ensure that we set up a situation where an organisation that has met the public benefit test still has an incentive to improve its delivery of benefits to the public in the future.

We aim to stimulate this process by establishing with different parts of the sector what the spread of good practice is in delivering public benefit, publicising this and enabling individual charities, where appropriate, to compare themselves with others. This would enable independent boards of trustees working in similar areas to share ideas about how they, and other charities, are achieving results. The improvement efforts which are already being made by many would be showcased more explicitly.

Issues concerning fee-charging charities

Charities may charge fees for the facilities or services they provide. Charities which charge relatively high fees must demonstrate accessibility to those facilities or services. It will not normally be possible to demonstrate public benefit through indirect benefits alone, such as savings in public expenditure through the provision of a service like education or health.

We think all charities should give an account each year of the public benefit they provide. For fee-charging charities where public benefit is not immediately obvious given the high level of fees charged, one suggestion we will explore is to expect those charities also to assess and report the value of the tangible benefits they bring, alongside the value of the tax breaks they receive.

The importance of review

It is important that the Commission implements the public benefit test robustly, and we are committed to doing this. We are confident that the combination of clear articulation of public benefit provided by individual charities and the spreading of best practice, coupled with the fact that there will be a review of progress to see what has been achieved—with the possibility that Parliament could revisit the issue.

Last updated: 23 Oct 2006

APPENDIX 3

CABINET OFFICE

OFFICE OF THE THIRD SECTOR

Charities Act 2006: Implementation Plan

Charities Act 2006: Implementation

This document sets out our provisional timetable for implementation of the Charities Act 2006 (the Act), and the fulfilment of other commitments made during its passage through Parliament. Our aim is to give charities (and others that will be affected by the Act) time to properly prepare for changes that will affect them.

The legislation received Royal Assent on 8th November 2006. The Act, and explanatory notes that accompany it are available on the website of the Office of Public Sector Information. Parts of the Act will come into force early in 2007, and subsequent provisions will roll out over the following two to three years.

Implementation will be led by the Office of the Third Sector in the Cabinet Office, working closely with colleagues in the Charity Commission and representatives from the sector itself.

In the first half of 2007, the sector will see:

- A plain English guide to the Charities Act;
- A series of regional events to explain the Act to charities in England and Wales;
- Initial reductions in the regulatory burden on charities, especially smaller charities;
- A modernised framework for the Charity Commission;
- Consultations with the sector begin to ensure clear guidance is available on the public benefit test.

Other key measures in the Act will follow. The full raft of deregulatory provisions will be brought into effect as quickly as possible, while other measures will require consultation and Secondary Legislation or guidance before they can be commenced.

For example, the new definition of charity, and the public benefit test, will not be brought into force until there is an accessible appeal right through the Charity Tribunal, and the Charity Commission has developed and consulted on its guidance on the operation of the public benefit requirement.

The timetable below sets out when we expect to bring most of the provisions of the Act into force.

More details about the implementation, including progress updates, will be available on the websites of the Office of the Third Sector and the Charity Commission.

First Commencement Order—early 2007

The main provisions that will be commenced by this Order will be:

- The new Charity Commission, its objectives, functions and duties *(sections 6*
- *& 7, schedules 1 & 2).*
- The requirement for the Commission to develop guidance and consult on the public benefit test *(section 4).*
- Interim changes to the registration threshold for small charities—which will be followed by an order to increase the threshold to £5,000 annual income
- *(section 10).*
- The relaxation of publicity requirements relating to schemes *(section 22).*
- The participation of Scottish and Northern Irish charities in Common Investment and Deposit Funds *(section 23).*
- Changes to the audit thresholds for unincorporated and incorporated charities *(sections 28 & 32).*
- The power for the Commission to determine the membership of a charity, and the power for the Commission to enter premises and seize documents under a warrant *(sections 25 & 26).*
- Changes to the restrictions on mortgages of charity land *(section 27).*
- Waiver of trustee's disqualification and the power for the Commission to relieve trustees and auditors from liability for breach or trust or duty *(sections 35 & 38).*
- The ability for charities to purchase trustee indemnity insurance *(section 39).*
- The power for unincorporated charities to modify powers or procedures *(section 42).*
- The reserve power to control fundraising by charitable institutions *(section 69).*
- Powers for Secretaries of State, the Minister for the Cabinet Office, and the National Assembly for Wales to give financial assistance to charitable, philanthropic or benevolent organisations *(sections 70 & 71).*

Second Commencement Order—second half of 2007

The main provisions that will be commenced by this Order will be:

- Provisions relating to mergers of charities *(section 44).*
- Statements indicating benefits for charitable institutions, professional fundraisers, and commercial participators *(sections 67 & 68).*
- Provisions relating to audit and accounting for charities, including group accounts and changes to the accounting regime for small charitable companies *(sections 29, 30, 31, 33, and an order under section 77, and schedule 6)*

Third Commencement Order—early 2008

The main provisions that will be commenced by this Order will be:

- The new definition of charity and the public benefit requirement *(sections 1, 2, 3, and 5).*
- The Charity Tribunal (section 8 and schedules 3 & 4).
- New powers for the Charity Commission—to remove or suspend trustees from membership of a charity, to give specific directions for the protection of charity property, to direct the application of charity property, and to give advice and guidance *(sections 19, 20, 21 and 24).*
- Remuneration of trustees providing services to a charity *(sections 36 & 37).*
- Powers for unincorporated charities to transfer all property, to replace purposes or to spend capital *(sections 40, 41 & 43).*
- The Charitable Incorporated Organisation *(section 34 and schedule 7).*
- Changes to Cy Près occasions and Schemes *(sections 15 to 18).*

Exempt and Excepted Charities

Provisions relating to the registration of certain 'excepted' charities, and provisions relating to 'exempt' charities, are not expected to come into force before 2008. This will enable those charities, the proposed principal regulators of exempt charities, and the Charity Commission, time to prepare for the changes *(parts of section 9, sections 11 to 14, and schedule 5)*.

While the Charity Commission is registering the large numbers of formerly excepted and exempt charities that it will have to register, the current law which enables the Charity Commission to exercise its discretion in relation to applications for voluntary registration will continue in force. Once those excepted and exempt charities that are required to register have been registered, the provision in the Act requiring the Commission to register charities that apply for voluntary registration will be commenced.

Licensing regime for public charitable collections

Before these provisions can come into force, work remains to be done in preparing and consulting on regulations and guidance. In addition the Charity Commission will need to equip itself to take on its new role in the scheme. Therefore it is not envisaged that the new licensing regime will come into force before 2009 *(sections 45 to 66)*.

For both these sets of provisions, we will update the implementation plan as soon as the timetable for their implementation is settled, following discussions with stakeholders.

Other commitments

There were several other commitments made during the passage of the Charities Bill:

- Preparation of a plain English guide to the Act, aimed particularly at small charities. We are working closely with the Charity Commission to produce this, and expect to publish it early in 2007.

- Consolidation of charity law will be a matter for the Law Commission. While we can't speak for the Commission we understand that it has accepted into its work programme the consolidation of charity statute law. We anticipate that much of the preparatory work will be done during the current session of Parliament but that the consolidation Act or Acts probably won't be enacted until the next session (2007/08).

- A review of the financial thresholds in the Charities Acts, to take place within a year of Royal Assent. The aim of the review will be to determine what scope there is for raising or simplifying existing thresholds. The thresholds can be changed by an order made by the Minister. Any proposals will be subject to consultation during 2007.

- A review of existing Secondary Legislation under the Charities Acts 1992, and 1993, with a view to identifying whether any existing regulations can be simplified. This review will take place during 2007 with any proposals for change subject to public consultation.

- A review of the impact of the public benefit requirement within three years of the public benefit requirement coming into force.

- An evaluation of the impact of the Charities Act 2006 within five years of Royal Assent is required by section 73. Ministers would appoint the person to undertake the review, which would report to Parliament on the impact of the Act.

Index

References are to Paragraph Numbers